THE NORDIC REGIONS AND THE EUROPEAN UNION

The International Political Economy of New Regionalisms Series

The International Political Economy of New Regionalisms Series presents innovative analyses of a range of novel regional relations and institutions. Going beyond established, formal, interstate economic organizations, this essential series provides informed interdisciplinary and international research and debate about myriad heterogeneous intermediate level interactions.

Reflective of its cosmopolitan and creative orientation, this series is developed by an international editorial team of established and emerging scholars in both the South and North. It reinforces ongoing networks of analysts in both academia and think-tanks as well as international agencies concerned with micro-, meso- and macro-level regionalisms.

Recent Titles in the Series

The New Regionalism in Africa
Edited by J. Andrew Grant and Fredrik Söderbaum

Reconfigured Sovereignty
Edited by Thomas L. Ilgen

Euro-Mediterranean Security
Sven Biscop

Transnational Democracy in Critical and Comparative Perspective
Edited by Bruce Morrison

Comparative Regional Integration
Edited by Finn Laursen

The Nordic Regions and the European Union

Edited by

SØREN DOSENRODE and HENRIK HALKIER
Institute for History, International and Social Studies,
Aalborg University, Denmark

Routledge
Taylor & Francis Group
LONDON AND NEW YORK

First published 2004 by Ashgate Publishing

Reissued 2018 by Routledge
2 Park Square, Milton Park, Abingdon, Oxon OX14 4RN
711 Third Avenue, New York, NY 10017, USA

Routledge is an imprint of the Taylor & Francis Group, an informa business

A Library of Congress record exists under LC control number: 2003054480

ISBN 13: 978-0-815-39803-5 (hbk)
ISBN 13: 978-1-351-14592-3 (ebk)

Contents

List of Figures

List of Tables

List of Contributors

ANDREAS P. CORNETT, PhD, Associate Professor, University of Southern Denmark, Soenderborg, Chair of the Nordic Section of the Regional Science Association.

SØREN DOSENRODE, Dr. Phil., Jean Monnet Professor of European Politics and Administration, Director, Institute for History, International and Social Studies, Aalborg University, Denmark.

ARILD GJERTSEN is employed as a researcher at the Nordland Research Institute in Bodø, Norway.

JAN ERIK GRINDHEIM, cand. polit., Associate Professor of European Integration and Public Administration, The Jean Monnet Project, Centre for European Studies, Agder University College, Norway. Adviser on regional development to Oslo Technopole.

HENRIK HALKIER, Associate Professor of British and European Politics at Aalborg University, Denmark. Director of the *SPIRIT* Doctoral School and Chair of the International Committee of the Regional Studies Association.

OLE B. JENSEN, MA, PhD, Associate Professor of Sociology & Planning, Urban Studies and Planning Division, Department of Development & Planning, Aalborg University, Denmark.

JØRN LEIN-MATHISEN, political advisor at the Norwegian Parliament. He is affiliated to the ARENA research programme at the University of Oslo, Norway.

KAISA LÄHTEENMÄKI-SMITH, Dr. Pol. Sci., Senior Research Fellow, Nordregio (Nordic Centre for Spatial Development), Stockholm, Sweden.

JAN OLSSON, Dr. Phil., Associate Professor of Political Science, Örebro University, Sweden.

TIM RICHARDSON, Dr., Senior Lecturer in Town and Regional Planning, University of Sheffield, UK and Visiting Professor in European Spatial Policy, Aalborg University, Denmark.

JOACHIM ÅSTRÖM is a PhD student of Political Science at Örebro University, Sweden.

List of Acronyms

A SEED	– Action for Solidarity, Equality, Environment and Diversity
ADCC	– Association of Danish County Councils
ADR	– Association of the Danish Regions
AEBR	– Association of European Border Regions
AER	– Assembly of the European Regions
BIC	– Business Innovation Centre
BSR	– Baltic Sea Region
CA	– County Administrations
CAB	– County Administration Board
CC	– County Councils
CEEC	– Central and East European Countries
CEMR	– Council of European Municipalities and Regions
CLRAE	– Congress of Local and Regional Authorities of Europe
CMEA	– Council of Mutual Economic Assistance
COR	– Committee of the Regions
CPMR	– Conference of Peripheral Maritime Regions
DU	– Distriktenes utbygningsfond (The Norwegian Regional Development Fund)
EC	– European Community
ECOSOC	– Economic and Social Committee
EEA	– European Economic Area
EFTA	– European Free Trade Area
EMU	– European Monetary Union
EP	– European Parliament
ERDF	– European Regional Development Fund
ERT	– European Roundtable of Industrialists
ESA	– European Surveillance Authority
ESF	– European Social Fund
ESPD	– European Spatial Development Perspective
EU	– European Union
FDI	– Foreign Direct Investment
GNP	– Gross National Product
He	– Hallituksen esitys (Finnish) = Government Proposal
IO	– Interest organization
IULA	– International Union of Local Authorities
LA	– Local Authorities
NGO	– Non-governmental organization

RDP	– Regional Development Programmes (RUP)
RETI	– Association of European Regions of Industrial Technology
RUP	– Regionale utviklingsprogrammer (RDP)
SEA	– Single European Act
SMEs	– Small and medium-sized enterprises
SND	– Statens nærings- og distriktsutviklingsfond (The Norwegian Industrial and Regional Development Fund)
TEN-T	– Trans-European Network for Transport
TEU	– Treaty on European Union
UK	– United Kingdom

Chapter 1

Introduction: The Nordic Regions and the European Union

Søren Dosenrode

Seen from the outside, the Nordic countries Denmark, Finland, Norway and Sweden may look relatively alike; they are all small centralized states without a federal tradition; all are very stable democracies with a tradition of minority and or coalition governments; three of them are monarchies, one talks of a 'Nordic welfare state model'; they have been co-operating for decades in the Nordic Council; and when any of the three that are members of the European Union (EU) – have held the rotating EU Presidency, they have all (more or less explicitly) referred to aspirations of supporting the emergence of a 'Nordic dimension'[1] in the Union. Thus it is fair to say, that they are often looked upon as a special block in Europe (cf. Kleven *et al.*, 2000, p. 94). This group of states and their regions is the focus of this book.[2]

At the sub-national level, the regions of the four states are all to varying degrees dependent on their central governments politically, economically and administratively, although their rights of self-government are guaranteed by law in two of them (Denmark and Sweden) and have a strong tradition in the other two (Finland and Norway). Until the end of the 1980s, the Nordic regions lived a very quiet life at the national level, not to mention the international one. But beginning with the Single European Act (SEA) and the reform of the Structural Funds in the 1980s, followed by both the Maastricht Treaty on the European Union and the subsequent development in the institutional and constitutional structures of the EU, Nordic regions – beginning with the Danish ones – have embarked on a more active course vis-à-vis the EU. The dynamics set free by the SEA in the last half of the

1 The concrete content of this 'Nordic dimension' has been less clear, but it includes aspects like transparency and 'openness' in the EU administration and decision-making process; bringing the EU closer to the citizens; being less formalistic and more pragmatic and so forth.

2 In this book we do not pay attention to the Faeroe Islands, Greenland, Svalbard, Jan Main and the Åland Islands, as their status as autonomous regions would make it difficult to include them in the same comparative framework as the other regions discussed here. Statistically their relevance is insignificant due to their share of the total population being less than one per cent.

1980s first resulted in some Danish regions beginning to establish tentative contacts with the European Community and were later institutionalised in the creation of the Committee of the Regions as the procedure by which the regions participate in the EU decision-making process. As previous surveys have shown that the regions of Austria, Germany and Switzerland (amongst others) have all been influenced by the European integration process (cf. Dosenrode, 1995), it is natural to ask the questions: *how has the European integration process influenced the role of the Nordic regions within their states,* and *how have they reacted to this*?

As this topic has not been treated systematically before,[3] this book consists of two parts: 1) a general comparative 'nation-by-nation' part in which the Europeanization of the Nordic regions is examined, and 2) a part in which three central topics (in five chapters) are analysed in depth.

In the general part, the Europeanization of the four states is analysed thoroughly. The reader is introduced to the regional systems of government followed by analyses of how the regions are Europeanized. Our working hypothesis is that Europeanization is both a *de facto* condition that the regions will have to live with, and a potential means to achieve two ends: (1) more resources, and (2) a more symmetrically interdependent relationship between the regional and state levels.

But what is meant by 'region' and 'Europeanization'? Concerning the concept of 'region', we have adopted a pragmatic attitude in that we let the individual contributors define their understanding of the concept.[4] While the four country studies have applied the same approach, concentrating on the first substantial sub-national level ie. *amter*, *fylker*, *län* and *maakunta*, it would have been wrong to choose a rigorist approach which would only cause problems when one had to define less traditional regions such as cross-border ones, e.g., the Øresund region.[5]

In the four national case studies, there is an underlying understanding of the concept of 'Europeanization' as the EU-related part of the general concept of internationalization. Europeanization is defined as the increasing degree to which the regions are influenced by, and involved in, developments going on outside their home country, but within the EU (Dosenrode, 1997).

In this definition, there are three implicit aspects: a) a passive, b) a mental and c) an active one.

---

3 Baldersheim and Ståhlberg recently published an informative article on the local level (Baldersheim and Ståhlberg, 2002), in which they analyse and compare the methods of co-ordination and integration in central – local relations in the four Nordic countries. The article is a good addition to this volume, if one needs a survey of the whole sub-national arena.

4 In chapter 6, Lein-Mathisen discusses the concept of 'region'.

5 The Union uses the 'nomenclature of territorial units for statistics' abbreviated 'NUTS' (after the French translation). This nomenclature operates with three levels: NUTS 1 which includes for example the German *Länder*; NUTS 2 which includes for example comunidades autónomas in Spain or regions in Ireland and NUTS 3 which includes the Danish *amter*, the Finnish *maakunta*, the Norwegian *fylker* and the Swedish *län*.

a) The *passive* aspect is characterized by the regions acting upon EU legislation which they have not been involved in laying down and which has been transferred into national law.
b) The second aspect, the *mental* one, is less tangible. It involves the awareness of Europeanization brought about by factors such as regions having civil servants responsible for EU matters, some regions having representatives in Brussels, some regions sending a democratically elected representative to the Committee of Regions, etc. These can all be seen as developments that influence some civil servants and (some) politicians to the extent that their traditional nationally focused mindsets are transformed and they think increasingly 'European'. One can talk of a growing awareness of the surrounding environment, a process of learning, which is difficult to track and will only be touched upon sporadically. The mental aspect is however important in that it can be seen as a precondition for active Europeanization.
c) *Active* Europeanization is characterized by the goal-oriented, conscious and voluntary participation of the regions in activities in which one or more of the co-actors are, directly or indirectly, of another nationality than the regions in question. As a working hypothesis we assume that the main motives for conducting active Europeanization are a) to secure resources to the region, and b) to diminish an asymmetric relationship to the central government.

This is a fairly 'down-to-earth' definition, but it has previously shown itself to be operational, and also useful as a basis for analysing the degree of Europeanization that the regions in a country have (cf. Cortelius, 2002).[6] Europeanization is both a fact (a given condition), and an opportunity for the region to diminish its dependence on the state.

To make a comparison possible, whilst at the same time leaving room for specific features, the four national studies deal with key issues such as:

- Mapping Europeanization in the regions;
- The administrative adaptation caused by Europeanization;
- The relationship between the regions and central government;

6 Lein-Mathisen also discusses 'Europeanization' in chapter 6. Claudio Radaelli has a more detailed, though not necessarily more easily operationalised definition of the concept: 'Europeanization refers to: Processes of a) construction, b) diffusion and c) institutionalization of formal and informal rules, procedures, policy paradigms, styles, "way of doing things" and shared beliefs and norms which are first defined and consolidated in the making of EU decisions and then incorporated in the logic of domestic discourse, identities, political structures and public policies. This definition stresses the importance of change in the logic of political behaviour. The latter changes through a process leading to the institutionalization in the domestic political system (at the national and/or sub-national levels) of discourse, cognitive maps, normative frameworks and styles coming from the EU' (2000, p. 4).

- The participation of the regions in the national part of the EU decision-making process;
- The relationship between the regions and the EU.

If a process of Europeanization is taking place, in what regional institutions does it take place and which forms does it take? Are those pushing the process forward mainly civil servants, as some Danish surveys indicate (cf. Kurt Klaudi Klausen, 1996), or is it the politicians, or the interest organizations of the region driving Europeanization forward or ignoring it, respectively? Have administrative adaptations happened?

An analysis of regional Europeanization cannot stop at the regions. We assume the eagerness in pursuing active Europeanization to be a sign of the regions aiming to diminish their asymmetrical interdependent relationship with the state, and thus we have to take a look at the relations between the regions and the state, and between the regions and the EU. Basically, we are dealing with an analysis with three levels and a multitude of interactions within and among these levels.

Although we assume a strongly asymmetrical interdependent relationship between state and regions, it still is an *inter*dependent situation. In spite of a few political parties questioning the utility of the regional level, the state needs the regions; the state would have to undergo radical changes if the regions were not there to implement laws, bring services to citizens, report back on needs and effects of the laws and rules made centrally, etc. In the classic unitary state, the regions are totally dependent on the national centre. But does this model hold true today? Probably not; in *causa Europa* it sometimes happens that the regions are better and earlier informed than the central government and thus are able to act before it (cf, chapter 2). Thus, we assume that the regions may be able to diminish their dependence, but how does the situation look in reality? Has Europeanization been a strategy in this respect? Have the regions been able to make the asymmetry smaller as a consequence of the EU regional impact? Answering these questions will involve looking at how the regions formulate and communicate their interests at the national and the supra-national level.

In the conclusion of each national case study the political consequences of Europeanization will be assessed. Did the regions gain more influence? Were they able to lessen the assumed asymmetric relationship to the state? Are there indications of whether the relationship is under change?

The second, thematic, part of the book analyses topics in depth that could only be treated less intensively in the first part. These thematic chapters cover a high-profile example of direct vertical contacts between the regional and the European level, direct horizontal links between regions in different countries, and a functional area of public policy that has become increasingly regionalised and Europeanized: first, the question of sub-national external relations is analysed in the chapter *Nordic Regional Lobbying in Brussels* (chapter 6). The examination of the flourishing regional offices in Brussels tries to identify trends and lessons in the first decade or so, focusing on one EU member state (Sweden) and another non-member state (Norway).

Then questions of inter-regional relations and transnational region building move to the fore in two chapters. In *Regional Perspectives on Integration in the Baltic Sea Region* (chapter 7) the author aims to assess the future position of the 'Baltic Rim' in the European system. The impact of the economic changes in Europe after the fall of the Berlin Wall in 1989 are analysed in relation to the integration process, which is seen as the single most important social force in the process of transition of the Baltic Sea Region. This is followed by a study of one of the most prominent examples of cross-border region building in the chapter *Constructing a Transnational Mobility Region – on the Øresund Region and its Role in the New European Union Spatial Policy* (Chapter 8). Here the role of the Øresund Region in the new spatial policy of the EU is analysed. Among other things, this chapter emphasizes the necessity of understanding the importance of the interplay between new representations of space, institutions and practices of European spatial planning and their potential contribution to European political integration.

Finally the impact of the European Structural Funds on the aims and organization of economic development policy in Nordic regions is examined. First, *Denmark of the Regions? Europeanization, Multi-level Governance and Danish Regional Policy Strategies* (chapter 9) presents Denmark as a somewhat extreme example of the general European trend towards abolishing national incentive schemes as the main part of spatial economic policy, in favour of various EU schemes. The chapter examines this transformation process in order to find out to what extent the changes have increased the ability of the regions to follow their own agendas. Looking more specifically at the organization of development policy at the regional level, *Europeanization and Beyond – Regional Development through Partnership in Norway and Denmark* (chapter 10) is a comparative study, analysing regional development through partnership in the EU member state of Denmark, and the non-member state of Norway. The starting point is the assumption that the various partnerships are influenced by a variety of factors, but that it nevertheless – or perhaps especially so – becomes important to distinguish between different kinds of 'partnerships'. Thus the aim of this chapter is to investigate the changing nature of partnership in regional policy in order to establish the extent to which a European model has been transferred, adopted or circumvented.

All of these topics are relevant for all four Nordic countries and occupy central roles both on the national and regional levels, and focus on the interplay between regional strategies and processes of Europeanization. By concentrating on specific areas of regional activity, the thematic chapters allow a more detailed and balanced picture to emerge of the position of the Nordic regions within the larger European arena. In the last chapter (11) some general conclusions are drawn.

This book is the result of a project on Nordic regions and the European Union which is the offspring of a workshop held by the Nordic Political Science

Association (NOPSA) in Helsinki chaired by the editors some years ago. We are grateful to our colleagues, and contributors to this volume who share our interest in the regions and the EU. We would like to thank Professor Timothy Shaw for his constructive comments, as well as the team at Ashgate for their fast and professional handling of the manuscript. Last but not least, we are very grateful to research secretary Julie Larsen at Aalborg University for her help and patience.

The federalist scholar Denis de Rougemont attached great importance to the regions in the process of European integration, and with him many in Brussels (whether he is right is another question). As a spiritual father of the Union's regional policy, we let him end the introduction by stipulating why regions must be important for the integration process:

> Wie die Personen die Gemeinschaft braucht, um sich zu verwirklichen, und wie das Gemeinwesen nach der Region verlangt, so verlangt die Region die kontinentale Vereinigung (1980, p. 281).[7]

Bibliography

Baldersheim, Harald & Stålberg, Krister (2002), 'From Guided Democracy to Multi-Level Governance: Trends in Central – Local Relations in the Nordic Countries', in *Local Government Studies*, Vol. 28, No. 3.

Cortelius, Malene (2002), *Europæiseringen af danske amter*, Aalborg Universitetsforlag, Aalborg.

Dosenrode, Søren (1995), 'Going NUTS – Amter, delstater og kantoner i Europa', in *Nordisk Administrativt Tidsskrift*, No. 2, pp. 149-167.

Dosenrode, Søren (1997), 'Power to the Regions?' in Lastenouse-Bury, Jacqueline, *L'Union Européene B l'aubre d'un nouveau siΠcle, Libre Amicorum*, Ed. Juridica, S.A. Madrid.

Klausen, Kurt Klaudi (ed.) (1996), *Erfaringer med Internationalisering i Amter og Kommuner*, Odense Universitets Forlag.

Kleven, Terje et al. (2000), 'Renewal of Local Government in Scandinavia: Effects for Local Politicians', in *Local Government Studies*, Vol. 26, No. 2, pp. 93-116.

Radaelli, Claudio M. (2000), 'Whither Europeanization? Concept Stretching a Substantive Change', *European Online Papers* (EioP) Vol. 4, No 8, http://eiop.or.at/eiop/texte/2000-008a.htm (printed out May 2003).

de Rougemont, Denis (1980), *Die Zukunft ist unsere Sache*, Klett-Cotta Verlag, Stuttgart.

7 'As man needs community to realise himself, and as the community requires the region, so do the regions require continental unification' (my translation).

Chapter 2

Denmark

Søren Dosenrode

Preface: A Theoretical Hors d'Oeuvre

We know from previous studies that the sub-central level in various European states has been affected by the European integration process (cf. von Dosenrode, 1997; Jones and Keating, 1995). But *how has European integration influenced the Danish regions*? This is the main question we seek to answer in this chapter. The institutional unit of analysis is the Danish regions, the counties. The institutions and the policy-making are central for answering the main question in this analysis.

When looking for a theoretical framework, we turn to Rhodes. In his study of British sub-central government, Rhodes makes an all-encompassing analysis; in this study we are more modest, concentrating only on the regions. Using Rhodes' definition of sub-central government (1992, p. 14) is a good starting-point for the analysis of the Danish case. But we have to expand Rhodes' definition, and include the relationships to both the EU institutions as well as other regional units abroad. Thus we look at *the areas of political activity concerned with the relations between central political institutions in Copenhagen and Brussels, and the sub-central political organizations and governmental units*.

It is from this perspective that we look at the process of Europeanization. The most important relationship of the county[1] as sub-central government is the one to the centre(s), but the analysis must also include what Rhodes defines as inter-organizational relations. When analysing sub-central governments, Rhodes suggests dividing the relations mentioned above into two groups, the territorial representational relations and the intergovernmental relations. The 'territorial representation' refers to '*the representation of ethnic-territorial units at the centre and the activities of territorially based political organisations*' (1992, p. 15). In the Danish case this group consists of the secretariat of the Association of the Danish Regions (ADR,[2] Amtsrådsforeningen i Danmark) and the four regional representatives in the Committee of Regions in Brussels. In this group we also find

---

1 In this chapter the Danish term 'Amt' and the English terms 'region' and 'county' are used interchangeably.

2 Until 2002 the official translation of 'Amtsrådsforeningen' was 'Association of Danish County Councils' (ADCC), but as a consequence of the policy-decision to regard the counties as the regional level in Denmark, the English translation was changed.

the regional offices in Brussels. When looking at the intergovernmental relations we will have to look at the central-local relations as well as the relations within and among the regions '*the relations between all forms of governmental organizations*' as stated by Rhodes (1992, p. 15). This 'catch all' definition is too broad and all-encompassing for our purpose; our focus will be the county council, the county administration and the co-operation with the local level, i.e. the municipalities. This modification stresses the importance attached to the involved institutions. It is not enough just to look at the relations between various units, if the aim is to understand the Europeanization of the Danish counties; we will also look at the institutions involved. At the different levels of analysis the emphasis will be different according to which institutions are considered the most important.

Thus the theoretical inspiration for this analysis will be a mixed institutional and policy approach. With this approach it is important to keep the *levels of analysis* clear. In the Danish case it is correct to look at three levels, defined according to principal relationships. Each level has its dominant relationships and actors.

The Danish governmental system contains two sub-central levels; the municipalities (primærkommuner) and the counties (amtskommuner).[3] The municipalities are only to a minor degree subordinate to the counties. The county-municipalities relationship belongs to the intra-regional level, together with the other relationships within the county. We have to bear in mind that the central administration of the county consists of various departments and is not necessarily homogenous, and that each department has its own contacts to, for example, the relevant actors in the municipality administration. This level would, in Rhodes' terminology, be the micro level. The institutional focal point is the central administration of the county, the region.

The second level concerns the relations of the regions to the two centres, the national and the supra-national: the meso-level. The two main relationships, county-state and county-EU, are placed on the same analytical level, as we deal with relations to centres with a state-like character.[4] But the nation-state, Denmark, is by far the most important context or frame for the counties. In the first set of relations, county-state, the institutional focal points are the Association of Danish Regions as well as the Danish EU decision-making and co-ordination process. The second part of the region-centre relationships are the direct relations between the region and the EU institutions. The institutional focal points are the Committee of Regions and the Representations of the Regions in Brussels.

---

3 To be correct, there is also the 'state counties' (statsamterne). These entities are directly subordinate to the Ministry of Interior and conduct mainly legal functions, within the area of family law (adoptions, divorces etc.) and will only be touched upon sporadically in this analysis.

4 E.g. Søren Dosenrode (2003) or James Caporaso (1996). The former argues that the EU today possesses its own statehood, the latter argues for considering the EU an international state.

The third level consists of the national as well as the supra-national socio-economic and political environment. It forms the context of the two previous levels. This macro level sets the frame for the actions of the other two levels, and includes variables such as the European integration process (economic and political factors), the development of the Danish welfare state, and the developments in the political system.

It can be of no surprise that the relations in question are fairly complex, not totally unlike the concept of 'Multi-level governance', as proposed by Gerry Marks *et al.* (Gerry Marks, Lisbet Hooghe, Kermit Blank, 1996).

After these theoretical remarks, we will now turn to the introduction, in which the Danish regions are presented and where the national and supra-national socio-economic and political frames are outlined. Then follows the section on intra-regional relations and one on regional relations to Copenhagen (state – region relations) and to Brussels (EU – region relations). To round up this case study, the question 'power to the regions?' will be discussed.[5]

Introduction: The Danish Regions – An Overview

The Origin of the Regions

Although it is possible to trace the ancestry of today's counties (amter) to the feudal system and later to absolutism, it was not until the end of the 18th century that the counties received administrative and political structures that show a certain resemblance to today's counties. The original main task assigned to the governor (amtmanden) was to govern a certain part of the King's territory, the Amt, according to the King's commands. At that time the legal duties of the governor were extended to include the organization of a rudimentary health system, as well as the improvement of the quality of the roads.

Later, the 'county funds' (amtsrepartitionsfond) were created with the governor as the chairman to secure the financing, and to systematize the governor's budgets. Following that, the yearly county tax (amtsskatten) was introduced. The year 1803 brought the creation of a county poor-relief (Amtsfattigkasserne) and 1814 the primary school-funds, thus establishing the administrative and organizational main-sectors of today's county administrations, i.e. public health-care, schools and infrastructure.[6]

5 The empirical material for the following analysis consists of a variety of texts from the Danish counties, the ADCC/ADR and the ministries in Copenhagen (ranging from internal memoranda to official reports and laws), as well as systematic interviews with political and administrative actors representing most Danish counties, as well as the ADCC/ADR and the Central administration, all collected systematically over a period ranging from September 1992 to May 2003.

6 As Norway and Denmark formed a double monarchy until 1814, it is not surprising that one traces the same developments in Norway (cf. chapter 4).

County councils (Amtsråd) were created in 1841, and with them the first signs of a local democracy; but it was the governor, who chaired the sessions and had the final word. An important aspect of the reform was that the county councils had a formal right to make submissions to the central government in Copenhagen, and the ministries (Kollegierne) were obliged to consult the county councils in all important questions relating to the regions.

Beginning with a 'local government reform' in 1970, followed by a reform of duties, a reform of the economic burden-sharing between state, region and municipality, and ending with a reform of the budgeting system in 1977, the 1970s brought several important reforms concerning the division of rights and duties between the local, regional and national level. It was the first comprehensive attempt to reform the local and regional level since J. B. S. Estrup's rejected plans of 1867.

The municipality reform included the counties and implied a dramatic reduction of the number of sub-national territorial units. The number of counties was reduced from 23 to 14, and the number of municipalities decreased from around 1300 to 277. The arguments for these reforms were of an economic and rationalization nature. The new units should economically and administratively be able to fulfil the new tasks assigned to them. These tasks were linked to the welfare-state idea. To be able to administrate all the new tasks, professional administrations at the local and regional level were needed. The result was a dramatic decentralization of tasks previously performed by the central administration in Copenhagen. To control the new larger regional units, the rights of the county councils were strengthened, and the governor lost his central position as the chairman of the county council to an elected county mayor (amtsborgmester). But decentralization as such was not in itself seen as a virtue, something to pursue. It simply turned out to be the best way of solving the accumulated administrative problems (Mikkelsen in Dafolo, 1995, p. 19).[7]

Pedersen *et al.* argue that the 1970 reform created three new power centres as well as a certain 'job-sharing' (1994, pp. 59f).

The first was dominated by the Social Democratic party and included the major organizations of the labour market; this power centre was mainly in charge of regional development, labour-force mobility, etc. The second power-centre was aimed to put the regions and the municipalities in charge of the distribution of social welfare, and it was dominated by the Liberals and the Conservatives. The third power centre was ruled by the Ministry of Finance, which was in charge of the national-economic co-ordination of the municipalities.

As Pedersen rightly remarks, conflicts are pre-programmed, as the state is in charge of the overall economic decisions, while the sub-governmental level is taking care of the welfare system (1994, p. 60).

---

7 Since the municipality reform, the regional councils have taken over several new tasks, which before were in the hands of the Central Administration in Copenhagen (Amtsrådsforeningen, 1993, p. 9).

In 1996 the Social Democratic government set up a commission, with the task of evaluating the existing division of tasks between state, counties and municipalities. Those who had hoped for a major change in the Danish governmental system were disappointed. The major conclusion of the committee was that the present division of labour was basically sound and there was no reason to make larger changes (Betænkning nr 1366, p. 227). But the counties were not on the 'list of protected species', and the liberal-conservative government decided in 2002 to set up a 'structure commission' with the task of making an analysis of the pros and cons of alternative models for structuring the whole public sector. The commission should, *inter alia*, assess the size of municipalities and counties; and assess the advantages of abolishing the counties (cf. kommissorium). The counties signalized a basically positive attitude towards an evaluation of the structures, but found the old wish of the Conservative party, to abolish the counties, less wise, arguing that it is important to have a politically responsible level between municipalities and state, to prioritize and make decisions instead of centralization. Also, the present situation is the cheapest (cf. Bemærkninger, and *Jyllandsposten*, 29 February 2003). At the time of writing – the middle of 2003 – it looks as if the counties will continue, but that their size will be reduced from 14 to between five and eight.[8] An upgrade of the counties' size would, in addition to giving them a larger economic basis, move them up in the EU-regional hierarchy. Similar to the 1970s reform, the main emphasis is on economics, not on democracy, etc., thus it seems as if a good opportunity to discuss, *inter alia*, a regional parliament has been missed, again. The 'structural commission' is supposed to deliver its report at the end of 2003.

The Regions in the State System

The Danish constitution guarantees the counties and municipalities the right to govern their own affairs (§82), under the supervision of the state. Thus there should not exist a traditional system of superiority/inferiority in the sense of Max Weber. The government needs a law if it wants to oblige the regions to do this or that. On the other hand, §82 is vague and does not stipulate borders and criteria for what this 'independence' means. In Denmark one talks of the 'municipality/county proxy' (kommunalfuldmagten). Apart from doing what the law tells the counties (and municipalities) to do, they are entitled to take their own initiatives as long as 1) they do not interfere with the free market forces, 2) they do not discriminate against certain groups of citizens, and 3) they do not interfere with policies of the

---

8 I support my guess with the following indications: the Minister of Interior has been quoted as declaring that he would like to reduce the 'state counties' (statsamterne) to five (cf. *Politiken*, 7 February 2003) and a report on the hospital system suggested that a popular basis of 400,000 to 700,000 persons per 'central hospital' was needed and the hospitals are one of the major responsibilities of the counties.

parliament (cf. Dosenrode, 2002, p. 292). The right to collect taxes is an important instrument for the counties and municipalities to safeguard their rights.

Traditionally the counties were superior to the municipalities; this relationship was to a very large extent abolished with the reform in 1970. It was the logical consequence of the fundamental principle of delegating tasks to the lowest possible level. Thus in an ideal world, the counties and municipalities would be complementary. The only leftover of the former supremacy of the counties over the municipalities is the 'council of supervision' (tilsynsrådet). This council consists of the state county governor (stiftsamtmanden) and four members of the county council. Its task is to check that the decisions made by the municipality councils are legally correct, and that the budget is made according to the rules applicable.

Table 2.1 Principles of regional administrative organization

	National Level	*Regional Level*	*Local Level*
Territorial Unit	Denmark	Regions	Municipalities
Governing Unit	Government	Regional Mayor	Municipality Mayor
Democratic Unit	Parliament	Regional Council	Municipality Council

The guiding principle of the reforms of the 1970s was to delegate tasks to the lowest economically possible level, i.e. the national, regional or the local level.

The duties of the county councils are reflected in their budgets. The average percentages are as follows: the public hospital and health-insurance sector comes out as a clear number one, as 70 per cent of the budget is ascribed to it, followed by education and culture (10%), social- and health-services (9%), regional planning, environment and roads (4%), administration (7%) (Amtsrådsforeningen, 2003, p. 14).[9] Over the past years, the state subvention to the regions has declined radically (cf. chapter 9), and now only constitutes four per cent of the counties' income, whereas 85 per cent of their income comes from income tax, and 11 per cent comes from tax on property (Amtsrådsforeningen, 2003, p. 13). Thus the counties are in reality self-financing, with a budget of approximately 80 billion DKK in 2003.

Although the 'Law on the governance of municipalities' (Loven om kommuners styrelse) gives the regions (and the municipalities) great liberties in how to organize their administration, most county councils have organized the regional administration very much alike. The law only imposes that the counties are to be led by a democratically elected county council, which is presided over by the county mayor. The county council has to form an economic committee as well as at least one other 'standing committee' for the administration of the region's affairs.

9 Compared to the expenses in 1992, one notices that the share of hospitals and health insurance as well as county administration have risen by five and three per cent respectively (Amtsrådsforeningen, 1992, p. 19).

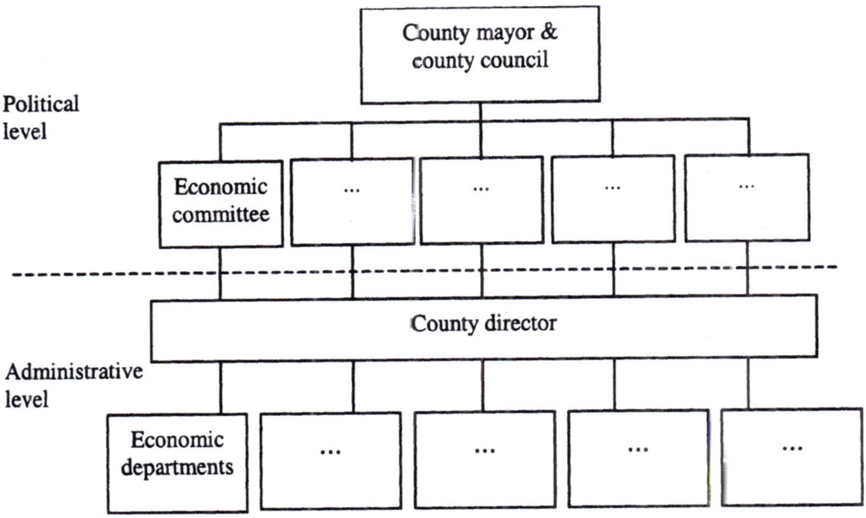

Figure 2.1 The Danish counties

Traditionally, the county councils have around five standing committees. The county administration is organized parallel to the political level. There is an administrative branch for each of the standing committees. The economic branch of the county administration is *primus inter pares*, and normally functions as the central administrative unit. The county mayor plays the role of a 'connecting link' between the county administration and the county council, as he is head of the former and chairman of the latter.

Compared to the Austrian or German *Bundesländer* the Danish counties have a primarily administrative nature, without a historic past as sovereign or semi-sovereign states. There is no tradition of federalism in Denmark (cf. Dosenrode, 2002).

The National (and Supra-National) Socio-economic and Political Frame

The *national* socio-economic framework is dominated by the Danish economy of negotiation. According to Pedersen *et al.* (1994, p. 34f) one of the most important political events at the beginning of the 1950s was the creation of the concept of a societal, a national economy. This new economy was to become the basis for the economy of negotiation. The economy of negotiation is the means to achieve the goal: Denmark as one (national) economy.

Today one can argue that the results of the development beginning in the 1950s has led to the development of a new, independent political system for decision-making and administration of the national economy. It includes a quasi-autonomous and partly closed set of institutions, a development very much in line with Helmut Willke's theories of the development of Western states (1992).

> [...] The national economic constitution does not include an absolute state. Neither does it include institutions with absolute power. The national economic constitution is something new: a national co-operation. An interplay has been developed among political parties and civil servants, government and interest organization and it has got its power centres in many places [...]. Institutions have been created and cross the borders between public authority and private interest, without [...] the state having deprived individuals, concerns or interest organizations of their fundamental independence, and without [...] the state being reduced to a weak and secluded guardian of liberty and morals. A strong state in a strong society [...] (Ove K. Pedersen *et al.*, 1994, p. 44, my translation).

The frame within which the regions will have to act is of large complexity and low transparency. To get influence, one has to be able to find the right fora, *and* to be admitted to them.

As mentioned previously, the EU constitutes the *supra-national* frame; a frame which today possesses its own statehood (cf. Dosenrode, 2003). The main purpose of the founding fathers of the present EU was to prevent a future war and to create the basis of a European federation. The means of the Christian Democrats Robert Schuman, Jean Monnet, Alcide de Gaspari and Konrad Adenauer was twofold; to deprive the two prime antagonists, Germany and France, of the means of a new arms race, by putting coal and steel production under a supra-national authority (European Coal and Steel Community), and to secure prosperity, thus preventing social unrest and new nationalism (European Economic Community). As the possibility of a war between France and Germany became more and more unlikely, the purpose of the European Community gradually changed towards a) a narrow liberal focus on prosperity, as the Single European Act (with the internal market programme) and the plans for the European Monetary Union clearly demonstrate, and b) the creation of a genuine Union.

Of special relevance here is that to be able to make the shift of ideology from Christian Democratic values to liberal ideas, it has been necessary to calm the potential losers, i.e. the periphery and especially the southern part of the Union. This is also a necessity, if a European federal state is to have any endurance. Thus the European regional policy was revitalized together with the gradual implementation of the internal market programme beginning in the 1980s.[10] This served the purpose of furthering integration through involving the regions, through

10 In the 2002-2006 budget of the Union, the Structural Funds as well as the Cohesion Fund count for approximately 34 per cent of the total budget. The admission of the new Eastern European member states in 2004 has rather severe consequences for the old member states, as the budget is not being expanded, and more needy regions are now joining.

institutionalizing the involvement of the regions, through the Committee of Regions, thus putting the member states under pressure.

Today there are a variety of differences between a 'normal' liberal democratic state and the Union, although the EU today has begun to look very much more like a 'traditional' state (cf. Dosenrode, 2003).

What is important in our case is to emphasize the complexity of decision-making, the constitutional fights between (and among) the European institutions on the one side and the member states on the other side, and that the regions play their part in this game often as allies of the Commission in its fight for power.[11]

The Intra-regional Relations

In the previous part, we looked at the national and the supra-national frame; now we turn to the micro-level.

At the regional level, within the county, Europeanization can be looked at in various ways: the institutional aspects of the county council and administration, the relationship between the county council and the administration on one side and the municipality on the other, and the county's relations to local business.

To start out, we will briefly discuss the concepts of Europeanization of the regional administrations and the regional councils. The concept of Europeanization is described rather arbitrarily, or rather, in the way that suits the individual author best. In this chapter, I understand the concept of Europeanization as the EU-related part of the general concept of internationalization. I define Europeanization as the increasing degree to which the regions are influenced, and are involved in developments going on outside their home-country, but within the EU (von Dosenrode, 1997, p. 395).[12] In this definition, there are three implicit aspects: a) a passive, b) a mental and c) an active (cf. chapter 1). The *passive* aspect is characterized by the counties acting upon EU legislation, which they have not been involved in laying down, and which has been transferred into national law. The second aspect, the *mental* one, is less tangible: that the counties have civil servants responsible for EU matters that some counties have representatives in Brussels; that some counties send a democratically elected representative to the Committee of Regions. All of these influence some civil servants and some politicians to think 'European'. One can talk of the counties' growing awareness of the surrounding environment. It is, to a certain extent, the precondition for the third aspect: *active* Europeanization is characterized by the active, conscious and voluntary participation of the counties in activities, where one or more of the co-actors are of a different nationality from the counties.

11 For a detailed discussion of the EU decision-making system, see von Dosenrode, 1997.

12 See Claudio Radaelli's definition in footnote 6, page 3.

Passive Europeanization of the Regions

The initiative to relaunch the basic idea of the founding fathers of the EU, a real common market, came up in the first half of the 1980s. The basic idea was that dismantling all trade barriers would further economic efficiency and prosperity in the participating states. The result was the Single European Act (SEA). The content of the Internal Market Programme ('1992') can be grouped into four pillars. The first concerns the 'four liberties' (free movement of labour, capital, goods and services), the second the adaptation of laws, the third initiatives that were to strengthen competition, and the fourth provisions on the common external customs (Nugent, 2003, pp. 298-305). This qualitative and quantitative leap forward was bound to involve the European regions.

The typical tasks of regions within the EU, including the Danish counties, are found within the fields of education, public health, infrastructure/public transportation (roads, harbours, etc.), social policy (old age, unemployment), environmental protection and regional development. These policy areas are particularly related to the implementation of the four liberties of the Internal Market. But the regions of centralized states, such as Denmark, were not significantly involved in the negotiations leading to the SEA and to the Treaty on European Union (TEU), although large parts of the SEA directly imposed new duties and extra work on them. This implies that the regions will have to live with this Europeanization even if they were not involved in the shaping of it.

Especially the competition rules of the SEA have had a lasting influence on the daily administration of the regional administration (Madsen, 1997). EU directives on public procurement lay down rules on procedure, time limits, publication, technical specifications, etc. which bind the public institutions when procuring something with a value of more than €200,000 (Bjørnbak, no year, p. 7). As this price-limit is fairly low, the EU procedure on public procurement is often used by the regional administrators, who, for practical reasons, have had to form special sections or groups to handle such cases.

These procurement directives give the EU a high visibility in the county administrations although the SEA and the following treaties have not caused big changes in the administrative structures of the county administrations. But all county administrations have created an economic development department (erhvervsafdeling), and very often the county's EU co-ordinator as well as the co-ordinator for social funds have been placed there. Thus an 'EU section' has been created in most county administrations.

As the SEA has been the driving force behind the revitalized European regional policy, the 'Open Process of Co-ordination' often referred to as the Lisbon Process, will potentially strengthen passive Europeanization in years to come. The process includes, *inter alia*, topics such as education and measures against unemployment, in other words central areas for the counties.

In the county administrations, 'European cases' are treated just like 'normal cases'. There are several reasons for that (Dosenrode, 2002, p. 300, and esp.

Dosenrode, 1995, p. 158f): 1) the majority of the county administration has no contact with the EU; when an EU directive reaches the county, it *looks* like a normal, Danish administrative regulation; 2) although 'regions' have been on the agenda since the middle of the 1970s due to the European Regional Development Fund and the Consultative Council of Regional and Local Authorities created in 1988, it has gained visibility since the Maastricht treaty created the Committee of Regions. The EU Regional Policy has been concerned with the national government and civil servants, not the regional government; and 3) it has not been considered necessary to change the normal working procedures, or structures, for that matter.

Mental Europeanization[13]

The mental aspect of Europeanization *is* very important. Awareness of European affairs has grown especially within the county administrations, but also in the councils of all counties, especially in those with an active policy of Europeanization. This new awareness has several implications. First of all, it is the first step in a process which eventually may lead to some kind of active Europeanization. Another very important implication is that the self-esteem of the county councils and administrations in their dealings with the national government (and the municipalities) has grown, thus diminishing asymmetric dependence. Civil servants also report that Europeanization has broadened their views of how to do things, thus creating greater flexibility and more effective administration (interviews, 1995 and 2003). A senior civil servant in the Association of County Councils expressed it like this: 'Europeanization has made it easier to be a county in Denmark' (Interview, 1995).

Active Europeanization

Active Europeanization is basically voluntary. Thus it is relevant to look for the motives of the county councils and administrations, for taking on an international activity.[14] A quotation from a discussion paper of the county directors (Amtsrådsforeningen, 1988, p. 37, my translation) set the reasons and priorities very clearly:

> The growth and well-being of the local economy is the crucial fundament for collecting taxes, for the extent of social welfare and the level of public services in the municipalities and regions.

---

13 Malene Cortelius discusses the degree of Europeanization in four Danish counties (2002, pp. 83-91).

14 Internationalization per se is nothing new. Since the end of the Second World War, the regions have concluded a number of 'friendship treaties', especially with Nordic regions. These agreements have had the aim of promoting understanding and friendship among the peoples, and have until lately only peripherally had a commercial aim.

Next in the list of priorities comes the wish to enhance the influence of the counties vis-à-vis the national and the supra-national level. This is followed by the staff-developing aspect (personaleudvikling) and the wish for better understanding amongst the peoples. The motives and their priorities are very clear. In the period 1992-97 the 14 county administrations were involved in 483 international projects (Amtsrådsforeningen, 1997, p. 5).[15] The level of activity varies strongly between the various counties: the county of Roskilde, for example, had one project in this period, whereas the county of Storstrøm was involved in 80 projects. Naturally, the administrative and political consequences vary as much among the counties.[16]

The changes in the regional development funds will have a great influence on the Danish counties, especially the peripheral ones. Until now they have benefited from being Objective 2 areas, but this is now changing as a consequence of the eastern enlargement of the Union. With no – or few – direct subventions from the Union, other ways of co-operation are being pursued, with an emphasis on knowledge sharing between regions in the old member states, as well as partnerships with regions in the new member states. The assumption from civil servants of the ADR is that there will have to be a trade-off which pays in the long run, otherwise the old states will lose their interest in sponsoring the poor regions. While there is a lot of logic in this reasoning, it runs counter to the state-project of the Union, where economic assistance to underdeveloped regions serves the aim of keeping the difference between the 'rich' and the 'poor' on an acceptable level to secure the cohesion of the Union.

The reason for this great difference in the level of activity among Danish regions is due to a variety of circumstances, but the economic situation of the county has a high explanatory power. It is no coincidence that the County of Nordjylland, which has had one of the highest unemployment rates, has seen EU programmes as one way of attracting resources to the region. Another important factor is the personal interest of leading civil servants and – to a lesser degree – the members of the regional councils. With no tradition of internationalization, facing a completely new field, it has to a large extent been up to the individual civil servants to take initiatives for internationalization or do nothing. The initiatives for active Europeanization mostly come from the civil servants, or to a lesser degree from private enterprise in the county, but rarely from the council, i.e. from the elected politicians. In a collection of essays written by municipality and county civil servants, it appears again and again that they are the active ones, and that they have to make politically binding decisions lying outside their traditional realm...

15 Unfortunately, no more recent figures are available, but civil servants of the ADR share the opinion that this development has continued, although no quantitative indicators are available.

16 Cf. the comprehensive survey of the international activities of the counties, published by the Association of Danish County Councils (International Cooperation Projects, Amtsrådsforeningen, 1997).

and that they do not like it (e.g. Christensen in Klausen, 1996). The reasons for this are seen in the better educations of the civil servants (foreign languages, etc.).

It appears that the international involvement of counties grew within the administrative branch before it received political interest and legitimation. Europeanization seemed to be politically uninteresting in the county councils for many years (Klausen in Klausen, 1996, p. 194), and in 2003 it has a high priority in only a few county councils. As Christensen remarked back in 1996, international activity is all right as long as everything goes well, but if one day an initiative fails, and it has large economic consequences, it would be a catastrophe, for the civil servant in particular, but also for the reliability of the county council as a democratically elected body (in Klausen, 1996, p. 36).

Regional – Local Co-operation

The county-municipality relationship should theoretically be unproblematic as it rests on complementarity. In reality it looks different, both concerning EU affairs and other policy areas. In spite of the fact that the large cities and counties would have obvious advantages if they co-operated on EU matters, co-operation is difficult. If one, for example, looks at the seemingly obvious idea of opening joint offices in Brussels, only two localities, Aalborg and Århus, succeeded in setting up such offices (cf. Amtsrådsforeningen, 2003a) and the region's main city co-operation was by no means without problems. The counties have preferred to work together with other counties, rather than with their main city (e.g. the County of Fyn has an office together with the County of Sønderjylland, not with the city of Odense). The County of Nordjylland cancelled its co-financing of an office in Brussels with Aalborg city for a period, and only joined again when the county of Viborg also joined. The same happened with the Organization of Municipalities and the Association of County Councils: after a few years together in Brussels, they split up. Now each has their own office. There are several possible explanations: the larger municipalities (Copenhagen, Odense, Aalborg, Århus) all have the necessary economic potential to 'do it alone'. These municipalities often feel that they can attract more investments, etc., if they embark on their own development policy instead of relying on the county, which has to look after *all* areas in the county, not only the prosperous ones. But by pursuing an active development policy, they often come into conflict with the county's overall development policy. Thus conflicts of interest are pre-programmed. If one pushed the argument, one could add that the municipalities have enjoyed a position of primacy over the counties for decades; the municipalities were present in the mind of the public, representing a lot of positive images such as local democracy, local trouble-shooters, etc. The counties, on the other hand, were remote and mainly associated with raising taxes and problems with the management of the seemingly ungovernable health sector. Since the SEA, some of the counties have been able to gain more positive credit (structural funding, etc.), thus potentially threatening the primacy of the municipalities. Some county civil servants expressed the view that poor co-operation on European questions was due to the fact that the counties have had too much success (interviews, 1995; 1997; 2003). Klausen explains the lack of co-operation on Funen and around the capital like this (in Klausen, 1996, p. 197 translated by the author):

> All initiatives for co-operation have stopped due to lack of political will, old traditional conflicts of interest as well as due to personal envy and resentments.

And in 2003 this still holds true in many places.

The Relations of the Counties to the Two Centres

Regional participation in the EU decision-making process is double-tracked, seen with the eyes of the Danish counties; the regions have their direct relations to Copenhagen as well as to Brussels. This has implications, not only for EU-related topics, but also for the general state-county relationship. Thus we start out by looking at the relationship of the counties to the government, i.e. the national level, including the participation of the counties in the Danish EU co-ordination and decision-making process. Then we turn to the Danish counties' direct connections to the EU.

Relationship to the National Centre

The relationship between the counties and the national centre is characterised by the interplay of factors, e.g. that Denmark is a centralized state, but that counties and municipalities formally have self-governance, and that the sub-national level controls more than 65 per cent of total public expenditures. This underlines why a system of negotiations is important. The three parties in this system are: the national government (and its central administration), the Association of Danish Regions (with its secretariat) and the Organization of Municipalities (with its secretariat). All three parties have democratic legitimacy, thus creating a system of shared statehood, or 'internal multi-level governance'.

There are a variety of formal and informal networks in which actors of different backgrounds negotiate the general problems of relationship and financial development, as well as concrete questions concerning new tasks that the sub-national level is going to take on, how to finance them, etc. One example is the 'budget co-operation' where state, counties and municipalities negotiate taxes, financial activities, etc. at the sub-national level within the framework of the national economy. The most important negotiations are undertaken under the direct supervision of the Ministry of Finance. This is a new tendency corresponding to the notion of Denmark as 'one large economy' i.e. a negotiated economy. Previously, the Ministry of Interior was the undisputed ***primus inter pares***, now it is the Ministry of Finance. The civil servants are leading actors – conducting all the preliminary negotiations, trying to find ways for compromises, etc., but they leave the field for the politicians to make the final decisions.

Who decides in the power relations between state and counties? The popular term 'negotiation' implies a certain degree of equality, otherwise one party could simply dictate; this in fact happened several times in the mid 1980s as well as in 2001, when the state used sanctions to force the sub-national actors to conform. But, generally, the rule of the game is very close, daily co-operation between the state and the sub-national actors. The Association of Danish Regions is heard every time the government prepares new rules or legislation concerning the counties. The civil servants of the ADR bring factual knowledge and legitimacy into the game, and they get influence in return. But the state is the unquestioned *primus*; in case of conflict the government can, for example, submit bills to Parliament which may create a new law forcing the counties to comply.

According to some authors, the relationships among state – county – and municipality are changing. Originally, there was a clear centralized national government granting the municipals self-governance; now it has changed to a system of co-governance with some kind of national confederation in which the important decisions are made through negotiations among the three parties listed above (e.g. Pedersen *et al.*, 1994, pp. 52-70). While this is exaggerated, it is clear that the state – sub-national level relationship is very close, and that there is a wide range of actors: the government with its officials, the organizations with their political leaders and civil servants, as well as members of Parliament and party officials.

A central actor in the government – county relationship is the Association of Danish Regions with its secretariat. Its tasks are to represent the counties in their negotiations with the state and the municipalities, to negotiate salaries, etc. for all the people employed by the counties and to advice and consult its members, the counties. The ADR's board is elected by the county councils, and all its members are themselves members of a county council, and has, as mentioned above, a great degree of democratic legitimacy. The board is assisted by a secretariat of approximately 95 academics. This secretariat is in a grey zone between administration and politics. It prepares and participates in the drafting of new legislation, and it is the secretariat that helps to implement new legislation in the counties. Within this secretariat, an international section has been created. It co-ordinates the international affairs of the ADR, runs and staffs the office of the Danish Counties in Brussels, assists the four county-elected members of the Committee of Regions, keeps an eye on the international activities of the counties and assists with advice if asked.

The secretariat of the ADR represents the counties on a day-to-day basis in the Danish EU co-ordination and decision-making procedure, to which we will draw our attention now.

The Participation of the Counties in the Danish Part of the EU Decision-making Process

Before turning to the participation of the counties in the Danish part of the EU decision-making procedure, let us briefly look at the EU decision-making process.

Decision-making in the EU is in the first and decisive phases (problem definition, agenda setting) dominated by the European Commission, with the legally founded quest for promoting the unification process. In these phases the Commission is easily influenced by all kinds of lobbyists, including regional representatives. In the later phases of the decision-making process (policy formulation) the member states are domineering, but depending on the conditions in the individual member state, the following implementation phase again opens up possibilities of regional influence.

What is important in our case is to emphasize the complexity of the decision-making, the constitutional fights between (and among) the European institutions on the one side and the member states on the other, and that the regions play their part in this game, often as allies of the Commission in its fight for power.[17] We return to the channels of influence of the counties later, but as figure 2.3 indicates, it is often possible for the regions to participate in the decision-making process at an earlier stage than the Danish state.

17 For a detailed discussion of the EU decision-making system, see von Dosenrode, 1997.

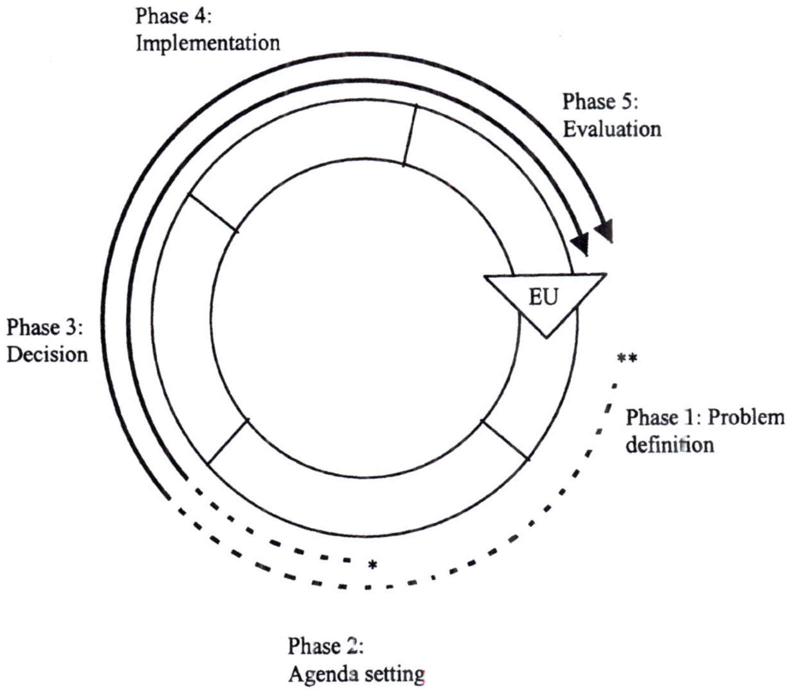

Figure 2.2 The EU policy cycle

Note: * Danish state, ** Counties
Source: I have adapted this model from the discussions of Adrienne Windhoff-Hëretier (1987), *Policy Analyse*, Frankfurt. One has to be aware that in reality the policy process is very much less linear and often 'messy'.

The *formal* part of the Danish EU co-ordination and decision-making procedure is built up around co-ordination and consultation committees on various levels with different actors. On the lowest level one finds the 'EU special committees' (EU-specialudvalgene); there were 35 in 2003. Their task is to co-ordinate the points of view of the involved ministries on a single issue or policy area The work at this level was expected to be of a specific and technical nature, but it includes very political aspects too. Since 1990 the ADR has been represented in approximately 13 of these committees by civil servants from its secretariat. It is not represented on any other level. The next level is the 'EU Committee' (EU-udvalget), a senior official co-ordination committee that has to co-ordinate the submissions of the 35 special committees and filter political from administrative issues and lead the former on to the government. The highest administrative level is the government, especially its Foreign Political Committee (Regeringens Udenrigspolitiske Udvalg). Its main task is to decide the Danish stand on issues that are negotiated in the EU. Before the government can participate in the meetings of the Council in

Brussels, it has to get the consent of the Folketing, or rather it has to ensure that there is not a majority against its stand. This is done in the parliamentary European Committee (Europaudvalget).

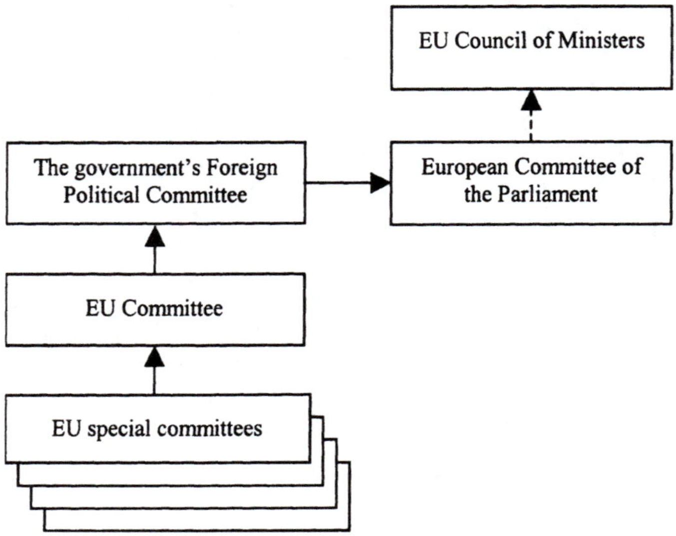

Figure 2.3 Denmark's EU co-ordination system

The formal structure does not reveal the whole truth about the Danish EU decision-making process. The rhetorical idea concerning the Danish EU co-ordination and decision-making system is a system where the government and the parliament jointly, i.e. the politicians, shape and decide the Danish EU stand. To find out who decides, one has to look at the involved networks. They are built around the formal structures described above. There are two important conglomerate networks in Danish EU policy formulation: the administrative – corporative network, and the parliamentarian network.[18] The administrative – corporative network consists of 37 sub-networks: the 35 special committee networks, the co-ordination network, and the ministerial network. The special committees sub-networks are the most important in the daily formulation of Danish EU policy. They *can* be involved at an early stage in the EU decision-making process. It is strong a sub-network, with authority towards the outside. The strongest are those with formal or informal contacts to the interest organizations (IOs). To co-ordinate the recommendations of the special committees networks, a co-ordination network has been set up around the EU Committee. Its tasks are important, but it rarely changes the recommendations of the special committees

18 For a detailed analysis of this approach as well as of the networks and their actors, function and power relations, see von Dosenrode, 1997 and Dosenrode, 2000.

networks substantially; words such as 'pragmatic' and 'informal' are characteristic of its approach. The third part of the network is the ministerial network. It bridges the gap to the parliamentary network and it prepares the negotiations in Brussels. Altogether we have a conglomerate network with fairly clear roles and functions. It is a strong network which decides most Danish EU policy.

The second important network is the parliamentary network, centred around the European Committee of the Parliament. The Committee's task is to control and influence Danish EU policy in the name of the electorate. The committee is the meeting point of the parliamentary and the administrative co-operative network. In spite of its high legitimacy, its real powers have been limited since the Danish 'no' to Maastricht in 1992, due to political considerations. The problem is that the Danish population is divided into two equally large groups concerning their attitude to Danish EU membership. This dividing line does not correspond to the usual political spectrum. Thus several political parties are internally divided on EU matters. This tended to paralyse the members of the Committee for several years,[19] but after the successful Danish EU presidency in the second half of 2002, it seems as if a certain amount of activity has returned, although it is still too early to tell.

The counties have, as mentioned, been represented in the EU special committees since 1990, but not in the other fora of the administrative – corporative network. Their experiences with these relations are, however, not as positive as their experiences with their participation in the purely national legislative process.

One of the purposes of the EU special committees is to hear the opinions of the parties involved; this was decided when the EU co-ordination and decision-making procedure was established shortly before Danish membership in 1972. But ADR representatives in the special committees share the opinion that since the second half of the 1990s the administrative culture has changed. The central administration is no longer as interested in the opinions of the ADR as it was at the beginning of the 1990s, and that gives the representatives an uneasy feeling of participating in a 'legitimation exercise'. They support this argument by the observation that they now get cases later than before and that their remarks are not incorporated in the final submissions unless they oppose vigorously. The nature of co-operation in the EU special committees used to be based on a culture of consensus. This has changed: now it is often the representatives of the ministries and of one or two of the interest organizations that write the submissions without listening to the ADR, unless the ADR protests vigorously. The result is that the ADR has begun to neglect the EU Special Committees in favour of other fora. When an issue is important to the civil servants of the ADR they have other possibilities to exert influence: a) they may ask for a political intervention from the chairman of the ADR, where he typically writes to the European Committee of the Parliament as well as to the Government b) much of the ADR's activities are now transferred to the European level and these channels are used frequently, or c) they may try to use

19 Cf. von Dosenrode, 1997, and Dosenrode, 2000.

the two new contact groups which have been formed, due to the pressure of the ADR.

As an input to the Danish discussion of the Intergovernmental Conference on the revision of the Treaty of the European Union in 1996, the ADR voiced their concerns as well as their ideas as follows (Amtsrådsforeningen, 1996): in the first phases of the policy cycle, the European Commission is too closed. The various working groups which the Commission consults do not possess the knowledge about Danish counties that is necessary in order to make adequate legislation in the following phases. Thus the ADR suggested creating Danish 'shadow groups', who could advise and help the Danish government's working group members. The problem with this suggestion is that the national governments do not necessarily have representatives in these early phases of the policy process, as mentioned above; the members of the working groups are chosen by the Commission according to their own priorities (cf. Dosenrode, 2000). The same problem turns up in the ADR's next suggestion that it should be possible for the counties to send 'national experts' to the Commission's working groups. Although there are often civil servants from the central administration participating in the working groups of the Commission, this is not a rule laid down in a legal text. In other words, the ADR implicitly asked for a changed and much more transparent EU policy process.

The ADR's suggestions concerning the later phase of the policy process, i.e. when the national governments are involved within the framework of the Council of Ministers, were – theoretically – easier to implement. Although the Danish EU special committees were supposed to be factual and non-political, this is not the case; the counties often feel pushed aside by the economic interest organizations present in the committees. Therefore, factual arguments on, for example, the economic and administrative consequences of new directives are not taken into consideration when the committee makes its submission to the higher levels in the network. Thus the ADR suggests creating what other states have, too: a political co-ordination committee including the government and the two sub-national organizations (Amtsrådsforeningen, 1996, p. 10). Such a committee would reduce the danger that representatives of the central state and of certain private interest organizations work together in the special committees networks and thus suppress the needs of the counties.

The creation of the so-called 'Ove Fick-Committee', named after the then chairman of the Parliamentary European Committee in 1995, was seen as a potential step in the 'right' direction. The European Committee of the Parliament has met two to three times a year with the Danish members of the Committee of Regions and the Danish members of the Economic and Social Committee to discuss topics of mutual interest – the Danish members of the European Parliament are invited, too, but seldom turn up. The network is a mix of politicians from various levels (Parliament, (EP), regions and municipalities), representatives of interest organizations (ESC) and civil servants. The ADR assesses these meetings as important, as they cross several political levels and facilitate a mutual understanding of each other's points of view. The problem with this committee is that there are no ministers in it and that it lies in the 'wrong' network. 'Wrong' network because the parliamentary network is still less influential than the administrative corporative network. In 2003 it still does not look as if a co-ordination group including the government, the counties and the municipalities is on its way, and the ADR does not press much any longer.

When the Open Co-ordination Process was introduced in 2000, the ADR got uneasy about this development. As mentioned above, several of the issues under this procedure are the duty of the counties, so if the government agrees to do something, for example, in the field of unemployment or education, it may very well be the counties which have to pay the bill for new obligations. With this background the ADR persuaded the government to establish a committee, presided over by the Foreign Office, and including all relevant ministries, the ADR, the Association of Municipalities as well as other interest organizations, with the task of keeping the organizations informed on the initiatives on the agenda of the European Council, which may end in a decision, where the Open Co-ordination Process is used.[20] This committee is considered as very useful, seen through the eyes of the ADR, as it gets information, and is able to give information, and thus is regarded as a valuable partner, with the influence it brings.

The latest initiative is the meetings of the ADR and the Association of Municipalities twice a year with the Permanent Danish Representation in Brussels. Before each new EU presidency the ADR and the Association of Municipalities meet with the Danish diplomats in Brussels, to exchange information on the coming presidencies' focal points. The ADR regards this as a very important source of information as well as a good opportunity to establish contacts with the relevant people sent out from Denmark to assist the representation.

The Relations to the Supra-national Centre

The ADR's final leap onto the European scene was accomplished by the opening of a joint county-municipality office in Brussels in October 1991. But already two years before that, a joint county-municipality EC-secretariat had been opened in Copenhagen; this joint venture lasted only until the end of 1993.

The activities of the Danish counties on the European level fall into four groups: 1) membership of the Committee of Regions, 2) direct contact with the Commission, 3) membership of European interest organizations, 4) regional offices in Brussels and lobbying. The first three groups of activities are prepared through the ADR and its secretariat, including its office in Brussels. The fourth group is run by individual counties.

---

20 The initiative to this committee came from the ADR, and they had wanted it to be exclusive for the public authorities ie. state, regions and municipalities. The Government decided to water it down by letting 'relevant' interest organizations in.

From a Danish county's point of view, two of the Committee of Regions' main achievements are to legitimize county contacts to the EU, especially to the Commission, and to symbolize the alternative to the Danish government. Both aspects are strongly supported by the Commission. The counties have become European actors.[21] In terms of actual power, one should not exaggerate the importance of the Committee of Regions,[22] but it serves well in a number of symbolic ways. Also, when a region is spokesman on a certain issue, it is able to draw on the Commission's civil servants and their expertise, thus getting very close contact with the Commission, often at an early phase of the decision-making process. Over the last few years, the work in the Committee of Regions has increased in importance for the ADR. Out of the nine Danish members, four represent counties, four represent municipalities and one represents the capital Copenhagen.[23] It is the secretariat of the ADR that, with the help of their office in Brussels, assists the representatives of the counties.

In the first decade of its 'European engagement' the Secretariat of ADR kept close contacts with the relevant General-Directorates of the European Commission, a practice that was facilitated by the Committee of Regions; they had become 'members of the family'. It was the impression of civil servants of the ADR's Secretariat that the Commission was attentive to suggestions and opinions. This has changed over the last few years. Although it occasionally happens that the ADR is invited to participate in the Commission's working groups, the main emphasis now is on the Committee of Regions. The Commission is today overburdened with lobbyists, thus the ADR gets much more out of using the privileges as part of the system. The problem is still that the ADR is not always aware that something is in the pipeline and it can therefore not always express its opinion. Thus one of the important roles of the ADR's office in Brussels is to monitor developments and to report back when something potentially interesting is going on.[24]

Corresponding to the growing feeling of being ignored in the Danish EU decision-making system, the ADR has started to concentrate on the European

21 '"Maastricht" obliges the consultation of the Regional Committee on policy proposals in the fields of education, employment, public health, culture, trans-European networks, and economic and social cohesion. At the request of the European Commission or at its own initiative, when specific regional interests are at stake, the Committee can forward "Opinions" (van der Knaap, 1994, p. 89). Peter van der Knaap has analysed and described the Committee. I refer to his analysis or to Thomas Wiedman's (2002).

22 A senior civil servant of the ADR with experience of the Committee said that it had problems creating a focus and thus often 'runs in too many directions, talking too much'.

23 Within the Committee of Regions, the nine Danish members feel an over-proportional power; this is because they are well prepared and always try to find a common Danish stand in spite of sometimes diverging interests between Danish counties and municipalities.

24 This problem is shared by the member states, and is a frequently heard complaint in the Danish central administration.

interest organizations. One civil servant in the ADR Secretariat expressed it as follows: 'If we only got our information from the central administration, we would have no influence at all'. The European interest organizations are often parties in negotiations with the Commission, and through them the ADR can influence directives and their implementation, without involving the Danish government (cf. figure 2.3). This strategy is used more and more: in some cases the ADR is meeting and negotiating more often in Brussels than in the relevant Danish EU special committees. 'That is our new way of working', said a representative of the ADR in 1997, and this was repeated in 2003.

Fundraising, or lobbying for the individual counties belongs to the realm of the individual counties. The ADR's work is politically and administratively oriented, working for all counties. The majority of the counties have chosen to set up an office in Brussels.[25] The counties around and in the capital – Copenhagen Frederiksborg and Roskilde have not. They are situated in areas of growth, take part in the Øresund region (cf. chapter 8), and never had the possibility of profiting from the Regional Funds. The task of the regional representations in Brussels is basically of a fundraising nature. They keep an eye on new EU programmes and report back to the county, they inform their county on what happens in Brussels, they help regional companies find European partners, etc.

Conclusion

On the intra-regional level Europeanization has had many consequences of varying significance for the different counties. Concerning passive Europeanization, the counties are implementing the directives coming from Brussels via Copenhagen, and they have to take the European dimension into consideration in many everyday situations. On the level of active Europeanization the majority of counties have adopted active strategies of Europeanization in an attempt to get more resources. They all (minus three: Copenhagen, Frederiksborg and Roskilde) have a section in charge of EU affairs and the majority have set up 'representations' in Brussels. Some have had an exchange of civil servants with the Commission, engage in system export, or in partnership projects, etc. The picture is that of a mosaic. Mentally, Europe has been moved much closer to the counties. In most county administrations the awareness of Europe has increased. Not all see 'Europe' as an opportunity, but most realize that there is 'something' outside Denmark. Especially as they have had to realize that a very significant amount of 'Danish' legislation of

25 The regions with a representation in Brussels are: Vestsjællands Amt, Storstrøms Amt, Funen, Sønderjyllands Amt, Ribe Amt, Ringkøbing Amt, Aalborg in co-operation with Aalborg City and Viborg county, Århus in co-operation with Århus City. Bornholm does not have an individual representation, but co-operates with six other Baltic islands in the B7 network. Frederiksborg, Copenhagen and Roskilde counties do not have representations (Amtsrådsforeningen, 2003a).

importance to the counties originates in Brussels. This awareness has in some instances led to higher demands when employing staff (e.g. language qualifications), and in some county administrations also to an increased openness to new ways of 'doing things', a new dynamism. The most affected parts have been the economic administration with its EU section. However, all these activities have not led to major changes in the administrative structure or practice.

One of the problematic aspects of this development is the slow growing 'EU awareness' of 'ordinary' members of the county councils. Until recently one could talk of a *de facto* exclusion of the elected bodies. Europeanization was – and partly still is – basically a matter for the administration and private business in the county. This is due to a lack of interest among regional politicians, perhaps combined with a lack of qualifications and lack of resources for getting involved with a new and less tangible field. A tentative estimate indicates that Europeanization has on the one hand strengthened the counties in their dealings with the municipalities, but on the other hand also opened up a variety of conflicts of interest, as some of the larger municipalities now have their own development policy with a strong EU connection.

On the national level, the Europeanization of the county – government relationship shows various tendencies. First, one has to keep in mind that the counties *are* involved in the Danish part of the EU decision-making process. Secondly, this involvement for a period developed in such a way that the counties perceived their influence as declining, encouraging them to seek other ways. Thirdly, the counties have for several years now been using the possibility of bypassing the central government. Europeanization has strengthened the counties in their dealings with the government and its administration as well as with the municipalities' organization.

In an EU context, Denmark has to a very large extent been a 'unitary actor', due to a strong Danish EU co-ordination and decision-making system. Danish firms and interest organizations have considered themselves too small to gain anything from individual initiatives in Brussels. It was easier to influence the stand of the national government, thus letting it do the job. This situation was beneficial both for the government and the interest organizations. The tendency for an increased direct involvement of the counties on the European level will in the long run weaken the state when negotiating in the EU system. But that is the natural consequence of leaving one party 'out in the cold'; the regions often feel that their interests are suppressed in the national EU decision-making system, thus they seek other ways of influencing the process. The European Union offers the Danish regions the possibility of negotiating, for example, matters of employment with the Commission, through the Euro-organizations, without involving the Danish level, although the result will be applicable on the national level, too. If one cannot reach one's goal in Denmark, there is a very attractive European option. The European card is played simultaneously with the national one. Bypassing of the national centre happens regularly.

Functionaries at the Commission often say that a development where the nation states are under pressure from above and below should be seen as something desirable... and that the regional policy encourages such a development in the direction of a 'Europe of Regions'. But seen with Danish eyes such a vision lies years ahead and is not desirable in the first place. Several interviewees expressed that they would like a more symmetric relationship with the national centre; the EU is good to further such a development, but the nation state Denmark would remain their primary frame of reference, thus let us repeat the already quoted words of a senior official of the ADR: *Europe has made it easier to be a county in Denmark.*

Bibliography

Amtsrådsforeningen (1988), *Fremtidens Amter* (diskussionsoplæg).

Amtsrådsforeningen (1992), *Amterne i Danmark.*

Amtsrådsforeningen (1996), *Den amtskommunale medvirken i EU-beslutningsprocessen – behov for nye samarbejdsformer*, marts.

Amtsrådsforeningen (1997), *International Cooperation Projects.*

Amtsrådsforeningen (2003a), De danske amter og kommuners i Bruxelles

Amtsrådsforeningen (2003b), Organiseringen af amternes internationale arbejde.

Amtsrådsforeningen (2003c), *Amterne i tal.*

Bemærkninger til udkast til kommissorium for strukturkommission (Bemærkninger), www.arf.dk/Strukturkommissionen/Kommissionen/BemaerkningerTilUdkastTilKommissoriumForStrukturkommissionen.htm (printed 21 April 2003).

Betænkning nr. 1366; Betænkning I og II om fordelingen af opgaver i den offentlige sektor.

Bjørnbak, Torkil (no year), *Amterne og Det indre Marked*, Storstrøms Amt.

Caporaso, James (1996), 'The European Union and Forms of State', in *JCMS* Vol. 34, No. 1, 1996.

Commission of the European Communities (1991), *The Regions in the 1990s*, Luxembourg.

Cortelius, Malene (2002), Europæiseringen af danske amter – et studie af danske amters forvaltning af EU's Strukturfonde, Aalborg University Press, Aalborg.

Dafolo (1995), *Kommunerne gennem 25 år*, Dafolo Forlag, Frederikshavn.

von Dosenrode, Søren (1995), 'Going NUTS – amter, delstater og kantoner i Europa', in *Nordisk administrativt Tidsskrift*, Vol. 76, No. 2.

von Dosenrode, Søren (1997), 'Networks in Danish EU Policy-Making', *European Studies Series of Occasional Papers*, No. 20, Aalborg University.

Dosenrode, Søren (2000), 'Danish EU Policy-Making' in Branner, Hand & Kelstrup, Morten (eds), *Denmark's Policy towards Europe after 1945*, Odense University Press.

Dosenrode, Søren (2002), 'Dänemark – DezentralizierterEinheitsstaat in eine Föderation', in *Jahrbuch des Föderalismus 2002*, Nomos Verlag, Baden-Baden.

Dosenrode, Søren (2003), 'The EUropean State' in Serdült, Uwe and Widmer, Thomas (eds), *Politik im Fokus: Festschrift für Ulrich Klöti.* Zürich, Verlag Neue Zürcher Zeitung.

Jones, Barry and Keating, Michael (eds) (1995), *The European Union and the Regions*, Clarendonn Press, Oxford.

Jyllandsposten, 29 February 2003.

Klausen, Kurt Klaudi (ed.) (1996), *Erfaringer med Internationalisering i Amter og Kommuner*, Odense Universitetsforlag, Odense.

van der Knapp, Peter (1994), 'The Committee of the Regions', in *Regional Politics & Policy*, Vol. 4, No. 2.

Kommissorium for Strukturkommissionen, (Kommissorium), www.arf.dk/Strukturkommissionen/Kommissionen/Kommissorium.htm (printed 21 April 2003)

Lastenouse-Bury, Jacqueline (1997), *L'Union Européenne à l'aubre d'un nouveau siècle*, Liber Amicorum, Euroius, ED. Juridica, S.A. Madrid.

Lovbekendtgørelse nr. 615 om kommuners styrelse i sin nyeste udgave fra 18. juli 1995.

Madsen, Poul Thøis (1997), 'Public Procurement and the Single Market', *European Studies Series of Occasional Papers*, No. 23, Aalborg University.

Marks, Gerry, Hooghe, Lisbet and Blank, Kermit (1996), 'European Integration from the 80s: State-Centric vs. Multi-level Governance', *Journal of Common Market Studies*, Vol. 34, No. 3.

Nugent, Neill (2003), *The Government and Politics of the European Union*, 5th edition, Macmillan Press, Houndmills.

Pedersen, Ove Kaj *et al.* (1994), *Demokratiets lette tilstand*, Spektrum, København.

Politiken, 7 February 2003.

Radaelli, Cladio M. (2000), 'Whither Europeanization? Concept Stretching and Substantive Change', *Europe Online Papers* (EioP) Vol. 4, No 8 (2000), http://eiop.or.at/eiop/text/2000-008a.htm

Rhodes, R.A.W. (1992), *Beyond Westminster and Whitehall – the Sub-central Governments of Britain*, Routledge, London.

Wiedman, Thomas (2002), 'Abschied der Regionen vom AdR – Der Ausschuss der Regionen vor der Zerrissprobe, in *Jahrbuch des Föderalismus 2002*, Nomos Verlag, Baden-Baden, pp. 541-551.

Willke, Helmut (1992), *Ironie des Staates*, Suhrkamp Verlag, Frankfurt am Main.

Chapter 3

Finland

Kaisa Lähteenmäki-Smith

Introduction: Europeanization and the Finnish Regional Level

The European Union's impact on the member states continues to attract attention both in terms of international relations and national policy-making, while the sub-national level and the impact of its 'Europeanization' is often viewed as the poor relation in terms of the overall 'Europeanization' debate. The increase in this level of interest can be partially explained by the considerable increases in structural funding made available after 1988 and the ensuing debates related to the role of the sub-national tier as a sphere of political action in the early to mid-1990s. Thus the sub-national level emerged as one of the areas on which the process of European integration has impacted most profoundly (Allen, 1996, pp. 230; Bongers and Chatfield 1993, pp. 78-80; Keating, 1998 and Balme, 1997). The notion of 'Europeanization' here refers to the total impact of the process whereby the sub-national level gained a greater awareness of European legislation, a growing willingness and ability to mobilize resources in the search for European finance, an increased ability to co-operate with other European local and regional authorities and expert agencies, and an increased capacity to directly lobby EU institutions; as well as reflecting a general realization of the increasing influence of EU ideas on sub-national policy-making (John, 1994a and 1994b; Kohler-Koch, 1998). Moreover, the impact of EU ideas and policy on the sub-regional level has been exacerbated in particular by the ongoing expansion of Union competence into new policy areas and in particular by the impact of European Monetary Union (EMU).

The notion of regionalization has played a role in many of the politico-economic trends of the last ten years. One obvious example of this being its perceived relationship to the wider process of globalization, which in its various guises has been closely connected to the development of the region as an economic and political, as well as a philosophical, entity (see for instance Lähteenmäki-Smith, 1999). Furthermore, regionalism and regionalization[1] provide ample test

1 In the literature the distinction between these two has been based on the notions of agency 'from below' and 'from above', i.e. between an ideology where the representatives of regions act and mobilize support to enhance their autonomy, as opposed to one where the central government or other higher authority (e.g. the European Commission) acts to subject the regional level to various administrative,

cases of the ongoing restructuring of relationships between the state, society, and citizen in their various guises.[2]

In the case of Finland, accession to the European Union in 1995 and the subsequent adjustment and learning process that this implied involved both an administrative and political, and perhaps even more tellingly, a functional restructuring of the sub-national regional level, as decision-making on all levels had to be adapted to the impact of European policy-making and to implementation of the *acquis*. What had been a centralized unitary state structure had to take into consideration the wide-ranging regional level planning and implementation functions brought about by the need to adapt to the European structural funds regime. This required policy responses that can best be described in terms of a process of the ongoing 'Europeanization' of Finland's administrative and political sphere.

Though the general need for reform and for a more active role for the regional and local levels became increasingly apparent in the run up to accession, other factors of a more parochial nature also played their part. As has been argued by Anttiroiko, these changes in the institutional framework brought about by EU accession were also accompanied by economic recession and in response to this by the elaboration of a new Finnish 'national strategy' that aimed at becoming one of the world's leading information societies. In the achievement of this goal the local level has played a key role (Anttiroiko, 1998). Different policy instruments were also forged in order to strengthen the utilization and promotion of expertise in the regions, as this was seen as a key instrument of the national strategy for success, as well as an essential instrument for regional competitiveness (e.g. the Centres of Expertise programme, which is both an instrument of national innovation policy and a regional policy measure included in the national regional policy legislation). The fact that there has been a gradual move towards a more flexible and responsive local government (ibid. 9) also applies to the regional level, as the challenges facing the local and regional levels – as providers of welfare services – have developed hand in hand in this context. Thus, the basis of the new approach to the

---

political and social policies (Keating, 1998). A similar distinction can be made with the concepts of 'internal' and 'external' mobilization (Loughlin, 1996; Négrier, 1998; Loughlin, Mathias and Reilly, 1998). In the Finnish case similar distinctions have been made between the provinces as central government representation in the regions (*maakunta*), first implying central control and bureaucratic approach to regionality, whilst the second refers to regional identity and active citizenship (Kirkinen, 1996, p. 113).

2 In this sense regionalism can be interpreted within the political ideology and framework of Giddensian 'life politics', emanating from the reconstruction of political identity and empowerment, thus seeing the resurgence of regionalism more as a matter of (life) style than actual empowerment or emancipation (Giddens, 1990; 1991; 1998). Regionalism and regionalization can hence be viewed as indicative of 'hybridization' of political practices (e.g. Nederveen Pieterse, 1995) rather than leading to political empowerment of citizens through their regional surroundings.

Finnish regional policy regime can be viewed in terms of outlining a response to the challenge of reconciling the enduring Finnish tradition of a powerful unitary state bolstered by strong local municipal autonomy with the need to move towards a compromise package that retained the strong national level steering functions while promoting the development of a functionally based regional level.

Although central government functions as a co-ordinating point in this process, and is increasingly concerned with an attempt to co-ordinate sector concerns and measures when it comes to regional development, the three decentralized levels hold a relatively autonomous status within a legislative framework that spells out the functions that each is to perform. The actors on the various territorial levels and their main areas of responsibility (relevant to regional development) are introduced in the following table.

Table 3.1 The multi-level regional governance structure in Finland

<table>
<tr><td colspan="2">CENTRAL GOVERNMENT
Ministries responsible for co-ordinating Structural Funds and national regional policy:
• Ministry of the Interior (national regional policy + European Regional Development Fund)
• Ministry of Labour (European Social Fund)
• Ministry of Forestry and Agriculture (European Agricultural Guidance Fund)
• Ministry of Trade and Industry (Business subsidies)
• Increasing emphasis on national and regional co-ordination of other sector activities with regional effects (Infrastructure, Transport, TENs, Higher education and innovation policies, Labour policy etc.)</td></tr>
<tr><td>STATE ADMINISTRATION ON THE REGIONAL LEVEL:
• 5+1 State provincial offices (lääninhallitus; representing state authority of seven different ministries at the regional level; headed by 'governors' appointed by the President)
• 15 Employment and Economic Development Centres (Työvoima- ja Elinkeinokeskus = TE-keskus)
• 13 Environmental Centres (ympäristökeskus)</td><td>REGIONAL ADMINISTRATION:
• 19 Regional councils (Maakunta) + Åland (an autonomous region)
• Responsible for regional development in their respective areas according to legislation</td></tr>
<tr><td>STATE LOCAL ADMINISTRATION:
• 90 administrative county districts (kihlakunta), administratively subordinate to the state provincial offices, responsibilities – police, prosecutor's and bailiff's offices, registrar's services
• 208 Labour offices</td><td>MUNICIPAL ADMINISTRATION:
• 446 municipalities
• Approx. 270 local and joint municipal authorities (e.g. in the fields of education and health care)</td></tr>
</table>

Typically the different administrative levels have their specialized roles in the regional development sphere, particularly when it comes to the management of the Structural Funds (one of the main reasons for solidifying the regional level in the mid-1990s, see e.g. Virkkala, 2002, p. 9). The Structural Funds methodology influenced the Finnish regional development sphere also more generally, as Finland moved into the era of the so-called 'programme-based' regional policy. This shift reflected important changes in terms of development ideology, public administration and its organization. Development programming was intended to improve prioritization and effectiveness of public policy in the regional sphere, though as time was to show, due to the complexity and multi-layered fashion of the administrative structures, it did not always serve the purpose of improving transparency and decreasing bureaucracy.

The post-EU-accession system was in particular intended to strengthen the regional level, which is, in its political organization, made up of representatives of the municipal level. In order to ensure the influence of the regional level in decision-making[3] the state regional administration for instance was to have an opinion procedure for the regional councils before making funding decisions on regional development measures. Whilst the state provincial offices became less powerful[4] as a consequence of the 1990s reforms, it is the Employment and Economic Development Centres that could be seen as 'competing' with the newly reinvigorated regional level. Recent debates have considered the merging of these two bodies in yet another administrative reform in order to do away with this tug of war situation and to further strengthen the regional level (e.g. Niemi-Iilahti, Stenvall and Ståhlberg, 2002).

The main question as to the impact of Europeanization on the regional level concerns the role of the regions. Indeed, to what extent have regions in fact emerged as actors in their own right or are they still predominantly objects of public policy (central government initiatives in the last instance)?

In the Finnish context, the notion of a region ('maakunta') can be defined via four dimensions: as a socio-geographic entity (a tier between state and municipality with a cultural and historical identity); as a political community (representing the articulated will of the citizens living in a certain region); as a functional entity (as the administrative entity taking care of assigned functions); and as a judicial entity (displaying its separate legal status) (Mennola, 1990, p. 104). These four dimensions act as constituent parts of the regional whole and are best understood in terms of a process of region construction or as the

3 Administrative reform was implemented in two stages, as the necessary reforms due to the EU accession were followed by more reforms in 1997, with the so-called 'Aluehallinto 2000' (*Regional administration 2000*) process that entailed major changes in the number and functions of state provincial offices and the establishment of the new state regional offices, i.e. Employment and Economic Development Centres representing sector authorities in the regions.

4 The role of the State Provincial Offices is extensive in terms of the sectors they represent, i.e. social and health sector, culture and education, police and rescue services, etc., though the functions are mostly connected to monitoring and control functions within these areas.

'institutionalization' of the regions (Paasi, 1996). As we shall see, all dimensions are constitutive to the region, though political concerns often determine which of them dominates the public debates at any one time. These four elements of regionality do however each contribute to the act of making visible key dimensions of regional transformation(s) (ibid. 32). The balance between the different aspects of regionality reflects the prevailing ideological and political trends and therefore it is hardly surprising that even today they are in a process of re-articulation.

Whilst the socio-geographical dimension is perhaps less problematic today than earlier when regional level was particularly weakly defined in Finland, the political and functional aspects are the most interesting ones today. One could even argue that the Finnish region (in the sense of 'maakunta') is strictly speaking neither political nor functional as, politically, the regional level is indirectly elected and in this sense subordinate to the local level with strong autonomy, and functionally the main focus has shifted from the local to the sub-regional level, i.e. to the local labour market areas or functional regions (*seutukunta*). The relationship between the regional and the local level is therefore particularly close. So far there are no direct elections on the regional level and therefore the local level is the political sphere for debate and participation. There has however been discussion even quite recently on the possibility of further reforms solidifying the regional level, establishing a directly elected regional level and of merging the regional councils and the Employment and Economic Development Centres (e.g. Niemi-Iilahti, Stenvall and Ståhlberg, 2002). The Kainuu 'experiment' where amongst other things the regional level becomes directly elected (2005-2012) is path breaking in this regard, though not necessarily directly applicable in other Finnish regions. As we shall see in the closer analysis below, even today the regional level does have an important role in regional development and as a strategic actor. Regional development responsibility is shared between the regions and the central administration. Whilst Finland lacks 'regional politicians' and therefore the regional level is in a disadvantaged position in relation to the national level as a sphere of political activity and debate, the regional councils are in charge of programming and planning functions in their constituency and as such are expected to reflect the interests of that constituency.

The Relationship between the Regional and the Central Government Levels

The Finnish governance system is marked by its historical duality, where the strength of the central government in the tradition of the unitary state is bolstered by the strength of the constituent parts on the *local* level, (i.e. the municipalities) all of which display a high degree of autonomy. Only recently then, and in particular in relation to EU accession, did the regional level become a serious player by breaking into this traditional duality by demanding more of a role and a voice for the intermediate, or regional, level.

The regional level now plays an important part in regional development functions, though the dominance of the central government level cannot be overlooked either, yet again making clear the duality of regional development as a policy issue in the Finnish administrative structure. The central government level defines the general objectives of regional policy for each electoral period/government, the most recent being the National Objective Programme for Regional Policy (of 9/11/2000). These general aims currently consist of the following:

- Aims at defining governmental regional policy for the coming years by targeting and co-ordinating regional development activities at the ministerial level with activities on the regional and local levels;
- Seeks to pay heed to the need to prepare for EU enlargement and for changes in EU Structural Funds support;
- Aims at promoting equality between citizens and the sustainable and balanced development of the regions.

More specific regionally targeted activities within these general policy goals in turn consist of the following:

- Launching a new 'Regional Centre Development Programme' (Aluekeskusohjelma, key issues: strengthening the urban centres as engines of growth, promotion of partnership-based co-operation and strengthening the 'knowledge-based vitality' of the 34 urban regions chosen for the programme);[5]
- Development activities in Eastern and Northern Finland (key issues: co-ordination and differentiation);
- Development activities in Western and Southern Finland (key issues: expertise and innovation);
- Development of the capital region (key issues: internationalization, national metropolitan policy, addressing the specific challenges of the capital region in terms of issues such as housing policy);
- Rural development (key issues: balanced service provision, urban-rural partnership, improved integration of rural policy into regional policy as a whole);
- Information society (key issues: expertise and availability of information technology (IT) infrastructure in all parts of the country);
- Regional innovation policy and Centres of Expertise (key issues: maintaining research and development (R&D) investment as a whole and expanding them geographically, the regional role of technology policy, drafting Regional Technology Strategies, further strengthening the Centres of Expertise and the role of the National Technology Agency TEKES);

---

5 For more information on this and other regional development initiatives and programmes in Finland, see www.intermin.fi.

- Business financing and services as an area for further development (key issues: state subsidies, seed financing, start-ups and other service and information activities targeting small- and medium sized enterprises = SMEs);
- Infrastructure development (key issue: improved accessibility);
- State services (key issues: formulation of a strategy for decentralizing the location of state services in the regions);
- Cross-sectoral co-operation and co-ordination (key issue: improving efficiency on different administrative levels);
- European regional and structural policy (key issues: preparing for EU enlargement and for the post-2006 and improving administration during the current financing period).

One of the key tasks that regional councils will be entrusted with is the drafting of a regional development programme, including strategic goals and objectives (updated at the beginning of the electoral period for the four-year period until the next election), as well as a financial plan (for one year at a time). This programme is supposed to include all of the different programmes and development initiatives, so in the final instance it is in the drafting process that central government co-ordination of the regional level is ensured. How this process is actually going to work in practice is still unclear, as this programming process is a novelty of the new legislation that came into force in January 2003. The methodology owes a lot to European Structural Funds planning, as the programme document is drafted in terms of a regional partnership. This goes some way to underlining the process-nature of planning and programming, as well as the interaction between programming and the social construction of the region.

It is however the regional councils that are in a central position here, as they define the objectives of development for the region in question and elaborate upon the implementation of these objectives. In elaborating these strategies regional councils need to take into consideration both public and private, as well as endogenous and exogenous factors: the opportunities offered by the EU structural funding programmes, as well as economic and political developments within the region itself. Regional trends in employment, financial opportunities and constraints, the development of the region's infrastructure and educational opportunities all have an impact on the environment within which these regional plans are developed.

As was seen in the table above, the political regional level (*maakunta*) co-exists with the state regional administration, with Finland being divided into six state provincial offices (Lapland, Oulu, Eastern Finland, Western Finland, Southern Finland and Åland). The administrative functions of the state administration in the regions remain wide-ranging, as they represent the public authority in seven different public policy areas. The provincial state offices perform functions in the areas of social and health administration; educational and cultural administration; police administration; rescue administration; consumer, competition and food administration; veterinary services and animal protection; judicial administration;

and activities in the area of sport and youth affairs. These functions are centred on the use and implementation of monitoring and control mechanisms, as they are responsible for controls, inspections and certain licences within the above-mentioned areas of activity. They do also have a role in development programming, as participants in the regional partnerships responsible for programme preparation.

The reform of the provincial state administration in the mid-1990s was based on the need to simplify the complexity of administrative structures and to enhance their efficiency. It can be argued that the administrative problems faced by the provinces predominantly relate to their complexity, and primarily to their desire to enhance efficiency and co-ordination. This is illustrated by the fact that there were 23 different types of administrative entities within their organization, all of whom were responsible for their own limited functions, thus making the structure insufficiently co-ordinated and ultimately, inefficient (He 148/1996). The aims of the reform process for Finnish regional administration were thus outlined as follows:

- Making the services more public-friendly;
- Enhancing co-operation and co-ordination between the various administrative bodies;
- Enhancing economic efficiency;
- Clarifying the administrative process and making it more transparent to the public;
- Enhancing flexibility between different administrative bodies;
- Moving the direct service-functions of administration closer to the customer; and
- Strengthening municipal self-rule (He 148/1996).

The mechanism employed in the implementation of these aims was the fundamental downsizing of the provincial administration, cutting the number of provinces from 12 to six (Law on Provincial State Offices, *Lääninhallituslaki*, 1997). The changes in regional administration in Finland have thus been important all through the 1990s, though this process as yet seems to be far from over, as we shall see in the section to come concerning the relationship between the state (central government) and the regions.

The 'Europeanization' of the regions could be expected to reflect the need for more democratic governance on the regional level, in line with for instance the European Union's White Paper on Governance or the Council of Europe's Charter of Local Self-Government. In this sense, and in terms of issues such as strategic agency and public participation, the relevant Finnish regional actor is thus the regional council (*maakunta*), where municipalities are institutionally organized into regional councils, nominated by the local municipalities in proportion to the relative strength of the political parties represented therein. The political organs on the regional level are nominated for the term of four years (the same period as the municipal councils). Each municipality holds a set number of seats and voting power, based on the rules of each regional council. The implementation tasks are the responsibility of the executive, which is based on the prevailing political power of each party. The indirectly elected nature of the regional level entails a significant problem when viewed in light of the European principles and ideals embedded in the Council of Europe's 'European Charter of Local Self Government', namely, the lack of direct accountability and of citizens' participation. This has been widely debated and two main responses seem to have emerged in light of such concerns. These responses favour in turn the strengthening of regional democracy and the bolstering of strong local autonomy. As an exceptionally homogenous unitary state Finland has a weak tradition of regionalism upon which to build in order to strengthen the democratically accountable regional level. The tradition of local autonomy is not democratically problematic: rather it seems to keep the decision-making focus where it should be, i.e. as close to the citizens as possible. There is however a clear tendency to seek efficiency gains and better policy delivery through regionalization, as many of the Finnish municipalities have small and ageing populations, and thus find it difficult to ensure the provision of those services that law obliges them to deliver. The average population of a Finnish municipality is less than 12,000 (Finnish Association of Local Authorities, 2 May 2002), which makes it easy to see that co-operation between municipalities is the only way to ensure that citizens receive the services that they need at a price that is reasonable.

It was noted above that many of the changes and pressures for further reform were precipitated by international pressure. The background to the current structure is however not the sole product of a process of Finland's adjustment to European integration. Indeed, as was also noted previously, it can be argued that Europeanization is a process that influences and is influenced by the surrounding national and regional environments, each with their own necessary internal dynamics. Thus for instance in the case of Finland many of the issues connected to European Union accession in terms of innovation, ideas and ideals in a regional context (i.e. programming, subsidiarity, accountability, co-ordination) had already been extensively discussed in Finland in the 1970s (Committee Report/ Komiteamietintö, 1974, p. 98). In particular co-ordination was repeatedly raised as one of the major problems within Finland's regional administrative structures. This can still be seen as one of the potential weaknesses of the European presence or 'voice' at the Finnish regional tier of government (e.g. Sisäasiainministeriö / Ministry of the Interior, 1994). Potential reasons for the relative weakness of the regional voice can best be explained by reference to the Finnish tradition of local government, which has left international connections largely to the central government. Though progress has been made in this respect in recent years, increased co-ordination and the fuller integration of the regional tier is still required.

It is first and foremost through their constituent parts (i.e. the member municipalities) that the regions are involved with European issues, both in terms of the direct impact of European legislation and with regard to its international repercussions. Most councils have, however, also formulated strategies for internationalization and Europeanization on their own, which reflect their regional interests and strengths (Berghäll and Aronen, 1998). Though these programmes are a relatively recent trend, they are based on longer historical co-operative structures and connections, and thus build on long-term aims and goals, which is in itself an important factor in pursuing successful internationalization. While the value of such documents beyond the rhetoric sphere could be questioned, they are another indication of the increased level of awareness among Finnish regions that internationalization is something that is of direct strategic importance to the competitiveness and attractiveness of their regions.

Finnish Regions and the European Union

The representation of regional interests in the EU context is largely dependent on internal mobilization, and thus relatively less dependent on the domestic legal and administrative order than is often the assumption. This has to do with the fact that regional interest representation and relevant policies are decreasingly a zero-sum game situation (Keating, 1998, p. 24). Yet the fact is that those regions with the best functioning connections to the national centre also tend to be in the strongest negotiating position *vis-à-vis* European politics (ibid.). In this respect the special status Helsinki holds in lobbying terms (as a region in itself rather than merely a capital of Uusimaa region) is compatible both with the traditional centralism of Finnish interest representation and the assumptions connected to recent developments in terms of Europeanization.

Since the type of institutional structure states pursue is of direct relevance to the representatives of the regions, developing and maintaining the connections between the regions and the state is also a matter of outlining general goals and ideals for integration. The fact that the Finnish government has placed special emphasis on developing the EU on an intergovernmental basis, with regional co-operation being pursued with neighbouring areas, to tackle the potential problems caused by disparities in standards of living and emerging ecological risks (Valtioneuvosto/Council of the State, 1998), is thus hardly surprising. This has however done little to discourage internal mobilization in this regard, as a result of which representatives of the Finnish regions have consistently aimed at developing more effective routes to influence in the wider European context.

In terms of regional mobilization and interest representation, both in its formal institutional guises and in terms of the more informal 'lobbying' type functions, Finland is only in the early stages of 'Europeanization'. This question will be approached though the study of three separate routes to influence, namely the direct, the institutional and the procedural. These in turn reflect three dimensions, active (political dimension, regionalism), passive (administrative dimension, regionalization) and reflexive (identity dimension).

Emphasis is increasingly placed on the necessity for direct links to European Union institutions and to co-operation partners. This represents the direct route to influence and is indicative of active regionalism within a certain regional sphere of activity. The main functions of the regional representations and offices in Brussels are a clear indication of the acknowledgement of the need to create direct connections between European institutions, member states and their regions and other partners. The functions of regional offices are both external and internal: establishing information channels between the region's 'home base' and Europe and enhancing information flows in both directions. Together with the active dimension there is however also a reactive dimension. Indicative of this dual nature was the establishment of a Brussels office for the Finnish association of local and regional authorities, which pre-dated Finnish EU membership (1992). The role played by this office was central in adapting the local and regional tiers of government to accession. Their functions centre on the channelling of information, knowledge and awareness regarding integration, thus accentuating the nature of integration as a learning process. The local authorities represented in Brussels not only act as lobbyists, but also form a part of the process of the construction of the region in terms of forming an important consensus-based link in the regional society concerned. This does not imply a harmony of interests, but rather it merely helps us to understand the process of reconciling effective strategies in the face of the continuing existence of particularistic and conflicting interests.

Other early entrants into the Brussels scene amongst the Finnish regional actors included the Ostrobothnia and West Finland offices. These are interesting cases of Europeanization in the Finnish context as they provide a common ground for a variety of regional interests, both in geographical and in functional terms. The Ostrobothnia regional office is supported by a consortium of interests, which in addition to the regional councils represent the largest municipalities, agricultural producers, chambers of commerce and other economic interests.

The Ostrobothnia regional office moreover is a good example of regional presence as a learning process. It was formed as a consequence of long existing close co-operative ties between Vaasa (the capital of Ostrobothnia region) and Kiel (the capital of Schleswig-Holstein). This resulted in 1994 in an agreement to allow Vaasa and the surrounding region to share Schleswig-Holstein's and Berlin's 'Hanse' office for exchange purposes. At first relatively short visits from regional representatives of various policy areas took place, then gradually the idea of establishing a more permanent region's presence within the framework of the 'Hanse' co-operation arrangements emerged. Thus in 1995 the decision was reached to employ a permanent person for this function.

The Finnish regional interests present in Brussels represent a geographically wide spectrum of regions. In addition to the Brussels office of the Finnish local authorities, there are a total of seven individual regions or municipalities represented in the Brussels regional lobbying sphere. They are as follows, the Helsinki EU-office, the West Finland European Office, the East Finland EU-

Office, the Lapland EU-Office, the City of Turku/South-West Finland EU-Office, and the South of Finland EU-office (Itä-Uusimaa, Häme and Päijät-Häme regions).

The structure and organization of the offices representing the Finnish sub-national presence in Brussels is extremely flexible. There has also been a variety of co-operative or even trans-border solutions such as that employed by the West Finland office (representing the Council of Tampere Region, Satakunta, Central Finland, South Ostrobothnia and Ostrobothnia), which has functioned as part of the 'Hanse'-office, or the East Finland EU-office, housed in the venerable *Scotland Europa* Centre. These examples indicate that Europeanization is a two-fold process whereby regions within Finland seek partners nationally in order to make their voice better heard internationally (and nationally) as regards EU questions. The alliances constructed within Finland seek new co-operative constellations in the EU sphere in order to find like-minded regions to co-operate with, only once the national level strategies and co-operative constellations have been identified and formed. In this sense it becomes obvious that Europeanization in terms of seeking to have a more active European role for the region does not bypass or replace national alliance building, though it may change the forms of this process.

Though the historical and political status of regions, as well as of regional administrations vary greatly across the European Union member states, and thus the opportunities for exerting influence differ accordingly,[6] some general conclusions can be drawn from the Finnish case. Though regionality does not allow for uniformity in regional strategies, some shared factors influence regional mobilization and the articulation of the 'regional voice' in the European Union context, highlighting important lessons to be drawn from individual experiences.

It can be argued that the internal and external dynamics of mobilization tend to coincide, occasionally conflicting, while at other times overlapping. What has been defined as the external mobilization of the regions (regionalization 'from above'), predominantly implemented through European Union policy instruments such as the Structural Funds has existed side by side, though not always in a harmonious relationship with the process of internal mobilization, described as regionalization 'from below'.[7]

---

6 These variations have been widely acknowledged as a factor hampering the emergence of a 'Europe of the Regions' (Kohler-Koch, 1998) debated in particular in the early 1990s in relation to the Maastricht strategy of the German Länder (Benz, 1998).

7 On the relationship between external and internal mobilization see Loughlin, 1996; Négrier, 1998, p. 29; Loughlin, Mathias and Reilly, 1998, p. 140 and Morata, 1998. The awareness of regionality as based on internal mobilization and consensus building became apparent in the interviews conducted with the representatives of the regional offices who see their role as that of 'middle-man' between the European Union and local/regional civil society, not only lobbying for finances for their region, but equally providing information and understanding of the EU and its dynamics in the region in question.

The presence and 'voice' of Finnish sub-national regional authorities and actors in the European Union context helps to highlight these potential openings, as well as the problems that the sub-national routes to influence entail, and the strategies that are available to these actors. The Finnish examples point to the fact that the direct and the institutional routes to the articulation of the regional actors' 'voice' coexist side by side, though the methods of transforming influence into policy implementation are not straightforward. The resources (human and material) of the actors still play a key role in determining the actual level of influence, and thus those with more resources are more likely to get their voice heard than those with fewer available resources. This is particularly valid, as an effective internationalization strategy requires the successful creation of a regional or local profile (Berghäll and Aronen, 1998, p. 74).

'Egalitarian' routes, placing all regional actors in a position of equality with regard to strategic power structures, and the ability to exert influence by participating in debates and through voting is not necessarily an effective means of influencing policy, as institutions accessible to regional actors, such as the COR tend to have only a marginal role to play in final decision-making (Christiansen 1996). Hasty judgements should however be avoided in the case of the COR, which is not only marked by the same dynamism as the European Union structure as a whole,[8] but more particularly can be seen as an evolving organization still in the early stages of the process of constituting its role as a part of the European governance structure. Though current expectations are not particularly high, it is however still viewed as an important forum for discussion, and if it can provide expertise on regional issues for wider use in the European sphere it can become a key actor in the articulation of the 'regional voice', and thus a key influence on the policies that affect the regions.

The role of the regional level in European decision-making has perhaps lost some of its impetus with the increased intergovernmentalism of recent debates, for instance as regards the debate on the European Convention set out to chart solutions for decision-making and the distribution of powers in a future European Union of 25+ member states. The working method of this broad-based European 'think-tank' is built on thematic working groups who are to outline possible future avenues for European polity in the making. Some of the key questions addressed by this body are:

- How is the division of competence between the Union and the member states to be organized?
- How can the European institutions' respective tasks be better defined?

8 Dynamism is often cited as one of the most characteristic elements of the evolving European polity as it evolves as an open-ended process. This also includes the complementary nature of the politico-institutional structure in relation to the constitutions of the member states; and its polycentric character contributing to the web-like nature of it in its multi-level structure. (See for instance Preuß, 1996, pp. 549-550.)

- How can the coherence and efficiency of the Union's external action be ensured?
- How can the Union's democratic legitimacy be strengthened?

When it concludes in 2003, the Convention will submit its proposals to the European Council and the following Intergovernmental Conference will then work forward on the basis of the draft Treaty for a European Constitution. The Convention has already contributed to public debate on European polity and policy, especially through the publication of the preliminary draft constitutional treaty (European Convention 2002). The ensuing debate has however concentrated more on the symbolism of a (possible) 'United States of Europe' and of an explicitly federal European entity. Little if any debate however has emerged in relation to the sub-national regional level as a relevant policy focus in this context.

The routes to influence indicate the opportunities for regional actors to influence policy-making in the European context. The direct route encompasses the 'lobbying' activities and co-operation schemes that link regional actors directly to other corresponding spheres of action, as well as to European institutions. The Union institutions themselves provide the institutional route in which regional actors and representatives have a role to play (most importantly in the Committee of the Regions, but also potentially in the European Parliament).[9] The constitutional or procedural route is formed by those rules, institutions and procedures that the European Union enshrines regarding the role of the regions as a part of the institutional structure. The rules pertaining to decision-making, the implementation of legislation and the right of appeal can be cited as examples here. The constitutional route is, in effect, constructed from an amalgam of the other two routes, as direct and institutional means of influence offer the best way for regional actors to try to increase their constitutional status within the European Union structure. What also needs to be considered here is the policy impact, particularly in terms of the internationalization or Europeanization of these regions. Structural policy includes areas that fall into this category, as many of the programmes include networking and cross-border co-operation.

It is important to bear in mind that EU membership entails more than just far-reaching legislative requirements and the adaptation required to implement them efficiently. A state's political and administrative culture is also influenced in various ways. The 'Europeanization' of the regions is a complex process that is manifest in a greater awareness of European legislation; a growing willingness and ability to mobilize resources in the search for European finance; increased co-

9 There are naturally non-EU-based institutions and organizations available for regional and local actors, such as The Standing Conference of Local and Regional Authorities of Europe (CLRAE, under the auspices of Council of Europe), the Assembly of European Regions (AER) and Council of European Municipalities and Regions (CEMR). These are however outside the scope of this paper, as the emphasis here is on the EU as a structure and tool of 'Europeanizing' the regions.

operation with other European local and regional authorities and expert agencies; direct lobbying of EU institutions; and the influence of ideas emanating from the EU on sub-national policy-making (John, 1994). Ideas such as 'subsidiarity' or 'programming' have in many cases changed practices on the regional and national levels in a way that has often empowered the regions in relation to the central administration in member states. This is particularly the case in member states with centralized and hierarchical administrative traditions such as Finland. This has required changes in the way regional representatives view their role and pursue their policy goals, as a more active role requires capacities for more assertive and informed actions.[10]

Regional Councils also strengthen their European presence through memberships (either individual or corporate) of European interest representation organizations. In the case of Finnish local and regional authorities this involves membership of associations such as the Association of European Border Regions (AEBR), the Assembly of the European Regions (AER), the Conference of Peripheral Maritime Regions (CPMR) and the Association of European Regions of Industrial Technology (RETI). Though most of these are organized within the EU framework, the AER is pan-European in nature.

It can be argued in general that though the European Union is naturally an important point of reference for these regions, pan-European projects should not be overlooked. Though the role of co-operation outside the EU framework, for instance within the International Union of Local Authorities (IULA) and its European subsidiary, the Council of European Municipalities and Regions (CEMR), is now decreasing in relevance, as regions and their strategies become more 'Europeanized' in the fashion described above, other routes to regional influence can still be utilized. As such, interaction in these forums can best be viewed as an important pre-accession phase, preparing the regions and states awaiting accession for the institutional and co-operative requirements of full EU membership.

Various trans-national groups appear to be a good option for the purposes of regional interest representation, in particular for those that are looking for contacts that are more intimate than those offering mere organizational or institutional links. As an example one can cite Northern Ostrobothnia and Oulu, who have for some years been affiliated members of *Scotland Europa*. Equally pilot programmes

10 This new multi-levelness has sometimes lead to over-reactions on the part of regional actors, as they have sought to influence EU actors in policies that would be more effectively influenced in the national sphere. The national government is still the main target of interest representation in the member states, though it is not the sole target. Sometimes such 'oversight' has been a conscious and necessary strategy where the national government has been unwilling to acknowledge and pursue regional demands and interests. Scotland and its 1980s interest representation strategy that sought to bypass the Westminster parliament, seen as unsympathetic to its needs, falls into this category.

launched with regions sharing similar interests and regional circumstances have also created interest in this regard. As an example of such projects one can cite the joint pilot programme for the Northern Peripheries that brings together northern peripheral regions from Scotland, Finland, Sweden and Norway.

Cross-border initiatives such as Interreg have become an important policy instrument in promoting cross-border co-operation between Finland and its neighbours, or rather they have solidified and brought new impetus to many of the co-operative constellations and close historical ties that have long existed in the European North. Currently Finland participates in seven Interreg initiatives.[11] These initiatives have given new impetus to both Nordic and Baltic co-operation. Side by side with the cross-border national dimensions there has also been a sub-national dimension to Nordic co-operation, as the Nordic countries have also long nurtured a structure of sub-national co-operation. This is based on both trans-national links in the Baltic context, inter-municipal connections and on co-operative ties between national administrations in regional planning and internal affairs.[12] The potential for co-operation is not necessarily hampered by the differences in national administrative and planning structures, though the differences of available funding, as well as unbalanced historical ties may potentially weaken incentives for co-operation. What is required is an expressed willingness to create and maintain co-operation even in the context of changing circumstances, such as differences in regional funding structures.

The way in which different member states pursue their European policy is not only a matter of forming 'government' positions *vis-à-vis* questions relating to the integration agenda. Such decisions have a profound impact upon the sub-national regional tier and on their potential strategies and responses to that process. As a relatively recent entrant to the EU, Finland has oscillated between its status as a 'new comer' and 'would-be-insider', thus at the same time attempting to be both a 'good European' and pursuing a policy marked by a relative conservatism and a status quo-orientation (Petersen, 1997, pp. 160 and 182). This applies to the implementation of regional policy as well as to other issues on the agenda.

As far as the role of the regions and the enhancement of the regional and local tier in the European Union structure are concerned, Finnish views have tended to be moderate, and status quo-oriented. This is hardly surprising considering the nature of the Finnish unitary state. In general it has been those member states with federal (or quasi-federal) politico-constitutional systems that have argued for a more marked role for the sub-national level. Germany as a federal state has been particularly predisposed to support the enhancement of the role of regional actors, and even of greater federalism within EU structures, whereas the Finnish

11 For more information on these programmes see Hanell, Aalbu and Neubauer, 2002.

12 For instance the Nordic Committee of Senior Officials for Regional Policy = NÄRP, which has included the representatives of national authorities responsible for regional policy and regional planning in the Nordic countries.

government remains more likely to favour national solutions and intergovernmental co-operation.

These differences were most clearly discernible in the 1996 IGC process, when the 'Europe of the Regions' theme was gathering momentum in some member states, in particular in Germany and Belgium. While the German government reflected the views of its own regional governments[13] in calling for the enhancement of the role of the Committee of the Regions, as well as for the right of co-decision for the European Parliament and the Council, (in decisions where the Council decides by majority vote), the Finnish government was more supportive of the status quo. The Finnish government moreover also rejected the strengthening of the European Parliament's position in the decision-making procedure relating to amending the Treaty, while also declining to support proposals to grant the EP power of decision over its own resources. In the Finnish view the Council should remain the central decision-making body, while the 'work of the Committee of the Regions as an advisory body should continue on its present basis' (Europa, 1997b). Since the conclusion of this particular debate attitudes have shifted even further towards entrenched intergovernmentalism on the part of most member states, and thus Finnish policy has become more preoccupied with the need to ensure that the voice of the small member states is not diluted by EU enlargement or by the initiatives of the larger member states.

Conclusions

Finland can be seen as strongly influenced by its historical and geographical background. This is equally valid in the case of the sub-national level, which can only be understood in its geographical and social context, whilst not leaving aside the other dimensions referred to in the introduction section. The socio-geographic dimensions are those that define the region on the most basic level, whilst as we have seen the political aspects are constitutive to many of the ongoing debates on regionality, as they define the region as a democratic entity. Judicial status has been outlined through the role of the regional level in legislation (e.g. regional development responsibilities) and the functional dimensions are those that seem to dominate as regions in their current form were largely forged for functional purposes (of administering the Structural Funds).

The Finnish regions represent many of the general traits of Europeanization: growing awareness of European integration and its impact, the need to adopt more active (though also reactive) strategies and to form new alliances and co-operative contacts. While all these dimensions require adaptive capacity, there are some

13 On the basis of the conclusions of the Conference of Ministers of European Affairs the Bundesrat adopted a decision on the preparations for the 1996 IGC in March 1995. These directly reflected the views of the *Länder*, since no substantial changes were made to the conclusions (Europa, 1997a).

specifically Finnish characteristics that can sometimes place (if not material, then 'psychological') restrictions on these strategies. The tradition of centralization, hierarchical structures and the natural emphasis on neighbouring areas in terms of co-operation are such persistent aspects of Finnish regionalism and regionalization. Yet the emphasis on adaptation and the need to view integration as a learning process can contribute to making this shift in strategic thinking easier.

Effective Europeanization and internationalization require competencies and the articulation of interests in ways that emphasize co-operation, co-ordination and differentiation in the domestic sphere. Thus regional strategies require working together when necessary, but also the establishment of practices, aims and connections specific to the region in question. Finnish regions are quite small actors when measured in population terms, which necessitates co-operation and co-ordination for reasons of cost-effectiveness and policy efficiency, though this should not undermine regional specificity. This need for co-operation has been one of the reasons behind co-operation initiatives between municipalities and functional regions in recent years. At times and especially for service provision purposes the functional regions are of a more appropriate scope than the regional councils. Does this imply then that the Finnish regions have only partially been empowered by the 'Europeanization process', whilst the municipalities remain the most powerful politico-administrative level below the strong central government level?

We can conclude that the regional level has been strengthened and solidified as a consequence of the 1990s administrative reforms. As long as the regional level is only indirectly accountable to the electorate Europeanization remains half-baked however. The regional level is important as a sphere for strategic development activity, but in order to emerge as a sphere for public debate and action, the regionalization process needs to be fully-fledged, i.e. it also needs to be implemented as a democratic process with regional politics, regional politicians and regional constituencies, i.e. the already accomplished administrative regionalization should also be accompanied by political regionalization.

National reforms and debates are, however, only one aspect of the Europeanization process. Side by side with them the international connections and adherences are also undergoing changes. Both in the national and the sub-national contexts we need to acknowledge that even the most long-standing historical ties and institutional structures (such as those of the Nordic Council) do not remain unaltered. Regional strategies today reflect the outward-oriented active adaptation aspect of the Europeanization process. Internationalization in this sense is increasingly a sub-national, as well as an intergovernmental process, and thus it is more accurate to speak of 'internationalizations', of which Europeanization of the regions is one important aspect.

Bibliography

Allen, David (1996), 'Cohesion and Structural Adjustment' in H. Wallace and W. Wallace (eds), *Policy-Making in the European Union*. Oxford University Press, Oxford, pp. 209-233.

Alueiden kehittämislaki. Annettu Helsingissä 12.7.2002, astuu voimaan 1.1.2003. (Law on regional development, passed on 12 July 2002, comes into force 1 January 2003). Available at: www.intermin.fi.

Anttiroiko, A.-V. (1998), *The Wings of Change. Restructuring the Local Government in Finland and Japan*. A presentation prepared for the international seminar 'Cities in the Age of Globalisation', University of Tampere, 25-26 May 1998. [http://www.uta.fi/~kuaran/japan.html], electronic document, 14 November 2002.

Armstrong, H. (1995), 'The Role and Evolution of European Community Regional Policy' in B. Jones and M. Keating (eds), *The European Union and the Regions*. Oxford University Press, Oxford.

Asetus alueiden kehittämisestä 17.12.1993, 1315/1993.

Balme, R. (1997), 'Regional Policy and European Governance' in M. Keating and J. Loughlin (eds), *The Political Economy of Regionalism*. Frank Cass, London, pp. 63-76.

Benz, A. (1998), 'German Regions in the European Union: from joint policy-making to multi-level governance' in Le Galés, P. and Lequesne, C. (eds), *Regions in Europe*. Routledge, London and New York.

Berghäll, E. and Aronen, Kauko (1998), *Kaupunkien kansainvälistymisen parhaat käytännöt*. Helsinki: Suomen kuntaliitto. (*The Best Practices of Internationalization of Municipalities*, report from the Finnish Association of Local Authorities).

Bongers, P. and Chatfield, J. (1993), 'Regions and Local Authorities in the Governance of Europe' in A. Duff (ed.), *Subsidiarity within the European Community*. Federal Trust, London, pp. 77-85.

Christiansen, T. (1996), 'Second Thoughts on European Union's "Third Level": The European Union's Committee of the Regions', *Publius: The Journal of Federalism*, 26:1, 93-116.

Commission of the European Communities (1996), *Baltic Sea Region Initiative*. SEC(96) 608 final.

Committee of the Regions (1996), Opinion of the Committee of the Regions on the 'Northern Dimension of the European Union and Cross-Border Co-operation on the Border between the European Union and the Russian Federation and in the Barents Region', OJC 337, 11 November 1996, 7-12.

Europa (1997a), Germany's Position on the 1996 IGC and the relevant documents. [http://Europa.int/en/agenda/igc-home/ms-doc/state-de/pos.htm], electronic document, 23 October 1997.

Europa (1997b), Finland's Position on the 1996 IGC and the relevant documents. [http://Europe.int/en/agenda/igc-home/ms-doc/state-fi/finn.htm], electronic document, 23 October 1997.

European Convention (2002), *Preliminary Draft Constitutional Treaty*, CONV 369/02, available at: http://european-convention.eu.int/

Giddens, A. (1990), *The Consequences of Modernity*. Polity, Cambridge.

Giddens, A. (1991), *Modernity and Self-Identity*. Polity, Cambridge.

Giddens, A. (1998), *The Third Way: The Renewal of Social Democracy*. Polity, Cambridge.

Hallituksen tiedonanto eduskunnalle 1995. (Finnish Government's Report to the Parliament on the Guidelines of Finnish EU-policy) [http:www.vn.fi], electronic document, 23 October 1997.

Hanell, T., Aalbu, H. and Neubauer, J. (2002), *Regional Development in the Nordic Countries*. Nordregio, Stockholm.

He 148/1996. Hallituksen esitys eduskunnalle valtion aluehallintoa koskevan lainsäädännön uudistamisesta. (The Government's proposal to the parliament concerning the legislative reform of regional administration.)

Helsingin Sanomat, 25 February (1997), 'Maakunnat haluavat pitää tukipäätökset Brysselissä'. ('The Regions want to keep funding decisions in Brussels', article in the main Finnish newspaper *Helsingin Sanomat*).

Hughes Hallett, A. and Scott, D. (1992), *Monetary Union and the Regions: Final Report*. Prepared for the Consortium of Scottish Local Authorities. COSLA, Edinburgh.

Ingebritsen, C. and Larson, S. (1997). 'Interest and Identity: Finland, Norway and European Union', *Cooperation and Conflict*, 32:2, 207-222.

John, P. (1994), 'UK Sub-National Offices in Brussels: Diversification or Regionalization?', *Regional Studies*, 28:7, 739-746.

Keating, M. (1998), 'Is There a Regional Level of Government in Europe?' in P. Le Galès and C. Lequesne (eds), *Regions in Europe*. London, Routledge, pp. 11-29.

Kirkinen, H. (1996), *Maakuntahallinto: kansanvallan uusi taso*. WSOY, Helsinki.

Kohler-Koch, B. (1998), 'La renaissance de la dimension territoriale en Europe: entre illusion et réalité' in E. Négrier et B. Jouve (dir.), *Que Gouvernent les Régions d'Europe?* L'Harmattan, Paris et Montréal, pp. 33-53.

Komiteamietintö (1974), Väliportaanhallintokomitean mietintö.

Laki alueiden kehittämisestä. 10.12.1993, 1135/1993. (Previous law on developing the regions, available at www.intermin.fi)

Laki saariston kehityksen edistämisestä. 26.6.1981/494. (Law on promoting development in archipelago areas, available in Finnish and Swedish at www.finlex.fi)

Le Galès, P. (1998), 'Conclusion: Government or Governance of Regions' in P. Le Galès and C. Lequesne (eds), *Regions in Europe*. Routledge, London and New York, pp. 239-267.

Loughlin, J. (1996), 'Europe of the Regions and the Federalization of Europe', *Publius: The Journal of Federalism*, 26: 141-162.

Loughlin, J., Mathias, J. and Reilly, A. (1998), 'Mobilisation régionale et échange politique au Pays-de-Galles et dans les West Midlands' in E. Négrier et B. Jouve (dir.), *Que Gouvernent les Régions d'Europe?* L'Harmattan, Paris et Montréal, pp. 135-159.

Lähteenmäki-Smith, K. (1999), *Globalization and Regionalization as Concurrent Phenomena in the European Governance Structure: Sub-National Regional Actors in the European Union: Four Scenarios*, PhD, University of Turku.

Lääninhallituslaki, 10.1.1997, 22/1997.

Mennola, Erkki (1990), *Maakunnan vapaus*. (*The Freedom of the Regions*.) Tampere University Press, Tampere.

Morata, F. (1998), 'Mobilisations différentielles dans l'Espagne des autonomres' in E. Négrier et B. Jouve (dir), Que gouvernent les régions d'Europe? L'Harmattan, Paris et Montréal.

Mäki-Lohiluoma, K-P and Oulasvirta, L. (2002), *Tuleeko neuvottelemalla tulosta? Valtion ja kuntien neuvottelujärjestelmästä*. (*Do Negotiations Lead to Results? Negotiation Systems between the State and Municipalities*.) Tampere University Press, Tampere.

Nederveen Pieterse, J. (1995), 'Globalisation as Hybridization' in M. Featherstone, S. Lash and R. Robertson (eds), *Global Modernities*. Sage, London, pp. 69-90.

Négrier, E. (1998), 'Que gouvernent les régions d'Europe? Échange politique territorialisé mobilisations régionales' in E. Négrier et B. Jouve (dir), *Que Gouvernent les Régions d'Europe?* L'Harmattan, Paris et Montréal, pp. 11-31.

Niemi-Iilahti, A., Stenvall, J. and Ståhlberg, K. (2002), *Iskukykyisempi Suomi. suomalaisen aluehallinnon kokonaisarviointi ja kehittämislinjauksia*. (A More Effective Finland: Evaluation of the Finnish Regional Administration.) Ministry of the Interior, Helsinki.

Paasi, A. (1996), *Territories, Boundaries and Consciousness. The Changing Geographies of the Finnish-Russian Border*. John Wiley and Sons, Chichester.

Petersen, N. (1997), 'The Nordic Trio and the Future of the EU' in G. Edwards and A. Pijpers (eds), *The Politics of European Treaty Reform. The 1996 Intergovernmental Conference and Beyond*. Pinter, London and Washington, pp. 159-187.

Preuß, U.K. (1996), 'Two Challenges to European Citizenship', *Political Studies*, 44:3, 534-552.

Regional Council of Southwest Finland (1997), 'Strategy for Internationalisation'. The Regional Council of Southwest Finland, Turku.

Sisäasiainministeriö (1994), *Aluetason kansainvälistä yhteistyötä selvittävän työryhmän mietintö*. (Finnish Ministry of Interior: Memorandum from the committee on international co-operation of the Regions.)

Statistics Finland (1998), *GDP and Employment* (1990-1998). [http://www.stat.fi/tk/tp_db/hg4_en.gif], electronic document, 9 December 1998.

Suomen Kuntaliitto (1998), *Kuntien ja alueiden toimistot Brysselissä*, Kuntaliiton Brysselin toimiston muistio. (The Brussels offices of municipal and regional authorities, Memo of the Finnish Association of Local Authorities.)

Valtioneuvosto (1998), (Finnish Council of State). *Government Programme*. 13 April 1995. [http://www.vn.fi/vn/english/index.htm], electronic document, 10 December 1998.

Virkkala, Seija (2002), 'The Finnish Cases – Combining Top-down and Bottom-up Partnership Formation' in A. Östhol and B. Svensson (eds), *Partnership Responses – Regional Governance in the Nordic Countries*, Nordregio, Stockholm, pp. 135-202.

Chapter 4

Norway

Jan Erik Grindheim[1]

The political and administrative unit in Norway equivalent to the regional level in the European Union and its member states is the county. The Norwegian name for county is *fylke,* with the *fylkesting* (county council) as the governing body of the county authority (*fylkeskommunen*) and the *fylkesmann* (county governor) as the state's representative in the county. There are 19 counties in mainland Norway, including Oslo being both a county and a municipality. The counties are divided into 434 municipalities, called *kommuner* in Norwegian, with the two largest cities Oslo and Bergen also divided into a fourth level of governance, *bydelsutvalg* (neighbourhood council). Region, however, is also used for functionally defined administrative units above the county level in the state hierarchy, for example health regions, or trans-national political and administrative units such as the Barents Region and this administrative level of government is increasing its power in Norway today.

This chapter begins with an introduction to the role of the regional, that is, county level, and its historical roots in the Norwegian political and administrative system. Then it shows how the membership negotiations between Norway and the European Union in 1994 was an impetus for change in the content and strategy of the Norwegian regional policy. Finally, I argue that the supra-state integration and sub-state regionalization that European countries have experienced over the past ten years particularly have caused a change in Norwegian rural and regional policy instruments from a centralized and territorial to a decentralized and functional approach.

Contrary to what other European countries seem to have experienced, however, the process of European integration and regionalization has not changed the top-down character of Norwegian regional policy in favour of a more bottom-up based policy of true regionalization. The county councils have lost considerable power in the last decade, in particular, to rediscovered or newly created regional bodies above the counties in the state hierarchy, which are mainly sector based and developed to foster principles of economic and administrative efficiency like sound practices, uniform approach and co-location rather than being placed under directly popularly elected political administration.

---

1 Thanks to Helene Ohm for valuable comments.

Norway in Brief

Norway is the only Nordic country without constitutional protection of the self-government of county and municipal councils. Nevertheless, local self-government is just as important in Norway as in the other Nordic countries and it has played a vital role in Norwegian political history, not least in the two referendums in Norway on membership of the European Union in 1972 and 1994. In both cases, there was a clear centre-periphery cleavage in which one of the main arguments was 'no to central bureaucracy, yes to local self-determination!'

Geographically, Norway is a long and narrow country with a scattered population in the north-west periphery of Europe. The 4.5 million Norwegians like to say that if you could swing the 1,750 km-long country down by its most southerly point, it would reach the Mediterranean. The area covered by Norway, including the northern islands Jan Mayen and Svalbard, is close to that of Great Britain or Italy. Outside mainland Norway, the polar region Dronning Maud Land, Peter I Øy and Bouvetøya at the South Pole are also under Norwegian protection but insofar as sovereignty over these regions is limited by international law, they will not be dealt with here.

Culturally, Norway has been a homogeneous country since the first parts of it were assembled as a political entity in the ninth century. There has been no regional claim for independence in its modern history. The only ethnic minority has been the indigenous Sami people in the north. The size of the Sami population has been reckoned at somewhere between 60,000 and 100,000, of which around 40,000 to 45,000 are believed to live in Norway. After strong oppression from the Norwegian nation-state in the nineteenth and twentieth centuries, the Sami people established its own parliament in 1988. Its political authority is based on a functional and not territorial definition. According to the Norwegian constitution, 'it is the responsibility of the authorities of the State to create conditions enabling the Sami people to preserve and develop its language, culture and way of life' (cited in Helander, 1992). In addition to the Sami ethnic minority there are around 300,000 immigrants in Norway. Most of them come from the Nordic countries, Europe or the United States and belong to the same Western cultural tradition as Norwegians, and also non-Western immigrants are in most cases culturally integrated into Norwegian society. Only in Oslo, have there been tendencies of functional and territorial concentration of various immigrant groups, primarily from Pakistan and Vietnam, which are the largest and fourth largest immigrant groups in Norway (Statistics Norway, 2002).

Politically, Norway is a constitutional monarchy and a unitary state. In unitary states, only one source of sovereign authority exists and all sorts of local self-government are in the end legally defined by the central state. The right to local self-government may be amended or withdrawn by the central government at will, 'so neither a means of adjudication regarding allocation of sovereignty nor methods of policy co-ordination between two sovereign levels of government are so necessary' (Roberts, 1997, p. 250). The Norwegian constitution dates back to 1814 when Norway was taken from Denmark and given to Sweden as a reward after the Napoleonic Wars. Norway gained full independence from Sweden in 1905 but already under what was called a personal union with Sweden, it took the first steps towards a fully-fledged modern democracy. On January 14, 1837, an act (*Formannskapslovene*) concerning local self-government in administrative counties and municipalities was passed in Norway. From 1884 secret ballots and a parliamentary system of government were introduced and universal suffrage was established in 1913. Direct elections at the regional level were implemented in 1976, when county councils also established their own administrative bodies and were granted the right to collect tax. In 1979 citizens of Nordic countries got the right to vote in local elections and in 1983, this right was extended to include also citizens of non-Nordic countries (Eliassen and Pedersen, 1985).

Today, there are three levels of government in the Norwegian political and administrative system with a fourth territorially defined political level in the two largest cities, Oslo and Bergen, and a fifth functionally defined administrative level between the counties and the state. In table 4.1 below, these two are not included and hence the county level should be seen as the regional political and administrative level in Norway.

Table 4.1 The levels of government and relationship between them in the Norwegian political system

	State	County	Municipality
National	Departments		
	Directorates		
Regional	County governor	County councils	
	Regional state offices		
Local	Local state offices		Municipal councils

Source: Building on Fimreite and Grindheim (2001, p. 81)

There is no hierarchical relationship between the counties and municipalities in the Norwegian system of local self-government, insofar as the county and municipal councils have equal power and authority in relation to the state. The county governor is the state's representative at the regional level and his/her main function is to control and supervise the municipalities. Only to a very limited degree does the county governor intervene in the policy and politics of the county authorities, which are subordinate to the ministries and directorates on a functional basis, that is, in relation to sector specific tasks.

The strong position of municipal self-government in Norway can also explain why the regional level between the counties and the state is so politically underdeveloped or non-existent in Norway but is strengthening its administrative power and authority. Whether this will change in the future is difficult to say but within the Norwegian state hierarchy, the counties have definitely lost much of their power and authority due to the creation of functionally defined administrative regions between the counties and the state. Some of it may be regained from a stronger international role of the counties in trans-regional programmes such as Interreg, etc. So far, however, what has come out of the increased focus on regionalization in Europe is mainly that Norwegian counties have developed an international perspective for increased trans-national co-operation and not for the strengthening of their power and authority within the Norwegian state hierarchy.

The History of Local Self-government in Norway

Already in the twelfth century, Norway was divided into 25 *fylker* (counties), an Old Norse word, and a derivative of *folk* (people). Early historians thought that *fylke* was the original designation of the territorial domain of differentiated tribes, meaning something like 'folkland', but as Olof Petersson (1994) has argued, administratively and politically the medieval *Things* (deliberative assemblies) were probably of greater importance for the development of the regional level than the *fylke*. The *Things* played an important role in the settling of disputes, passing of sentences on law-breakers and the election of kings at an early stage. The local district constituted a rudimentary form of self-government and *Things* were held both within smaller districts and whole regions.

As the administration of justice was gradually taken over by a centralized system of law courts and Norway became a hereditary monarchy in 1260, the *Things* diminished in importance and only the administrative structure was maintained to enforce the centralized power of the King. With the introduction of absolutist rule by the Danish King in Norway in 1660 what was then called *len* (the former *fylke*) changed name to *amt*, which is the term still used for counties in Denmark, and the local vassal was transformed into the King's officer in the region under the name of *amtmann*.

In the eighteenth century the *amt* – and above that in the administrative hierarchy the four *stiftamt* – extended its importance once again as the King was forced to establish some kind of public assistance for the increasing number of poor people, following a strong growth in the Norwegian population. Together with the bishop, who headed the parallel but in Protestant countries integrated ecclesiastical power structure, the *stiftamtmann* (the King's officer in the *stiftamt*) was given the responsibility to set up what was called 'school and poverty commissions' for the poor in the parishes. These commissions consisted of a representative from the local authority (*lensmann*), the vicar and two of his assistants (called *ombud*) and two representatives of the peasants in the local community (Nagel, 1991). The commissions were paid for by local farmers but in many cases also the *amt* and the *stiftamt* had to support them when the costs were too high. In the towns and villages, school and poverty systems were based on a larger degree of voluntarism but as this system proved to be insufficient, town councils were soon also allowed to collect taxes for this purpose.

The school and poverty commissions were the main pillars of the Norwegian system of local self-government when the act on local executive committees (*Formannskapslovene*) was sanctioned in 1837 (Steen, 1968), and during the nineteenth century, health, social welfare and schooling were going to be even more important for local communities to be engaged in. The reason for this was the fear of politicians of the new democratic nation-state to introduce any kind of central public support or even regulation of the economy that could bring out the taste of the former Danish 'Guardian State' (Grindheim, 1986).

In 1918, Norwegian counties were renamed *fylke* and the state's representative in the *fylke* was now to be called *fylkesmann*. However, local self-government was still mainly to be based on the municipalities. From 1890 to 1920, Norwegian municipalities went through a process of strong expansion – in particular in relation to health, social welfare and schooling. Together with voluntary social welfare organizations and private actors, local politicians and what Rune Ervik and Stein Kuhnle (1993) have called socio-political intellectuals at both the local and the national level, initiated new social welfare services and school reforms later to be taken over by the state and made universal for all citizens at the national level. A new time of growth in local self-government came in the years 1940-60 but after this, the national level once again strengthened its position versus the local level of government by focusing on the regional level (Seip, 1991).

Bringing the Counties Back In

In the 1960s, Norwegian counties were given an active role in the development of a better psychiatric health care, the set-up of new hospitals and nursing homes, and in secondary education. As a result, the ratio of expenses between the counties and the municipalities changed from 10%-90% in 1950 to 30%-70% in 1978 (Grønlie, 1987). However, the county councils were still only indirectly elected entities without autonomous political power. They consisted of mayors of rural municipalities and the county governors, with the mayors of the cities included from 1964, and direct elections were not introduced before 1976.

The most important change in the politics of local self-government in Norway since then is a pilot project on increased local self-government introduced in 1987 which lasted until 1992 called *frikommuneforsøket* (the free municipality experiment). It followed the implementation of a new income system for the counties and municipalities in 1986 and was a project in which 20 municipalities and four (later six) counties were given a time-limited exemption from national rules and regulations to develop autonomous strategies to improve their services by becoming more efficient and more democratic. For instance the city council of Oslo and the county council of Hedmark introduced a parliamentary system of government instead of the traditional system of power sharing. For the four counties the project was first directed towards the field of trade and industry/business development and primarily concentrated on how the northern county of Finnmark and the county of Nord-Trøndelag in mid-Norway, with extra subsidies from the national level, could develop and implement a local regional policy based on their own goals and priorities. Second, how the northern county of Nordland and the southern county of Aust-Agder could improve their services by new models of co-operation between the politicians and the administrative personnel of the county and the state. The result was the development of new organizational structures for the relationship between the state and the counties. Before the 1980s central planning had dominated this relationship but the pilot project got an increasing number of counties to introduce new political and administrative routines, such as strategic planning, agreements of intent and project organisation, and it led to a stronger consciousness in Norway for an autonomous regional policy (Fimreite, 1997).

The top-down character of this pilot project illustrates how integrated the idea of local self-government traditionally has been in the national policy of the Norwegian state. But when we study the relationship between the counties and the state, much has changed in the 1990s due both to internal processes of de-bureaucratization, decentralization and democratization of the traditionally rule-orientated and centralized Norwegian state-model (Grindheim, 1994), and to external processes of supra-state integration and sub-state regionalization in Europe (Grindheim, 1998; 1999). Hence, following Udo Bullmann, we could say that in a historical perspective, Norway has moved from a *classic unitary* state to a partly *devolving unitary* state on a continuum in which *regionalized unitary* states and *federal* states are the next two values on the variable:

- *Classic unitary states* have sub-national government only at the local level. Regional structures may exist for administrative purposes, but are strictly subordinated to the central state;
- *Devolving unitary states* have undergone a process of reform to establish elected regional authorities above the local level. The regional tier enjoys a certain degree of constitutional protection and autonomy;
- *Regionalized unitary states* are characterized by the existence of a directly elected tier of regional government with constitutional status, wide-ranging autonomy and legislative powers. Most of the regions here are also larger in size than in devolving unitary countries. These countries have gone furthest down the road of regional devolution among the unitary states in the EU;
- *Federal states* involve a constitutional sharing of powers and the coexistence of sovereignties. The regional tier exists in its own right and cannot be abolished or restructured unilaterally by the central government (Bullman, 1997, p. 1).

Taking the Counties Out? Bringing Regions In?

In Norway, as in other European countries and in the political and administrative system of the European Union, there are also special administrative units called regions at a higher level than the county to which it seems to be a trend today to transfer power. Top-down in classic unitary states, bottom-up in federal political systems and through the system of subsidiarity in the EU. Region is for example used by the Norwegian Army for the organization of national defence, the Directorate of Labour for the division of the labour market, and the Norwegian National Coastal Administration for the conduct of sea-transport in Norwegian waters or Norwegian road authorities for transport on land. Recently, the Norwegian Public Roads

Administration (*Statens vegvesen*) was reorganized from a county-based to a regional structure of five units. Most interesting in relation to the role of the counties, however, is the total reorganization of the hospital sector newly implemented by the Ministry of Health in Norway.

In June 2001, the Norwegian Parliament (*Stortinget*) resolved that from January 1 2002 all public hospitals in Norway should be taken over by central government and operated as Health Enterprises under state responsibility within five health regions. Even though the reform is commonly known as the Hospital Reform, it included most municipal specialist health services within both somatic and psychiatric health care and the ambulance service, and was a functional and administrative reorganization of formerly territorially and politically based structures. Its most serious consequence was the total dismantling of the role of the counties in Norwegian health and social welfare policy. It broke with a more than 30-year tradition of hospitals being owned and run by the counties in Norway.

Already in 1974, however, Norway had been divided into five health regions, 'to reflect the fact that as far as specialist medicine was concerned one needed a large catchment area in order to secure high-quality services at an acceptable cost' (Ministry of Health, 2003), but regional co-operation in this system was based on voluntary participation by the counties. The objectives of the new reform were to give Norwegians better and more equal health services, improve the running of hospitals through what was to become known as unambiguous management, and to create a clear division of responsibility. The vision was to introduce a new form of functional organization of the Norwegian health and hospital services – 'better suited to meet the challenges of the medical technology of tomorrow' (Hellandsvik, 2003, p. 5). Needless to say, the reform had a devastating effect on the political and administrative legitimacy of the counties. Overnight, they went from being the most important service providers in the health sector to being left with secondary education and a rather undefined role as partners in regional development. Today one of the main issues in the debate on the future role of the counties in Norway is if there is any role for them at all.

Looking at figures from 1998, when hospitals were still the responsibility of the counties in Norway, budgets show clearly the importance of this sector at the county level (see figure 4.2). The health and welfare sector stood for more than 60 per cent of the budgets, followed by secondary education (24 per cent), transport and communication (eight per cent), central administration (three per cent), culture (two per cent), and business and environmental issues, what is now called regional development (two per cent).

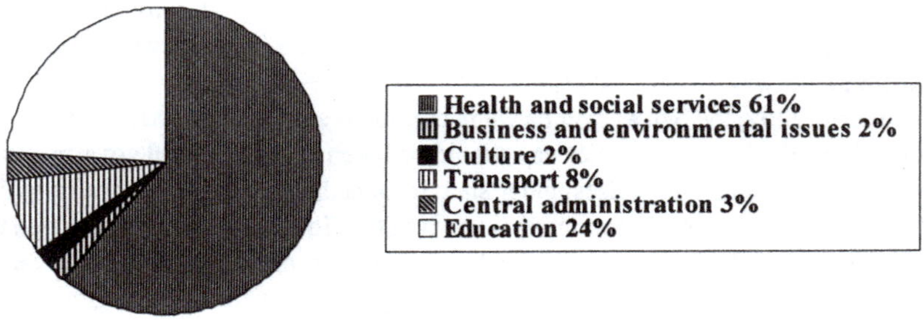

Figure 4.1 Gross public expenses of Norwegian counties 1998 (percentages)

Source: NOU, 2000: 22, p. 431.

Europeanization of Norwegian Regional Policy

The dispute over the future political and administrative role of the county level in Norway has not been focused solely on the changes brought about by the Hospital Reform and the idea of a regionalization at a higher administrative level of this sector from 1974. At the beginning of the 1990s, when Norway negotiated membership of the European Union and one of the main questions was what to do with the traditional centralized Norwegian rural and regional policy instruments, huge differences in the income structure of Norwegian counties appeared and, with that, knowledge about a system of subsidies incompatible with the rules of the EU. Taxes, for example, varied from NOK 3,952 per capita in Nord-Trøndelag to NOK 6,614 per capita in Akershus, and state subsidies were transferred in a proportion of 5:1 for non-earmarked subsidies and 3:1 for those earmarked to the two counties, a variation making it necessary to develop a comprehensive policy of equalization of expenses among the counties, plus extra subsidies for the counties in the northern part of the country (NOU, 1996, p. 1).

The subsidy policy, however, was not only incompatible with the rules of the EU. It was also criticized internally in Norway for conserving conditions the way they were and not bringing needed changes to what increasingly was understood as a dependency of particularly the peripheral districts of the north to the central state. The average rate of subsidies from the state was higher than the counties' income from fees and taxes, but again, there were big differences. In 1994 only the eastern counties of Akershus, Buskerud and Vestfold, and the western counties of Rogaland and Hordaland, had a positive ratio between fees and taxes on the one hand and state subsidies on the other. In Akershus 29 per cent of the income came as state subsidies, in Rogaland 37 per cent, while in the most northern county of Finnmark the state counted for 63 per cent of the income and in the western county of Sogn og Fjordane and the northern counties of Nord-Trøndelag, Nordland and Troms the figure was between 55 and 58 per cent

(NOU, 1997, p. 8). The result of the debate on the disproportionate economic relationship between central and peripheral counties in Norway led to a radical change in regional policy in the 1990s. The most important reason for this change was the negotiations on membership between Norway and the European Union before the referendum in 1994.

In the Norwegian government's regional statement to the parliament – put forward by the Ministry of Local Government and Labour as a parliamentary report in 1988–89 – regional policy was given a *centralized* and *territorial* definition as:

> the total public contribution to promote geographic balance and safe living conditions in all parts of the country. Both regional planning and district policy are parts of the regional policy. *Regional planning* is the physical and economic survey planning which takes place in all counties and municipalities. *The district policy*[2] has as its goal to develop trade and industry and local communities in the poorest developed parts of the country (St. meld. nr. 29, 1988–89, p. 5, translation by author).

While the next regional statement four years later was called 'City and land hand in hand' (*By og land hand i hand*) and focused on a *decentralized* and *functional* based policy for regional development:

> With an extensive regional division of labour the added value in one region will depend on functions in other regions, and the total national added value will be dependent on the collaboration between the different regions (St. meld. nr. 33, 1992–93, p. 5, translation by author).

The first statement had a geographical framework based on the counties and municipalities as its point of departure, the second took geographical areas with a common labour and service market – independent of administrative borders – as its starting point. According to the Ministry of Local Government and Labour, the change was brought about as a result of alterations in the international environment – in particular the supra-state integration and sub-state regionalization of Western Europe and the integration between east and west in Europe (St. meld. nr. 33, 1992–93, p. 16). In the next regional statement 'About the District and Regional Policy (*Om distrikts- og regionalpolitikken*) from 1996–97, after the majority of the Norwegian electorate had turned down the government's membership agreement with the EU, it was particularly the role of the counties that was emphasised:

> In a further development of the Norwegian district and regional policy in which the regions play an important part in the shaping of goals and strategies, it is primarily the county level that will be the natural unit to build on. [...] Co-operation across the county borders must

2 In Norway, the concept 'district policy' has traditionally been used for the centralized and territorially based regional policy, or what today is called 'rural and regional policy instruments', and does not refer to any particular level of government in the Norwegian political and administrative system.

> be stimulated when natural in relation to functional labour, market and service regions (St. meld. nr. 31, 1996–97, p. 8, translation by author).

It was the regional statement from 1992–93 that set the overall framework for the development of what was called an 'EU-adapted' Norwegian regional policy strategy in the 1990s and implemented by the Ministry of Local Government and Labour in January 1994, after being sanctioned by the European Surveillance Authority (ESA) according to the European Economic Area (EEA) agreement. The aims of the strategy were first to improve knowledge about the problems of the districts and towns in Norway to develop a cohesive regional policy, and second to present an analysis of how the Ministry could organize this policy in the best way possible. In 1996 the Minister of Local Government and Labour Gunnar Berge said:

> Regarding the regional policy, we should aim at a development in step with the mainstream of EU's regional policy. Not because this is important in itself, but because I think it represents important elements in relation to the responsibility of the regional level for regional development, in our case the responsibility of the county (Berge, 1996, p. 3, translation by author).

From Centralized District Policy to Decentralized Regional Policy

The immediate result of the new approach was a redefinition of the geographical field of operation for the rural and regional policy instruments in Norway. The political basis for the revision was laid in 1992 when a majority of the representatives of the parliament had asked for a concentration of the geographical field of operation for what was then known as the Regional Development Fund (*Distriktenes utbyggingsfond* – DU). DU had been set up in 1960 as a state-run organization for regional policy organized by what was at that time called the Ministry of Local Government. But in the 1980s the responsibility for this policy had been decentralized to the county and municipal levels and concentrated on a new goal and means-oriented management strategy at the expense of the traditional rule-oriented and centralized *distriktspolitikk* (district policy), as it was called in Norwegian. The idea was to make DU responsible for the trade and industry targeted instruments while long-term planning and the means utilized by the municipalities in regional policy still was to be managed by the Government and the Ministry of Local Government and Labour. The policy failed, however, as it caused a new wave of centralization of rural and regional policy instruments at a time when the regional imbalance and its challenges called for the opposite strategy (St. meld. nr. 29, 1988–89).

As part of the change in the traditional rural and regional policy instruments, a new instrument called The Norwegian Industrial and Regional Development Fund (*Statens nærings- og distriktsutviklingsfond*) was set up in 1993. It was based on the old DU structure, an industrial fund (*Industrifondet*), a fund for small and medium-sized enterprises (*Småbedriftsfondet*), and the Norwegian Bank of Industry (*Den Norske*

Industribank A/S). Its aim was to play an active role in the development of trade and industry in rural areas by making the traditional territorial and centralized rural and regional policy instruments more cohesive, efficient and user-friendly for local businesses (St. meld. nr. 31, 1996–97). The only short-term alterations that came through, though, were a reorganization of the local branches of the Bank of Industry into regional offices for SND and an increase in the number of offices from three to five. The long-term result was the development of a two-tier system at the regional level in Norway with SND and the counties (Berge, 1994). As long as the administration of risk loans, guarantees and subsidies was kept at the Ministry of Local Government and Labour and the Ministry of Trade and Industry, however, it became clear that in the short run this arrangement also was too centralized. The role of the counties in regional policy did not change to meet the new challenges pointed out in the regional statement of 1992–93 and it soon became clear that SND had to be reorganized only two years after it had been set up.

According to the magazine 'Municipal Report' (*Kommunal rapport*) (1995), a survey among the users of SND had shown that they were not satisfied with the services provided. Consequently, the permanent secretary of the Ministry of Trade and Industry Anne Breiby had to point out that SND had not been established for the politicians of the county and municipal councils but as an instrument to be used primarily by small and medium sized enterprises. She based her argument on the conclusion of a report delivered in 1995 by a committee called *Steine-utvalget*, which had been established to reconsider the organization of the SND as a result of the criticism raised against it for being too centralized and inflexible. The commission suggested that SND had to:

- Establish local offices in each county to distribute the business subsidies and to counterweight the political power of the county councils in this part of the district policy;
- Leave the responsibility for the development of regional business plans to the county councils;
- Set up business councils in each county to improve the collaboration between SND and the county councils.

The committee, the Norwegian Federation of Trade Unions (*Landsorganisasjonen*) and the Confederation of Norwegian Business and Industry (*Næringslivets Hovedorganisasjon*) supported the alterations suggested because they thought this would give a less bureaucratic, more user-friendly and comprehensive regional policy.[3] The political legitimacy behind it was derived from Minister Berge and the Labour Party government he was part of in 1995:

> As a result of both national and international changes, the regional policy will be faced with considerable tasks in the time to come. More than before it is necessary that we get the best

3 Taken from http://www1.kr.kommorg.no/kr/Arkiv/95_10/SND.html.

developmental effect possible out of the total regional political efforts. In particular there are three areas that stand out in the future development of regional policy: (1) reinforced regional co-operation across national borders, (2) better co-ordination of the total public contribution for regional development, and (3) further development of the means and administration directed towards trade and industry development in the regions (Berge, 1995, p. 9, translation by author).

Regional Development Programmes

Following this development, the introduction of what was called regional development programmes (in Norwegian: *regionale utviklingsprogrammer* shortened RUP) in the regional statement from 1996–97 was to become the most important change in the political context of Norwegian counties at the end of the 1990s. The purpose of these programmes was to establish a more efficient regional policy anchored in a more binding relationship between challenges, comparative advantages and planning of each region. Goals and strategies were to be formulated at the county level but in accordance with national goals for the rural and regional policy instruments. The county councils were supposed to work out the development programmes in close collaboration with regional governing bodies, labour and trade and industry to develop a partnership-model, a political statement clearly taken from the idea of the 'Europe of the Regions' programme of the EU, as we can read from the parliamentary report St. meld. 31, 1996-97, page 8:

> This development should be seen as a continuation of the experiences drawn from the preparations in 1994 for a possible membership of the EU through the work on Goal 6,[4] the pilot project on increased local self-government of the counties in Aust-Agder and Nordland, the work on Interreg and the models for collaboration developed in other countries. Better consultation, collaboration and co-operation at the regional level give a better exploitation of resources and integration between sectors. In addition, it provides a basis for better interaction between central, regional and local government (translation by author).

How the regional development programmes (RUPs) were organized in practice can be seen from table 4.2 below, where there is an overview of the budgets for 2000 in relation to RUPs in three Norwegian counties.

---

4 This was supposed to have included the four northern counties of Norway: Nord-Trøndelag, Nordland, Troms and Finmark and an understanding with the president of the Sami Parliament.

Table 4.2 Regional development programme budgets in three Norwegian counties 2000, in million €*

	Nordland**	Oppland	Rogaland
Preparations for business development	2.21	1.54	0.68
County specific means	4.01	1.68	0.49
Transfers to preparations for business development	1.64	0.54	***
Rural Development Fund (*Bygdeutviklingsfondet*)	0.41	2.8	
Subsidies for peripheral areas	13.1	3.56	1.31
Targeted risk loans for peripheral areas	6.36		0.94
Grants for setting up new businesses	1.35	0.82	0.67
Funds for regional co-ordination		0.41	
Subsidies for peripheral municipalities	0.54	0.13	
Subsidies for Interreg funds	0.54		
Transformation and innovation funds		0.68	
Municipal business funds		0.79	0.31
Norwegian Labour Market Administration (aetat)	1.67	0.03	
Others (municipal and state projects, etc.)	1.01	0.58	
Total	**32.84**	**13.56**	**4.4**

* Conversion rate from NOK to € 7.3.

** Nordland is in northern Norway, Oppland inland east, Rogaland sea-ward west.

*** Blanks mean not in the 2000 budgets.

Source: The Auditor General of Norway (2001-2002).

As the table shows the different entries of the three regions' budgets are mainly economic transfers from the central state to the county level. This is a special characteristic of the Norwegian model of regional development programmes: local self-government policies are integrated in a national strategy for what is called a comprehensive regional policy. It illustrates how strong the tradition of centralized rule is in Norway, as noted also in the Parliamentary report St. meld. nr. 31, 1996-97:

> To achieve a good co-ordination between the democratically elected bodies and the state bureaucracy at the county level, it is important that the county governor actively participate in the work. To guarantee coherence with national goals in the district policy and the regional policy for trade and industry, the programmes are supposed to be sanctioned by the central government (p. 8, translation by author).

Even though regional development is seen as the main task of Norwegian counties today, as the hospital sector has been taken over by the state and more and more of the counties' tasks are functionally organized in relation to administrative sector policies, few know for sure what the future role of the counties will be. On 1 January 2002, Norwegian counties were made responsible for:

- Secondary schools;
- Dental services;
- Child welfare institutions;
- Family welfare institutions;
- Institutions for alcohol and drug addicts;
- County roads, regional and local public transport;
- Preparation for business development;
- County planning;
- Museums and other cultural services and cultural heritage.[5]

The trend, however, is that the national level is increasingly strengthened through continuous territorial and functional reorganizations, that is, power is taken from elected political bodies at the county level and given to sector organized administrative bodies representing the state at the regional level. The principles for how and what to solve at which level of these and other tasks is based on six criteria:

- Elected bodies at the local and regional level should have the responsibility to decide what issues are to be treated in accordance with local and regional discernment;
- The state should be responsible for standardized tasks based on rules and regulations;
- The state should be responsible for tasks in which national co-ordination is needed for sound practices;
- Tasks should be solved at the lowest efficient level possible;
- The county should not develop into a super-ordinate authority;
- Changes in the division of labour between the different political and administrative levels should contribute to the reduction of bureaucracy.[6]

These criteria are so broadly defined it is difficult to say if they are strengthening or weakening the role of the regional level in Norway today. From the same Parliamentary report as the above quoted criteria are taken, we can read that the counties are supposed to play a central role in the future partnerships for regional development, but how the counties should be organized is not decided. In the Parliamentary report *Kommune, fylke, stat – en bedre oppgavefordeling* (Municipality, county, state – a better division of tasks)[7] it is argued that the future organization of Norwegian counties should be based on the following criteria:

- *A functional regional level.* The counties should make up functional and sustainable units to be able to take care of regional development tasks. The

5 St. meld. nr. 19, 2001-02, ch. 3.
6 St. meld. nr. 19, 2001-02, ch. 3 (translation by author).
7 St. meld. nr. 31, 2000-01, ch. 9 (translation by author).

territorial organization of the counties should contribute to securing a good co-ordination of resources within naturally coherent areas;

- *A real and meaningful democracy.* The county authorities shall be democratic arenas and give good opportunities for the citizens to participate in and influence the development of the regions;
- *Good user orientation.* People shall be able to make use of services provided by the nearest county authority;
- *Efficient use of resources.* The county authority should take advantage of economies of scale and make sure that regional tasks are solved in the most rational way within naturally coherent areas. The territorial organization of the counties should contribute to the most efficient use of resources, knowledge development and co-ordination within the state institutions in the counties.[8]

So far, most of the counties have discussed possibilities for mergers of counties into larger regions: Rogaland, Hordaland and Sogn og Fjordane in the west, Aust- and Vest-Agder and Telemark in the south, Telemark, Buskerud and Vestfold in the south-east, and Østfold, Oppland, Hedmark and Akershus in the eastern part of Norway. None of them, however, have been implemented. The county should therefore still be seen as the main regional political and administrative unit in Norway and in figure 4.3 and figure 4.4 below, we see how a typical county authority is organized in Norway today. The example is taken from the western county of Hordaland:

8 State institutions in the counties are mainly the responsibility of the county governor, whose tasks may vary between counties, but which for example in the southern county of Vest-Agder are in charge of emergency planning, social and family affairs, municipal affairs, other legal matters, environmental protection, farming and forestry, health care and education as of 1 January 2003.

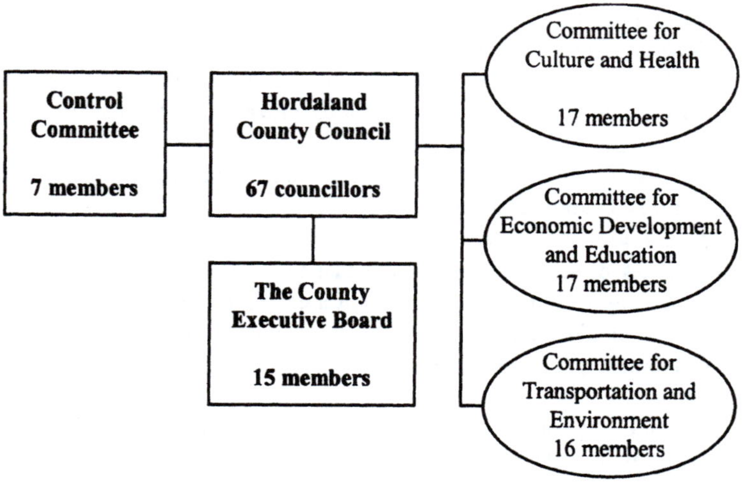

Figure 4.2 The political structure of a Norwegian county authority

Source: Hordaland County Authority, 2003.

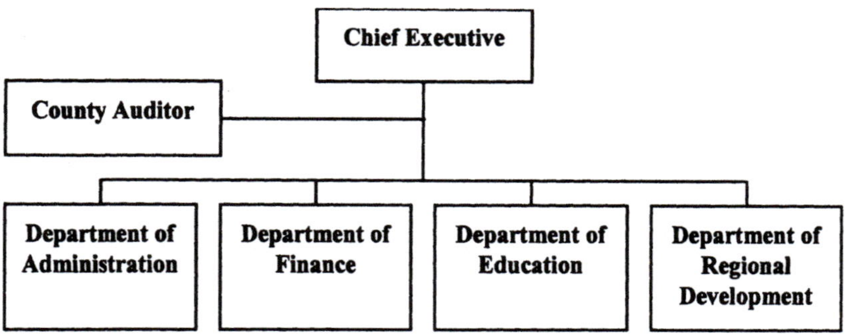

Figure 4.3 The administrative structure of a Norwegian county authority

Source: Hordaland County Authority, 2003.

One question remains, however. That is how the Europeanization of Norwegian regional policy has influenced the policy of counties themselves. Has led to a stronger bottom-up character of regional self-government in Norway?

Counties as Independent and International Actors?

The development of the Norwegian district and regional policy has traditionally been influenced by the regional policy of the other Nordic countries but after both Finland

and Sweden joined the European Union in 1995 the regional policy of the EU has become more important for Norway. Over the past decade, both the Labour Party governments and the coalition governments of the non-socialist parties in Norway – at present consisting of the Christian People's Party (*Kristelig folkeparti*), the Conservative Party (*Høyre*) and the Social Liberal party *Venstre* – have emphasised the need for Norway to participate in or at least to match the regional programmes of the EU. However, not being a member of the EU, Norway cannot take part in the structural and regional funds of the Union or other programmes specially designed for its member states. One exception is the Interreg programmes, where Norwegian governments since 1995 have given financial support to Norwegian counties participating in targeted projects under the different programmes.[9] Furthermore, analyses of the strong and weak sides of the regional areas pertaining to goals, strategies and actions have been discussed and developed in co-operation with the European Commission while implementation has been taken care of by the regional level through a partnership-model with the county councils as co-ordinating units.

How to organize the relationship between Norwegian counties and counties in the Union when the new regional funds for 2007-2013 are implemented is more difficult. As the negotiations between Norway and the European Commission about the European Economic Area Agreement (EEA) showed in the first months of 2003, it has been difficult to agree on what contributions countries like Norway should pay as non-members of the Union and whether a higher fee could give extended access to the programmes such as Interreg, etc. Nevertheless it is clear that, yes- and no-membership governments alike are determined to continue the interregional co-operation programmes with the EU, as State Secretary of the Norwegian Ministry of Foreign Affairs Kim Traavik (2003) has emphasized during negotiations with the European Commission over Norway's relationship with an enlarged European Union. However, as has been clearly demonstrated in the past, being a non-member of the EU brings with it some special needs and interests for Norway in the development of the future interregional programmes.

In addition to the overall goals of the Interreg IIa-programmes for example, it was also important from a Norwegian point of view to strengthen the economic role of the border counties and regions towards their counterparts in other countries particularly after Finland and Sweden joined the EU and got access to the Union's structural and regional funds. In the Interreg IIc-programmes the most important objectives were to take care of the national and regional interests in the two areas – with the purpose of promoting a sustainable economic growth that also takes into consideration social and environmental factors in the regions. Most striking, though, has been the problematic issue in the Norwegian debate on local self-government of how to give the counties a more independent political position in the state hierarchy on international issues. As former Minister of the Environment Thorbjørn Berntsen has argued, in theory the planning processes of the counties is a good tool for the development of larger regional co-operative structures, but 'in practice the county councils are often

9 For an overview, see www.interreg.no.

squeezed between strong state services and municipalities with the means to implement the policies' (Berntsen, 1996, p. 7, translation by author).

According to a 1995 report on trans-border regional co-operation in Europe and the role of Norwegian county councils, 'international co-operation with foreign regions is beginning to be a part of the political efforts for trade and industrial development in Norwegian county councils' (Farsund, Meissner and Nødland, 1995, p. iii, translation by author). Looking closer at the figures, however, the argument in this report that 'practically all counties can show some kind of activities in this area' was dubious from an empirical point of view at the time it was issued. Today, however, Norwegian counties are much more engaged in international co-operation, although few concrete results have been achieved from the many trans-border, trans-national and interregional co-operation projects. On the other hand, looking at how the programmes for such international co-operation are organized and what their aims are, the results are quite good for many Norwegian counties.[10]

Increased independent international engagement of Norwegian counties can also be measured by their presence in Brussels, where for example the Norwegian Association of Local and Regional Authorities has had their own office for many years and where today there are three county regional offices and four on the way.[11] Still, the most important change at the regional level in Norway over the last decade seems to have been in the way the content and strategy of Norwegian rural and regional policy instruments have changed since the negotiations between Norway and the EU over membership at the beginning of the 1990s.

Conclusion

Norwegian regional policy has changed over the past ten years from a mainly territorial and centralized district policy delimited by the nation-state, to a more functional and decentralized regional policy defined by the processes of supra-state integration and sub-state regionalization in Europe. Part of this process for Norwegian governments has been to emphasise the need for Norwegian counties to develop links with counties and regions in neighbouring countries. But few Norwegian counties seem to have taken advantage of the possibilities given by the new programmes for intra-national and trans-border regional co-operation in Norway, the Nordic region and in Europe to improve their power as local self-governing bodies. The main reason for

---

10 There are overviews and analytical articles, etc. of Norwegian participation in these programmes and regional policies of the EU in general at www.interreg.no. For a more academic analysis, see Andersen (2002).

11 The first county to establish a Brussels office was the south-western county of Rogaland, followed by Trøndelag from mid-Norway, and finally the northern county of Nordland. On the way are the Oslo Region (the City of Oslo and the County of Akershus, plus maybe one or more of the surrounding counties), a West-Norwegian office with the City of Bergen at its centre, a South-Norwegian office set up by the two Agder Counties, and an office for the inland eastern counties of Hedmark and Oppland.

this is the strong tradition of central control with local self-government in Norway – in particular at the county level. During the 1990s, it looked as if the counties should strengthen their political power over the central state as a result of the negotiations over Norwegian membership of the European Union and the adaptation to EU regional policies but due to recent major administrative reforms in Norway, primarily in the health and hospital sector, this process has now been reversed.

Bibliography

Andersen, Tron Lande (2002), *Fylkeskommunenes internasjonale engasjement*, internal report 25 June 2002. Oslo: Kommunenes sentralforbund.

Berge, Gunnar (1994), 'Regional- og distriktspolitisk redegjørelse', statement by the Minister of Local Government and Labour Gunnar Berge to *Stortinget* 10 May 1994, 13/94. The Ministry of Local Government and Labour, Department of Regional Policy.

Berge, Gunnar (1995), 'Regional og distriktspolitisk redegjørelse', statement by the Minister of Local Government and Labour Gunnar Berge to *Stortinget* 16 May 1995, H–17/95. The Ministry of Local Government and Labour, Department of Regional Policy.

Berge, Gunnar (1996), 'Regionalpolitikk i et internasjonalt perspektiv', lecture by the Minister of Local Government and Labour, Regjeringens kontaktkonferanse med fylkeskommunene (*The Government's Contact Conference with the County Councils*). Oslo: 29-30 May.

Berntsen, Thorbjørn (1996), 'Regional planlegging i lys av internasjonale utviklingstrekk og nasjonale utfordringer', lecture by the Minister of the Environment Thorbjørn Berntsen, Regjeringens kontaktkonferanse med fylkeskommunene (*The Government's Contact Conference with the County Councils*), Gamle Logen. Oslo: 29th May.

Bullmann, Udo (1997), 'Regional Integration in the EU – a German Perspective', paper delivered to Conference *'Local and Regional Integration in the EU'*. Odense: 7-8 March.

Eliassen, Kjell A. and Pedersen, Mogens N. (1985), *Nordic Political Facts*. Oslo: Tiden Norsk Forlag.

Ervik, Rune and Kuhnle, Stein (1993), 'Sosial kunnskap, risiko og sosialpolitikk', in Ervik, R. and Kuhnle, S. (eds), *Kunnskap, risiko og sosialpolitikk. Institusjonelle perspektiver på skandinavisk utvikling*. Bergen: Alma Mater.

Farsund, Arild, Meissner, Rudolf and Nødland, Svein Inge (1995), 'Regional samarbeid over landegrensene i Europa. Norske fylkeskommuners alliansebygging for næringsutvikling'. Stavanger: Rogalandsforskning.

Fimreite, Anne-Lise (1997), 'Kommunene', in Fimreite, A-L. (ed.), *Forskerblikk på Norge. En oppsummering fra satsningsområdet: Ledelse, organisasjon og styring*. Oslo: Tano Aschehoug.

Grindheim, Jan Erik (1986), *Velferd eller veldedighet? En analyse av frivillige organisasjoners rolle i utviklingen av alkoholistomsorgen i Norge*. Bergen: Institutt for sammenliknende politikk.

Grindheim, Jan Erik (1994), 'Towards a 'New State' in Social Policy? Changing Perspectives of the Norwegian Welfare State', in Bucar, B. and Kuhnle, S. (eds), *Small States Compared: Politics of Norway and Slovenia*. Bergen: Alma Mater.

Grindheim, Jan Erik (1996), 'Funksjonell integrasjon eller territoriell konsolidering? Nordiske regioner og EUs regionalpolitikk', paper delivered to Working Group 5 on 'The Nordic

Regions and European Integration', Nordic Political Science Association Congress. Helsinki 15-17 August 1996.
Grindheim, Jan Erik (1998), 'Europeisk regionalisering og norsk regionalpolitikk i 1990-årene – aktører, strategier, prosesser', *Norsk statsvitenskapelig tidsskrift*, 14(1) / 98.
Grindheim, Jan Erik (1999), *Regionaliseringen i Europa og norsk utenrikspolitikk*, report 1/99. Oslo: The Norwegian Ministry of Foreign Affairs.
Grønlie, Tore (1987), *Folkestyre i by og bygd, norske kommuner gjennom 150 år*, Næss, H.E. *et al.* (eds). Oslo: Universitetsforlaget.
Helander, Elina (1992), 'The Sami of Norway', written for The Norwegian Ministry of Foreign Affairs, http://odin.dep.no/ud/nornytt/uda-309.html.
Hellandsvik, Paul (2001), 'New Health Organization in Norway. Government Run Hospitals. Consequences for Research and Health Services'. Oslo: Ministry of Health.
Jervell, Sverre (1998), *N@RGE foran oppbruddet. Datateknologien, europeiseringen og regionaliseringen er i ferd med å omforme hele det norske samfunnet*. Oslo: Europaprogrammet.
Kommunal rapport (1995), http://www1.kr.kommorg.no/kr/Arkiv/95_10/SND.html.
Ministry of Foreign Affairs (1998), 'Demographic Data, Health', http://odin.dep.no/ud/publ/97/statistikk/en/kap 10.html#msd1.
Ministry of Health (2003), 'The Norwegian Hospital Reform – Government Assumes Responsibility for Hospitals'. www.odin.dep.no/shd/sykehusreformen/.
Nagel, Anne-Hilde (1991), 'Innledning. Kommunene og velferden', in Nagel, A-H. (ed.), *Velferdskommunen. Kommunenes rolle i utviklingen av velferdsstaten*. Bergen: Alma Mater.
NOU 1996:1, *Et enklere og mer rettferdig inntektssystem for kommuner og fylkeskommuner*. Oslo: Statens Forvaltningstjeneste.
NOU 1996:5, *Hvem skal eie sykehusene?* Oslo: Statens Forvaltningstjeneste.
NOU 1997:8, *Om finansiering av kommunesektoren*. Oslo: Statens Forvaltningstjeneste.
Petersson, Olof (1994), *The Government and Politics of the Nordic Countries*. Stockholm: Fritzes.
Riksrevisjonen (2001-2002), *Riksrevisjonens undersøkelse av regionale utviklingsprogrammer*. Dokument nr. 3:4, Oslo: Riksrevisjonen.
Roberts, Geoffrey K. (1997), 'Federalism, Devolution and Local Government', in Roberts, G. and Hogwood, P. (eds), *European Politics Today*. Manchester: Manchester University Press.
Seip, Anne-Lise (1991), 'Velferdskommunen og velferdstrekanten – et tilbakeblikk', in Nagel, A-H. (ed.), *Velferdskommunen. Kommunenes rolle i utviklingen av velferdsstaten*. Bergen: Alma Mater.
Statistics Norway (2002), *Innvandring og innvandrere*. Oslo: Statistics Norway.
Statistics Norway (2003), *Statistikkbanken. Offentlige finanser*. Oslo: Statistics Norway.
Steen, Sverre (1968), *Lokalt selvstyre i Norges bygder*. Oslo: J. W. Cappelens Forlag as.
St. meld. nr. 29 (1988–89), *Politikk for regional utvikling*, Kommunal- og arbeidsdepartementet. Oslo: Statens Forvaltningstjeneste.
St. meld. nr. 11 (1991-1992), *Norge trenger storbyene*, Kommunal- og arbeidsdepartementet. Oslo: Statens Forvaltningstjeneste.
St. meld. nr. 33 (1992-1993), *By og land hand i hand. Om regional utvikling*, Kommunal- og arbeidsdepartementet. Oslo: Statens Forvaltningstjeneste.
St. meld. nr. 31 (1996-1997), *Om distrikts- og regionalpolitikken*, Kommunal- og arbeidsdepartementet. Oslo: Statens Forvaltningstjeneste.

St. meld. nr. 19 (2001-2002), *Nye oppgaver for lokaldemokratiet – regionalt og lokalt nivå*, Kommunal- og regionaldepartementet. Oslo: Statens Forvaltningstjeneste.
Traavik, Kim (2003), 'Norsk regionalpolitikk kontra regionenes Europa', lecture given at Samfunnsviternes fagkonferanse, 6 February 2003. Oslo: Ministry of Foreign Affairs.

Chapter 5

Sweden

Jan Olsson and Joachim Åström

Introduction

This chapter examines the interaction between two forces that shape politics in the contemporary Swedish system: Europeanization and regionalization. How do Europeanization and regionalization relate to each other? According to many researchers these two tendencies can be seen as being convergent and mutually reinforcing (Johansson, 1995; Keating, 1995). The Europe-of-regions thesis stresses the importance of European integration in the process of regionalization. This would mean that Europeanization has a major influence on regional initiatives for increasing self-government and decreasing regional dependence on the state.

Other researchers question that Europeanization is the major driving force behind regionalization. Those researchers who are sceptical of the Europe-of-regions thesis have a more comprehensive and complex view of what the driving forces are and what the likely future developments might be. Regionalization is seen as a process of continuing decentralization within the frame of the nation-state rather than as a consequence of Europeanization. According to this view, state and region can be characterized by mutual dependence and co-operation as well as by tension and conflict (Andersson, 1990; Johansson, 1995; Åström, 1997). This would mean that regional initiatives are to a large extent related to an intra-national framework of problems, divergent from Europeanization.

The main thesis suggested here is that these forces cannot be assessed in isolation, independently from one another, nor from a perspective of convergence between them. Rather, Europeanization and regionalization should be captured and studied as forces relative to and overlapping each other, but never harmonious. The implication of this argument is a plea for pluralism and a picture of indeterminacy regarding the mutual and multiple effects of Europeanization and regionalization. For instance, instead of referring to a single regional order, we are witnessing today the emergence of a variety of new regional orders.

The chapter is divided into three basic parts. First, we give a short description of the Swedish political system as a historical background. In the second part, we focus on the regionalization process in Sweden by briefly describing the process and by focusing on some frontline experimental regions. The regions we have chosen are the four regions that are experimental regions in the formal sense that they have been included in a national project supervised and evaluated by the Swedish government. These are: the County of Skåne, the West Sweden Region, the County of Kalmar and the County of Gotland. We also analyse the County of Jämtland, because it showed an early interest in taking part in this national project of regional experimentation, but has had continuous problems on the way. In the third part we analyse Swedish regionalization from an intra-national framework. In the fourth part we discuss the relationship between Europeanization and regionalization on the national as well as the regional level. The empirical data that this chapter is based on comes from studies made by the authors and from secondary research.

The Political System of Sweden

Sweden is a unitary state with a strong self-government tradition of local authorities and county councils. Since 1995 Sweden has been a member of the European Union. In the political system of Sweden there are 289 Local Authorities (LA) and 21 County Councils (CC). These two types of self-government institutions are popularly elected. They have major decision-making competences (general competence) and taxation power. Local Authorities also have planning monopoly of land. There are no formal hierarchical relations between County Councils and Local Authorities. Both are self-government institutions, but with different functions.

Local Authorities are responsible for a number of traditional welfare policies, such as compulsory and upper secondary schools, child-care, social security, care of elderly, etc., but also local industrial policy and environmental protection. This extensive responsibility makes it reasonable to talk about Local Authorities as local states (Pierre, 1994). The County Councils are mainly responsible for health care. Other areas are regional traffic and culture.

Local Authorities are organized nationally in the Swedish Association of Local Authorities, and County Councils in the Swedish Federation of County Councils. Both these national organizations are very important when it comes to national policy-making which will affect local and regional levels. Their common goal is to promote and strengthen the position of the self-government institutions.

The Swedish state has 21 regional organizations called County Administrations (CA), which comprise the same geographical area as the County Councils. Thus, Sweden has two types of regional institutions in the provinces. The County Administration is led by a board of politicians appointed by the County Council, so that the political opinions of the province will be reflected in the board: County Administration Board (CAB). The chairman of the County Administration Board (CAB) is the governor of the County, who is appointed by the Swedish government. Thus, the County Administration is not just an instrument of the national government. In fact, during the 1980s the County Administration became more of a voice of the regional level. However, this might change in the years to come as a result of new and stronger regions, probably in the way that the CAs will be more instruments of the national government again (Ehn, 1998). This complexity can be interpreted as an expression of institutional power competition and compromises. In the national debate this institutional complexity has been called the 'regional mess' (SOU, 1995:27).

Thus, Sweden has three popularly elected political levels; four levels if we include the EU. The regional level is somewhat of a 'forgotten' political level. Leading politicians of the County Councils (CC) are often unknown to the citizens they represent. Despite this, the voting frequency is high. This is mainly the result of a relatively strong party identification among Swedish citizens as well as the fact that the local, regional and national elections all occur on the same day. Citizens also have difficulty in separating the popularly elected County Council from the County Administration (the state bureaucracy in the region). This should be weighed with attention to the fact that about 85 per cent of the County Council budget is earmarked for health care. Swedish citizens have a great deal of confidence in the health care system but this sentiment is directed mainly toward the services of professional groups (doctors, nurses, etc.) rather than toward the efforts of politicians or political parties. Strategically important topics for policy-making such as regional development have, traditionally, been dominated by the CAs. Thus, the Swedish County Councils have been depicted as popularly elected, politically anonymous health care organizations with relatively weak politicians and strong professional groups and administrators (Montin and Olsson, 1994; Montin, 1994; Olsson, 1996).

Revival of the Regional Issue

The regions' role in the administrative system of Sweden has been discussed more or less since the early 1960s (Krantz, 2002). However, in the 1990s there was a revival of the regional issue. In 1991, the Swedish government set up a committee to investigate the regional organization of the political system and to make a study of perspectives and alternatives for a structure of the future. It was completed in 1992 ('Regional Roles') and presented three alternative models for future regional organization in Sweden. These models have had an important effect on debate and experimental design during the last ten years.

Regional Responsibility of the State is a model that emphasises concentration of the state's regional areas of competence to one organizational unit per region, that is, the CA. Thus, the role of the CAs as regional representatives of the central government would be strengthened, implying an increased emphasis on national goals. *Local Authorities in Co-operation* is a decentralized model where local authorities would be delegated the major responsibility for regional public services. This means that the CCs would no longer be necessary and that some tasks would be decentralized to the local level. Issues of a trans-municipal character would, according to this model, best be handled with the assistance of different types of municipal unions. *Regional Parliamentary Democracy* is a model where public issues on the regional level would be directed toward popularly elected regional parliaments. Issues presently handled by the CAs would be transferred to new and stronger regional parliaments (SOU, 1992:63).

These three alternatives were well suited to the existing institutional interests in Sweden. The state, the local authorities and the CCs got their own models, so to speak. These 'logical' alternatives led to rather strict positions among institutional interests in the 1990s, implying difficulties in finding other types of solutions.

After the 'Regional Roles' study, the Swedish government set up yet another called The Committee of Regions. In its final document, 'Regional Future' (SOU 1995:27), it proposed that the regional responsibility for development and some other traditional issues of the state should be transferred to the existing CCs in each Swedish county by the year 1999. However, the Swedish government made a political judgement that implementation of the study proposal would not be possible, based on the mixed reactions from organizations which had it for consideration. This setback notwithstanding, four regions were still strongly interested in changing the distribution of political responsibility for regional issues as well as in taking initiatives of their own in starting organizational experiments for a defined period of time. These were the Counties of Gotland, Jämtland, Kalmar and Skåne. The Swedish government in turn was affected by this show of regional initiative and proposed, in a Government Bill (Government Bill 1996/97:36, 'The Regional Political Organization') that four experiments involving strong regional self-government would commence on 1 July 1997. An important demand from the Ministry of Civil Affairs was that the local and regional institutional interests (the CAs, the CCs and the local authorities) should agree to this experiment. The strategy of the Swedish government was that the experimental work of these regions would offer experience and knowledge which could contribute to a comprehensive regional reform in Sweden within the next couple of years.

In Jämtland, the institutional interests could not live up to the consensus demand. Short after the proposition was presented by the government the politicians in Jämtland decided not to carry through the reform, the outcome was to wait and find a better way towards regional self-government. Thus, Jämtland did not join the project. In parallel with the processes described above, a regionalization process had been going on for several years in the west of Sweden. A new region, called the County of West Götaland, was formed on 1 January 1998 by a fusion of three former counties. This new region took part in the national experimental project in 1999. This means that we have four formal experiments in the Swedish regionalization process.

The four experimental regions are basically testing to take over traditional state responsibility for some policy areas. These include responsibility for developing a strategy for the long-term development of the county, that is, a regional development plan for the county, as well as decision-making power concerning some economic measures of regional development. The increased responsibility for regional development also includes management and co-ordination of the regional growth-agreement (a state sanctioned regional partnership-model for development of Swedish regions). Further, the regions are also allowed the decision-making power when it comes to long-term planning for regional transportation infrastructure, as well as allocation of state subsidies to cultural institutions of the region (this does not hold for West Götaland) (Johansson, 2000, p.13). Moreover, the experiments include a testing of new forms of democratic organization and governance. For two regions, Skåne and West Götaland, it is also about creating larger regions by amalgamating counties (Johansson, 1998, 1999 and 2000).

Regional Experiments in Practice

What can we learn from the regional experiments in practice? What types of strategies and solutions have been chosen in the regions? In the County of Kalmar the self-government institutions formed a *regional alliance*, that is, the LA and the CC. The alliance has 13 members, that is, the Local Authorities of the County and the County Council. The alliance is governed by a regional council consisting of 45 members elected from popularly elected politicians of the County. The model that is tested in Kalmar means that the Local Authorities appoint two thirds of the seats, while the County Council appoint one third (Jerneck and Sjölin, 2000; SOU, 2000:85, p. 65).

In the Region of Skåne, the process started in the same manner as in Kalmar, but Skåne took the process some steps further. On 1 January 1997 the new bigger region, called the County of Skåne, was established by a fusion of the County of Malmöhus and the County of Kristianstad. In time for the 1998 election, a popularly elected regional parliament was established with 149 seats, called the Regional Council. The creation of this new political institution meant that the two former County Councils were terminated (Jerneck and Sjölin, 2000; SOU, 2000:85, p. 59).

On 1 January 1998 the County of West Götaland was formed by a fusion of three counties: the County of Gothenburg and Bohus, the County of Älvsborg and the County of Skaraborg, except for the Local Authorities of Habo and Mullsjö. Before the new region was established the regionalization process was managed by a non-profit association called The West Board. It consisted of 27 politicians who had been appointed by the organizations of the political parties in Local Authorities and County Councils. The board was reorganized in December 1997 and was replaced by a temporary council. From 1 November 1998 the region was represented by 149 popularly elected delegates on a regional council (SOU, 2000:85, p. 63).

In the County of Gotland, the biggest island of the Baltic Sea, it is the Local Authority of Gotland that is the self-government institution. Gotland does not have a County Council and there was no need to create a new regional self-government institution. Thus, this institutional concentration gives Gotland good conditions for co-operation. For a long time there has been a co-operative tradition depending on the fact that the Local Authority of Gotland is also responsible for issues which traditionally are handled by county councils, (such as health care, regional public transportation and culture). The Council of the Local Authority consists of 71 popularly elected delegates. In Gotland the regional experiment is solely about transferring tasks from the County Administration to the Local Authority (SOU 2000:85, p. 69 and ch. 7).

In all the experimental regions, the role of the CA-institution was supposed to be dramatically changed. It was, in the sense that CA-boards were abolished. In every other region in Sweden the CA-institution still has a board of politicians chosen by the CC, with the governor as the chairman. The role of the CA in the experimental regions is supposed to be reduced to co-ordinating state activities in the region and controlling national environmental and regional goals. Further, the CA is supposed to evaluate achievements and inform the government about the conditions in the region. The CAs will probably be more instruments of the national government again, rather than a voice of the region. The state will henceforth support the regional development through assisting the regional self-governing institutions. Considering the central role that the county governor has traditionally played in co-ordinating regional development, this will mean a much more important change for the CA than the reduction in resource allocations would indicate (Ehn, 1998, p. 168; Silenstam, 2000, p. 263). However, the conclusion drawn from the final report of the official evaluation from the Parliamentary Committee of Regions is that the division of responsibility between the CA and the self-government institutions is more or less unclear in all the experimental regions. There are old traditions and routines that have to be challenged to make a difference and it will take time (Johansson, 2000).

In the County of Jämtland politicians in the region decided in the autumn of 1998 to make a new effort to overcome disagreements between institutional interests. This time, the regional issue should be handled by the political parties. In June 1999, all political parties of the region agreed to develop an application to the Swedish government about setting up a popularly elected self-government institution on the regional level. The idea is that it will have the same type of responsibilities as the new regional self-government institutions in Skåne and West Götaland. In a more long-term perspective Jämtland has also shown an interest in taking over labour markets policy from the state and that the new institution shall have a co-ordinating role for upper secondary schools in the region. This new initiative or project in Jämtland is managed under the title Region Jämtland 2003 by a board of 21 members from the political parties. The tasks of the board are to spread information about the project, trying to make citizens involved in the plans and to develop a proposal for an organizational solution. In May 2000 Region Jämtland sent a formal application to the government about setting up a regional parliament, which is planned to start working from 1 January 2003. All political parties were behind this application, except for the Conservatives. Again, full consensus was not achieved (SOU, 2000:85, p. 110f).

However, this Jämtland initiative seems to be late. The Swedish parliament decided in January 2000 to terminate the experiment at the end of 2002, but to give all self-government institutions the opportunity to create co-operative institutions (or a regional alliance) in the period 2003-2006. The Kalmar model seems to be the favourite of the Swedish government. This means that Jämtland has to follow in the track of Kalmar, so to speak. In an overview of plans of regional co-operation made in the spring of 2002 there were two regions being negative (the County of Västerbotten and the County of Örebro), two not being able to because of intra-regional disagreements (the County of Västmanland and the County of Kronoberg) and the rest of the regions being on the move but at different speeds. Jämtland continues with a co-operative body even though there is no consensus in the region. The majority sees this body as a temporary solution and still hopes for a popularly elected regional parliament in 2006 (Kommuaktuellt, nr 9, 14/3, 2002, p. 17). However, the ongoing experiments in Skåne and West Götaland will continue for the next term of office (2002-2006). Thus, being fast and decisive seems to pay off.

Regionalization from an Intra-national Perspective

Swedish regionalization is not an expression of traditional Swedish policy-making as we knew it during the golden years of post-war expansion. For instance, the amalgamation of municipalities was uniform in nature, national programmes were implemented in a top-down manner and functional aspects such as demographic and territorial conditions were given myopic attention (Gustafsson, 1984). Today, the regionalization policy of the Swedish government has been more bottom-up in its orientation and has been guided by an explicit *experimental strategy*, which stresses the importance of regional co-operation and accepts quite big differences in solutions between regions.

Instead of policies characterized by instrumental rationality (anticipatory action), they are characterized by institutional behaviour, focusing on what is appropriate to do in the specific region (March and Olsen, 1989). Instead of top-down planning the new strategy encourages process-oriented, experimental learning from below. Instead of focusing narrowly on functional arguments, more weight has now been given to cultural aspects and people's feelings of identity and belonging. This is not a new or sudden shift in Swedish government policy as it relates to the question of regionalization. It is rather a matter of a gradual transformation which began in the 1980s, moving away from proactive government policies and towards more reactive policies. We have seen this transformation at work with regards to different policy areas and in many political issues, such as industrial and developmental policies, as well as in the regulation of local self-government (Jacobsson, 1989; Montin, 1993; Olsson, 1995).

The explicit experimental strategy of the Swedish government may be seen as a pragmatic way of handling the issue of regionalization given the existing circumstances. Divergent interests are probably easier to handle in an incremental way rather than in line with a rationalistic model. Experiments may offer answers to important and difficult questions. However, it is also possible to interpret the experimental strategy as an expression of political weakness – a consequence of not being able to formulate a straightforward or coherent policy in the short run. The experimental strategy could, seen from this perspective, be interpreted as a means of keeping or even increasing the government's political influence rather than as a strategy for learning by experience. Which interpretation best corresponds with reality is hard to say. However, there is some empirical evidence which indicates that the latter interpretation comes closest to the truth. The Ministry of Civil Affairs, sponsoring the experiment, met some resistance from other ministries which preferred centrally co-ordinated policies. Out in the separate regions, politicians and civil servants have noticed the emergence of double messages depending on which ministry they turn to. For example, at the same time as the Ministry of Civil Affairs moved the responsibility for regional development from the CA to self-governing institutions, the Ministry of Industry and Trade gave the County Governors in all Swedish regions instructions to co-ordinate regional efforts to stimulate economic growth. Thus, the lack of co-ordination has been striking during the process and the division of roles between authorities of the Swedish government (such as the CA) and the self-government institutions of the regions continues to be unclear (Åström, 1997; SOU, 2000:85).

Another important characteristic of regionalization in Sweden is its *tendency towards elitism*. This is notable in the processes involved in building new regions as well as in the new Structural Fund planning (Montin and Olsson, 1994; Fröjd and Åström, 1996; Olsson and Jakobsson, 1997; Olsson, 2003).

We see obvious signs of elitism in the experimental work with new regions. Empirical studies show that there are leading politicians or public officials involved in the process of building new regions. In a study of the problems and challenges that have been dealt with by politicians in the County Council of Bohuslän, the regular politicians mentioned different concrete questions related to health care service, traffic, education, etc. It was only among leading politicians that planning for a new region in West Götaland was mentioned as an important issue worth devoting a lot of time to (Olsson, 1994; Montin and Olsson, 1994). The leading politicians in the same region also have difficulties mobilizing their party members (Fröjd and Åström, 1996). A large portion of the population (approximately 60 per cent) did not even hold an opinion concerning the suggestions for a new regional organization in West Götaland (Malmström, 1994).

In the Structural Fund planning a limited number of regional public officials dominate over the planning framework set up by the Commission. CA public officials control the planning processes by organizing the process and having a dominant influence on the definition of regional development problems as well as by being the ones to formulate basic goals and strategies. Among the political parties and politicians there are a few leading politicians who exert a certain amount of influence albeit more through passive control than through pro-active involvement. Political parties do not mobilize to any extent at all and interest organizations and social movements do not have any real access to the planning process. The limited number of actors involved in the Swedish planning process is partly due to time restrictions and is not unique for Sweden, even though there are important differences in terms of actor composition between, for instance, Sweden and the UK. In Sweden politicians were included in partnerships from the very beginning, which took quite a long time to achieve in the UK. However, both cases are characterized by elitism and democratic problems in many senses (Bache and Olsson, 2001).

A third important trait, which is relevant when it comes to choice of strategies and solutions, is the *dominance of institutional interests* over other actors such as political parties, both in regional development and in regionalizing projects. These are not characterized by traditional conflicts between political parties along a right-left wing scale for instance.

Even though a limited debate regarding reform of the regional level in Sweden has been ongoing since the 1960s no significant changes in this direction have been made. In the 1980s and 1990s this aspect of the regional issue grew in importance. In the process of decentralization to the regional level arguments for better co-ordination and democratization gathered force. The continuing decentralization process had not been accompanied by a corresponding development in the regional democratic government. In order to engage the citizens, it was considered important to give local and regional politicians the responsibility for regional development. The continuing decentralization process also led to co-ordination problems at the regional level. The expression 'the regional mess' was used to describe a situation where some work was duplicated, while other tasks were not being attended to at all (SOU, 1995:27). It has been generally believed in the four experimental regions that these problems can be sorted out and that the regional organization will become more effective and democratic by increasing regional self-government.

As we described in the introduction, the clearly expressed positions competing with one another are similar to the three models that were formulated by the state-financed report 'Regional Roles'. However, over the past years, the institutional positions do not seem to be as rigid as in the beginning of the 1990s. Local Authorities and CCs have much in common, particularly concerning the question of democratic renewal and in relation to the central state. Today, it seems to be more about diverging interests between the self-government institutions and the Swedish government. The Conservative Party in Sweden is the only party which advocates the abolition of the CCs. The other parties are more pragmatic in their approach. However, the Conservative Party has quite a low profile on this and strong conservatives in the experimental regions act in favour of the new regional self-governance.

From the intra-national perspective we can also interpret regionalization in Sweden as a competitive race between major urban areas such as Skåne (Malmö/Lund), West Götaland (Gothenburg) and the Stockholm region. This can perhaps even be understood as an interregional competition – of course not of a zero-sum character – between Stockholm and the south-east coast of Sweden.

Thus, we have discussed three important characteristics of Swedish regionalization from the intra-national perspective: the experimental strategy, tendencies toward elitism and strong, diverging, institutional interests. We will now continue by focusing on our second thesis, that is, the Europe-of-regions thesis.

Europeanization and Regionalization

The Europe-of-regions thesis stresses the importance of European integration in the process of regionalization, that is, Europeanization has a major influence on regional initiatives for increasing self-government and decreasing regional dependence on the state. How can we understand these forces in the Swedish context?

The regional issue in Sweden was really revitalized in the early 1990s. However, the European integration process and plans for membership came before the agenda setting of the regional issue. The Swedish government was an important actor in this phase. The Social Democratic government made a sudden policy change concerning Swedish EU membership. In a government bill instituting measures against acute problems for the Swedish economy in 1990, it was said in a short sentence that a Swedish membership of the European Union was an important goal in the years to come (Olsson, 1999, p. 47). In 1991, the Swedish government set up, on the initiative of the Swedish Association of Local Authorities and the Swedish Federation of County Councils, a committee to investigate the regional organization of the political system and to make a study of perspectives and alternatives for a structure of the future. Thus, Europeanization of Sweden, initiated and controlled by the Swedish government, was a basic driving force behind the revitalization and growing importance of the regional issue.

Europeanization also seems to be an important driving force on the regional level. However, European integration impacts differently on different regions. First, there is a *mental aspect* accompanying Europeanization. In all regions, contacts with the EU have increased which have helped some regional politicians and bureaucrats to think in more European terms. The rapid increase of EU offices in Sweden is perhaps the most obvious expression of an increase in European mentality. This in turn has led to a more comparative style of thinking. In looking at the regions of Europe, it is apparent that discussions concerning the regions and regional self-government have been legitimized (Åström, 1997). However, interactive dialogue and exchange of ideas is facilitated by short distances between locations. The spreading of new ideas often takes place between neighbours (Schmidt, 1986). The geographical position of the regions is therefore of importance. In Skåne, with a relatively short distance to Central Europe, the mentality aspect of Europeanization is more real, especially in comparison with Jämtland which is considerably more distant from Central Europe.

Second, there is a *passive aspect* of Europeanization, which is clearly expressed in EU-related regional policy. The Commission steers the work of Structural Fund planning using several different means and Swedish regions seem to have adapted in a somewhat passive manner. The Structural Fund plans must be arranged according to a certain decisive structure; the Commission approves the plans after negotiations with the national government and the Commission is also involved in formulating the principles for evaluation. The focus on EU regional policies is understandably preoccupied with less developed regions where social and economic problems are more severe. In comparing the five regions, Jämtland, Gotland and Kalmar are allotted substantial amounts from these funds, while Skåne and West Götaland receive considerably less. Despite this, a majority of the population in the three economically weaker regions have been negative to Swedish EU-membership. This may seem paradoxical, but is an expression of a general pattern of popular attitudes in Sweden: populations in peripheral regions with weak economies are more negative to the EU compared to the few big urban areas of Sweden (Olsson and Jakobsson, 1997; Olsson, 2003).

The mental and passive aspects of Europeanization do not have to play an important role in regional initiatives. Yet, the mental and passive aspects may be of importance where they concern active and voluntary participation on the part of different regions in activities where one or more of the co-actors bear another nationality. According to those pleading for self-government, membership in the EU accentuates the need for regional engagement and activity in order to make use of the opportunities that the EU offers. In Gotland and Kalmar where the Structural Funds are of importance, a common argument for regional self-government is that the work involved with these funds would be better co-ordinated and more effectively handled if decision-making were decentralized. In this manner, Europeanization has increased the problems with the old structure, as we described earlier. In Jämtland, the discussion about regional self-government has concerned European integration only to a minor degree, despite the fact that it receives allocations from EU Structural Funds and has established EU contacts. The population of Jämtland was, in addition, one of the most negative to EU-membership among Swedish regions. Jämtland is a peripheral region far from the EU, with historical and cultural relations to the Tröndelag region of Norway (Åström, 1997).

In Skåne, European integration is a very important part of the argument for self-government. Here, the importance of the European Community is not related to regional Structural Funds but, rather, to the opportunities available for inter-regional co-operation which transcend national boundaries and which are legitimized and encouraged by the institutions and ethos of the Community. Initiatives are taken increasingly to broaden, not only the integration process taking place over the strait of Öresund, but the integration process with Northern

Germany as well (Gidlund and Sörlin, 1993; Åström, 1997; Baldersheim and Ståhlberg, 1999). In Kalmar and Gotland it is also argued that inter-regional co-operation can offer the regions new resources and help them find solutions to regional problems. Up until now, the CAs and central ministries have orchestrated these contacts largely without the involvement of the regional politicians and it is often argued that the time has come for inter-regional co-operation to be managed from the regional and not the central level (Åström, 1997).

Thus, there are really important differences among Swedish regions, which can be summarized in the following way: relatively economically independent regions close to Central Europe and with a relatively Europeanized mentality tend to regionalize to a larger extent than regions neither relatively economically independent nor having a Europeanized mentality. In other words, regionalization in Sweden is very much about modernization and economic development in urban regions. The 'modernizing regions' are obviously Skåne and West Sweden and to a lesser extent Kalmar. Leading actors in West Sweden, for instance, see their region as being part of a trans-border growth-region from Oslo, along the Swedish west coast including West Sweden (Gothenburg) and Skåne/Öresund (Malmö-Copenhagen) (Interview in Gränsbrytning, 9 December 2002).

Conclusions and Implications

We can conclude that data lends support both to the Europe-of-regions thesis and the intra-national framework thesis. However, the leading impression is that both are too simplistic. Europeanization does not have a general applicable validity for Swedish regions, but may be interpreted as an important triggering off mechanism for the national policy on regional experiments. In that way, Europeanization has had an *indirect* effect on all regions to different degrees. In a more *direct* sense, we have seen that Europeanization and regionalization are interrelated forces that work in a really complex way. Europeanization seems to be an important regionalizing force in urban regions, like Skåne and West Götaland, but is more of a problem and obstacle in peripheral regions far from Central Europe. The European dimension seems to be a hopeful challenge for the modernizing regions, which tend to diminish tensions between institutional interests in the regions.

From the intra-national perspective we want to stress the importance of regionalization as a competitive race between major urban areas such as Skåne (Malmö/Lund), West Götaland (Gothenburg) and the Stockholm region. Further, it seems as if regionalization does not have the same obvious meaning to other Swedish regions, being far from Central Europe in many aspects and having a weaker economic development with no prospects of recovering through Europeanization or economic globalization. This means that those regions will depend more or less on the Swedish state and how this relation should turn out in the regionalizing process is a complicated matter that tends to result in different positions among institutional interests within the regions.

The power relation between the Swedish state and the regions shifted during the 1990s in favour of the regions, mainly because of the open and experimental government strategy and the inspiration of the regions of Europe-of-regions thesis. This window of opportunity was used, in particular, by strong urban regions, like Skåne and West Götaland. They took the lead in the regionalization process and they still have it. However, the Swedish state will probably continue to hold a strong position in relation to Skåne and West Götaland, even though they are allowed to regionalize to a larger extent than other regions in Sweden. The two forces of regionalization and Europeanization do not have to undermine the position of the state. We should not forget that the EU is a co-operative effort between states. Some researchers even argue that Swedish national interests have been augmented by the European integration process. Co-operation between states means that the states must formulate a national position for all the relevant issues – a position which must also include issues for which no national position previously existed (Jacobsson, 1993). However, this does not mean that the Swedish state will maintain an unchanged historical position in Swedish society. The Swedish state has already attained a new role. Today it has decentralized many of its functions and EC integration has clarified the way that central state administrations now possess a more free and creative role than they had just a decade ago (Olsson, 1999; Jacobsson, 1993).

The Swedish state must now concentrate on a limited number of functions while decentralizing many others. Even if horizontal structures grow stronger, vertical and hierarchical structures live on together with these new structures. Decentralization and centralization normally occur together in differing composites (Elander and Montin, 1990). Decentralization of functions outward to the regions may well be accompanied by centralization of control, even if this is not done in an explicit way. The degree of control over the experimental regions has not yet taken shape and some features in the process indicate that the development towards regional self-government is not a straightforward matter: different regions are interested in different issues; there are strong, diverging, institutional interests; and it is difficult to know what the intention of the Swedish government really is, even though the government Bill and parliamentary decision from January 2000 may be interpreted as a first step towards a more restrictive policy on regionalization.

The latest phase in the process, where the government stops the possibility of new regional parliaments in favour of a more informal regional co-operation, may be interpreted as a new and more restrictive policy. Perhaps this is a first step forward in order to secure the initiative and control of the Swedish state in time for a more comprehensive and formal solution of the Swedish regional structure. The regional issue will be a very important one in the coming years and it would not be surprising if the process continues towards fewer regional models and more clear policies from the central level. From a local and regional democratic perspective, this can easily be interpreted as elitism. Whether or not it is viewed as democratic or non-democratic is another issue, which depends on what democratic viewpoint we have as a normative yardstick.

Consequently, we do not believe in the sudden death of the traditionally strong Swedish nation-state. Instead, one conceivable development would be the mutual evolution of dependence between state and region where the regional position may become stronger than it was previously. At the same time, important differences between regions would be maintained and may even increase. It may not be possible for Sweden to reach a uniform national system of regional self-government. Paradoxically, the experimental project of the Swedish government may even act as one of several forces that hinder the construction of a coherent national system for governing the regions. At this point in time, the regions that have joined the project develop at differing speeds and have different ambitions. What effects an institutionalized fragmented regional structure could have on Swedish society in the future is an interesting question which we do not intend to speculate on in this chapter.

Bibliography

Andersson, J. (1990), 'Skeptical Reflection of a Europe of the Regions: Britain, West Germany, and the European Development Fund', *Journal of Public Policy*, 10, pp. 417-447.

Bache, I. and Olsson, J. (2001), 'Legitimacy through Partnership? EU Policy Diffusion in Britain and Sweden'. Scandinavian Political Studies, Vol. 24, No. 3.

Baldersheim, H. and Ståhlberg, K. (eds) (1999), *Nordic Region-Building in a European Perspective*. Aldershot: Ashgate.

Ehn, P. (1998), *I skärningspunkten. Landshövdingarna och den centrala och regionala samordningen*. Rapport till den Parlamentariska regionkommittén (SOU, 1998:168).

Elander, I. and Montin, S. (1990), 'Decentralisation and Control: Central-Local Government Relations in Sweden'. *Policy and Politics*, Vol. 18, No 3, pp. 165-180.

Fröjd, S. and Åström, J. (1996), *Regiondebatt och partiarbete i Västsverige*. C-uppsats i statskunskap. Örebro: University of Örebro.

Gidlund, J. and Sörlin, S. (1993), *Det europeiska kalejdoskopet*. Stockholm: SNS förlag.

Government Bill 1996/97:36, *Den regionala samhällsorganisationen*.

Gustafsson, A. (1984), *Kommunal självstyrelse*. Malmö: Lieber förlag.

Jacobsson, B. (1989), *Konsten att reagera. Intressen, institutioner och näringspolitik*. Stockholm: Carlssons förlag.

Jacobsson, B. (1993), 'Europeiseringen av förvaltningen'. *Statsvetenskaplig tidskrift*. 1993, No 2.

Jerneck, M. and Gidlund, J. (2001), *Komplex flernivådemokrati. Regional lobbying i Bryssel*. Malmö: Liber.

Jerneck, M. and Sjölin, M. (2000), 'Regionalisering och flernivåpolitik – Kalmar och Skåne län', in Johansson *et al.*, *Regional försöksverksamhet – tre studier*. SOU, 2000:64.

Johansson, J. (1995), *Europeiska Regioner. Regionforskning i empirisk och normativ belysning*. Kumla: Kommanditbolaget Kumla Tryckeri.

Johansson, J. (1998), *Regional frihet och statligt ansvar – en principiell diskussion*. SOU, 1998:166.

Johansson, J. (1999), *Regionreform på försök – första stegen mot en ny regional samhällsorganisation*. SOU, 1999:103.

Johansson, J. (2000), 'Försök med en ny regional samhällsorganisation – demokrati, flernivåpolitik och regional mobilisering', in Johansson *et al.*, *Regional försöksverksamhet – tre studier*. SOU, 2000:64.

Keating, M. (1995), 'Europeanism and Regionalism'. In Jones, B. and Keating, M., *The European Union and the Regions*. Oxford: Clarendon Press.

Kommunaktuellt, nr 9, 14/3 2002, p. 17.

Krantz, T. (2002), *Makten över regionen. En idékritisk studie av svensk regiondebatt 1963-1996*. Statsvetenskapliga föreningen i Uppsala, 149.

Malmström, C. (1994), 'Inget folkligt stöd för regionparlament!' In Nilsson, L., *Västsverige i fokus. SOM-undersökningen i Västsverige 1993*, No. 12, Göteborg: SOM-institutet Göteborgs universitet.

March, J.G. and Olsen, J.P. (1989), *Rediscovering Institutions. The Organizational Basis of Politics*. New York: The Free Press.

Montin, S. (1993), with Fridolf, M. and Sköldborg, T., 'Radikala organisationsförändringar i kommuner och landsting' *SOU 1993:73*. Stockholm: Allmänna förlaget.

Montin, S. (1994), *Politikerrollen i olika landstingsmiljöer – En medborgarundersökning*. Örebro: Novemus.

Montin, S. and Olsson, J. (1994), *Demokrati och legitimitet i landstingen*. Örebro: Novemus.

Olsson, J. (1994), *Organisationsförändring och politik – En fallstudie av Bohuslandstinget*. Örebro: Novemus.

Olsson, J. (1995), *Den lokala näringspolitikens politiska ekonomi. En jämförande kommuntypsstudie*. Örebro: University of Örebro.

Olsson, J. (1996), 'Landstingskommunalt förändringsarbete – en fråga om demokrati?' *SOU, 1996:169*. Stockholm: Norstedts Tryckeri AB.

Olsson, J. (1999), *EU och demokratin – från svensk horisont*. Lund: Studentlitteratur.

Olsson, J. (2003), 'Democracy Paradoxes in Multi-level Governance: Theorizing on Structural Fund System Research'. *Journal of European Public Policy*, Vol. 10. No. 2.

Olsson, J. and Jakobsson, E. (1997), *Politisk demokrati och EU-integrerad regionalpolitik*. Örebro: Novemus.

Pierre, J. (1994), *Den lokala staten. Den kommunala självstyrelsens förutsättningar och restriktioner*. Stockholm: Almqvist and Wiksell.

Schmidt, S. (1986), *Pionjärer, efterföljare och avvaktare. Innovationer och deras spridning bland de svenska primärkommunerna*. Lund: Kommunfakta Förlag

Silenstam, P. (2000), 'Länsstyrelsens nya roll i Kalmar, Skåne och Västra Götalands län', i Johansson m.fl., *Regional försöksverksamhet – tre studier*. SOU, 2000:64.

SOU, 1992:63, *Regionala roller*. Stockholm: Allmänna förlaget.

SOU, 1995:27, *Regional framtid*. Stockholm: Fritzes.

SOU, 2000:85, *Regionalt folkstyre och statlig länsförvaltning. Slutbetänkande av den Parlamentariska regionkommittén (PARK)*. Stockholm: Fritzes.

Åström, J. (1997), *Regionpolitiska försök i 90-talets Sverige – en jämförande studie*. D-uppsats i statskunskap. Örebro: University of Örebro.

Chapter 6

Nordic Regional Lobbying in Brussels

Jørn Lein-Mathisen

Developing Sub-national External Relations

Since the late eighties Brussels has seen something of an epidemic. Sub-national regions have established regional 'representations' in the European capital. Whether called representations, information offices, delegations, mini-embassies or antennas; they are all examples of sub-national external relations, commonly known as regional offices. Although the Nordic regions have less of a tradition for bold regionalism, they have eagerly taken up this new informal channel of information and influence.

In this chapter I am looking into how the Nordic regional offices are using this newfound tool of sub-national external relations. What are their objectives? Is there a special type of Nordic regional office? Can we identify trends over these first years, pointing to the years to come? Are the Nordic regional offices part of the strong European regionalism that the German *länder* have been representing? And not least, are the Nordic regions there to stay?

The European presence of the Nordic regions today can be summarized as follows, using the names they themselves use in Brussels.[1] This contribution focuses on the first two countries, Sweden and Norway, one being an EU-member, the other still only being a part of the European Economic Area (EEA).

Table 6.1 The European presence in the Nordic regions

Nation-state	Regional offices	Total
Sweden	B7-The Baltic Sea Islands, Central Sweden, City of Malmö, North Sweden, South Sweden, Stockholm, West Sweden, East Sweden	8
Norway	Stavanger, Mid Scandinavia (Trøndelag), Nordland, West Norway, Oslo	5
Finland	City of Turku & South-West Finland, Helsinki, East Finland, European North Lapland – Oulo, Rovaniemi – Lapland, South Finland, Tampere Central Region, West Finland	8
Denmark	Copenhagen, Aarhus, Odense, EU Vest (Ribe), North of Denmark, EURA – Ringkøbing, South Denmark, Storstrøm, West Zealand	9

1 There is no 'official' list as these offices have no formal status. Several of the regional offices keep lists. We are using here the list of Niederösterreich dated 21 February 2003 as well as adding upcoming developments.

Framework for Discussion – The State of Research

Definition of 'Region'

Until now we have not defined the highly indeterminate term 'region'. Many definitions exist, ranging from large groups of nation-states to the smallest sub-national areas. Examining the various forms and competences of regional and local government in Europe one finds a wide diversity in competencies and sizeable variations. The average French municipality has 1,500 inhabitants, the Norwegian 9,000 and the Irish 43,000 inhabitants. However, the term 'region' has been given a more precise content for the sake of statistics, NUTS. But despite the aim of comparable size, each level still contains a large variety of area, population, economic weight or administrative power.

Regional space can, according to Keating, be seen as territorial, functional or political space.[2] Functional regions will often have capacities of planning and programming, especially in aspects of economic development. Regional strength can best be analysed, following Keating, across seven dimensions: institutions, capacity to formulate a policy, competences, power of integration, financial resources, the intergovernmental system, and relationships with the market. However, not even this functional understanding of 'region' applies fully to the 'regions' represented in Brussels. For this discussion I thus suggest the following working definition of 'region': 'Any sub-national area, or combination of adjoining areas represented by a 'coalition of the willing' consisting of *any* combination of sub-national territorial, political or functional actors within this geographical entity'.

This working definition covers multi-level entities where the regional authority, as well as local authorities, are taking part in parallel, as long as they together represent one single geographical entity. A notable exception is national associations of local and regional authorities as they represent all regions of a given country, operating as a national actor, even though they represent regional interests. Following the inclusion of 'any actor' one will find regions represented by among others a research institute or a land development agency (Stavanger), specific schools or conference centres (Aalborg), or the local or regional farming association (Vaasa). The extreme case would be Manchester with the airport being the dominating partner.

This 'coalition of the willing' of different regional actors seems to correspond with the observation that 'the region is not a natural entity, but a social construction, in a given space'.[3]

---

2 Michael Keating: 'The Invention of Regions, Political Restructuring and Territorial Government in Western Europe', ECPR-workshop, Oslo, 29 March to 3 April 1996, p. 8. This must be distinguished from Soldatos' use of territorial segmentation of different levels of governments and functional segmentation between different actors within the same level of government (Soldatos, 1990, pp. 36-40).

3 J. Agnew (1987), *Place and Politics. The Geographical Mediation of State and Society*, London: Allen and Unwin. R. Balme (*et al.*) (1994), *Le territoire pour politiques:*

Aspects from the Theoretical Literature

The academic interest for sub-national external relations and its causes has been surprisingly limited. Some academics have been dealing with the North American situation, and then in the early 1990s applied this to Europe. However, much of this literature has focused on either the constitutional aspects of sub-state external relations, or on the more functional aspects of the interplay between federalism and external relations.[4] Both of these mainly focus on the political implications of official representations which can be found mostly in democratic federal or decentralized systems – such as in the US, Australia, Canada, Switzerland, Germany, Austria, Spain and Belgium.[5] Although none of the Nordic states are federal states, parts of this literature will provide a relevant background for understanding the Nordic regional offices.

The phenomenon of 'many voices' in sub-state external relations consists of several interlinked concepts. Soldatos speaks of 'segmentation', referring closely to Fry's 'many voices' in foreign policy; often seen in terms of Hooghe's multi-level governance.[6] The external activities of the sub-state actor are coined 'para-diplomacy' by Soldatos, initially 'micro-diplomacy' by Duchacek.[7] Soldatos also points out that although such sub-state external relations are not new as such, there is a new qualitative and quantitative development: designated channels for external relations with substantial financial resources allocated, and also the wide scope and volume of interaction with larger number of partners. Given our European perspective we might add the dramatic rise in number of sub-national representations in Brussels. Soldatos identifies three sets of causal factors for sub-national external relations: domestic causes at the level of federal units, factors at the federal level, and thirdly external causes.

Hooghe refers to 'sub-national mobilization' and 'multi-level governance', giving a framework with an arena where not only member states and the EU institutions are

---

variations europeennes, Paris: l'Harmattan. Both cited with the words of Keating, 1996, p. 7.

4 Cf. Hacking (1993), 'Introduction' in Hacking, Brian (ed.), *Foreign Relations and Federal States*, – as well as Craven, Greg (1993), 'Federal Constitutions and External Relations', p. 9.

5 Duchacek (1990), 'Perforated Sovereignties: Towards a Typology of New Actors in International Relations', p. 5 – in Michelmann, Hans J. and Soldatos, Panayotis (eds), *Federalism and International Relations – the Role of Subnational Units*, Oxford.

6 Hooghe (1995), 'Subnational Mobilisation in the European Union' in *West European Politics*, July 1995. Panayotis Soldatos (1990), 'An Explanatory Framework for the Study of Federated States as Foreign Policy Actors', in Michelmann, Hans J. and Soldatos, Panayotis (eds), *Federalism and International Relations – the Role of Subnational Units*, Oxford, 1990. Fry, E. H. (1980), 'The International Relations of Sub-national Governments: Coping with the "Many Voices" Phenomenon of an Interdependent World', Corfu, Round Table Presentation, International Political Science Association, September 1980 – as referred in Soldatos p. 35.

7 As referred in Soldatos p. 52.

taking part in the decision-making process, but also sub-state actors – contrasting both the realist intergovernmental model and the functionalist supranational model. Her model reflects a pluralist anarchy, and does not foresee a uniformly open playing field; whoever wants – and has the resources – may take the initiative, corresponding very much to the world of the regional offices.[8]

All of these perspectives explain certain aspects of the regional offices and we will return to them in the analysis. However, a newer concept pulls all these aspects together in Keating's idea of 'New Regionalism'. This is based on the historical bourgeois regionalism and its forces of regional economic development. From this he develops his 'New Regionalism',[9] based on four factors: economic restructuring, globalization, transformation of the nation-state, and European integration. This trend has been developing since the late 1980s. Its focus is on the horizontal functionality and growing interdependence of regions, more than on the traditional vertically functional region, dependent on the nation-state.[10] In this way this concept provides a most useful framework for analysing the new sub-national external relations.

Research on Regional Offices

There have been several studies analysing different aspects of the regional offices. Here we will limit this overview to some of the basic defining characteristics. Zumschlange makes the basic distinction between regional offices organized under private law, as ASBL, non-profit associations, versus under public law when sending an official representative.[11] A further typology is suggested by John using organizational mode as the variable:[12]

- Single Local Authority Office;
- The Consultant;
- The English Model; or the consortium;
- Scotland/Wales/Northern Ireland.

Dosenrode distinguishes between three main tasks of the regional offices:[13]

- Catering for economic interest (contacts, marketing, info on EU-funding);
- Information on EU-policies and actions;
- (Cultural) presence and representation.

---

8 Hooghe (1995, pp. 175-198, especially p. 191) and Gren (1993, p. 16).

9 Only in 1993 leading scholars were not accepting this model, discussion with Jörgen Gren, 8 June 1996.

10 Keating, op.cit., pp. 3-5.

11 Zumschlange (1989), 'Berichte und Kritik – Die Informationsbüros der Bundesländer in Brüssel' in *Die Verwaltung*, Vol. 22, No. 2/1989, pp. 232-233.

12 John (1995), *A Base in Brussels – A Good Investment for Local Authorities?*

13 Dosenrode (1995), 'Going NUTS: amter, delstater og kantoner i Europa'.

Gren goes on to point out a general dichotomy of results of this regional lobbying:[14]

- Direct results: funds, location of European institutions, company establishments;
- Indirect results: interregional co-operation, regional awareness in the EC, comprehension of the EC in the region.

Many regional offices focus on EU funding and interregional co-operation. For further understanding of this role of the regional offices, it is useful to touch upon the term 'cobweb'. The philosophy underlying the many EU programmes is to develop a cobweb of individuals and organizations of all types, exchanging experience and best-practice and thereby increasing the overall level of competence in Europe. The idea is that the European citizen should examine his or her own experience and then identify ways to contribute. A prime example often cited in earlier literature is the 'Four Motors of Europe'.[15] However, this bottom-up process is often not started at the local level itself. Projects are often directly motivated by the EU programmes and initiated by the regional office.

This piece attempts to go beyond the official answers about the objectives for establishing – and even more interesting, upholding – regional offices; especially offices representing regions in the small Nordic centralist nation-states. I will focus on the more practical aspects and ask whether there are different types of offices, possibly even a Nordic type as the Nordic background is common. Finally, we will question the future of Nordic regional lobbying, trying to identify trends among the regional offices. But first we need to set the scene, questioning the likely strains put on the relationship between the national authorities and its sub-national entities undertaking such new initiatives. And for this it may prove useful to take a quick glance beyond the Nordic regional offices.

Legal Framework for Nordic Regional Offices

History tells us that in past centuries external relations were the sovereign competence of the nation-state; all diplomatic relations were covered by the national foreign office. However, today interstate relations are not confined to matters related to war and

14 Gren (1993), *Regional Lobbying in the European Community – A Manual*, pp. 61-63.

15 This is one of the most cited examples of regional development and co-operation, consisting of Lombardy, Catalonia, Baden-Wurtemberg and Rhone-Alpes. The network was created in 1988 with the purpose of promoting technological collaboration, research and development, and economic and cultural exchanges. The network has been highly successful; it is also known as 'il Quadrige'. Other examples that are often used in the literature on regional development include 'The Blue Banana', 'The Green Banana' or 'The Sunbelt'. Other regions and researchers have created mosaic-, star- or grape-models. Cf. Gren, Veggeland, Farsund. However, none of these terms are used in Brussels' world of the regional offices. The Aalborg office was not aware of Rhone-Alpes being part of the 'Four Motors' when relocating to the same Brussels premises as them.

peace. Neither technology, environmental problems nor people are effectively hindered from moving across the borders of today's Europe – rather the opposite.

In several countries this has caused a fight over external competences between nation-states and regions. The regional office for 'Europaregion Tirol' in autumn 1995 was searched by police as part of a case questioning the lawfulness of Italian regions establishing offices abroad. However, in February 1996 a law was passed in the Italian parliament, on the initiative of the Süd-Tiroler Volkspartei, stating that external relations of sub-state actors were indeed legal.[16] The Spanish *comunidades* were allowed by the Spanish constitutional court to have foreign representations, although not to individual nation-states.[17] Even what to call the regional offices can cause problems: in Germany there was a row between some regions and Bonn when in 1995 they started using the term 'Vertretung' (Representation) instead of 'Informationsbüro'.

In the Nordic countries discussions on the question of competences have taken place, with differing outcomes. The legal framework in Norway for sub-national international activities is very clear: the national level has neither power, nor interest, to stop the regions establishing representations abroad. However, the view has been discussed in the ministries that Norway is not a large enough country for several, possibly competing, representations abroad, all financed by public institutions.[18] In parts of the Norwegian Foreign Service one can still find remnants of the 19th century idea that the foreign office alone should be responsible for all (official) contact abroad.

The Swedish starting point in 1995 was a marked negative sentiment towards sub-national actors on the European scene. A year after entry into the EU; the officer for regional policy at the Swedish EU representation held a strongly negative view on local initiatives in Brussels.[19] However, major developments on the regional level have taken place in Sweden following its entry into the EU, see the chapter five for further discussion. For our purposes two developments should be mentioned specifically: in 2001 a new law legalized export of services by local authorities, in effect legalizing local foreign policies. This law is a direct effect of EU membership and has according to interviewees caused a mental shift on the local level.[20] This development has been furthered by the *regionforbund* regionalization process from 1 January 2003, giving formal authority to regions, especially in the field of regional

16 Süd Tiroler office, 11 June 1996. Thomas Klau (1996), 'Europe Enters the Age of Regions', *European Voice*, 30 May to 5 June 1996. Parliamentary questions asked 12 February 1996, published in OJ-C 26 July 1996.

17 Basque delegation, 7 June 1996. The law is 165/94, published in BOE 25 June 1994. The Basque delegation was decided on in 305/94 of 20 June 1996 published in BOPV 132 of 12 July 1996.

18 During the winter 1995-96 the Norwegian Export Council in Brussels was asked to represent a region. This was declined after a discussion in the foreign office of who should or could represent Norway abroad.

19 Discussion with Norsjö municipality of Sweden, 16 February 1996.

20 Linköping, 4 April 2003.

development. Until this the elected county councils, *landsting*, had to report to the foreign office when undertaking economic agreements or commitments such as opening a Brussels office. However, the *länsstyrelse*, the state-appointed regional authorities found practical arrangements around this – as when the Mid Sweden office was part-financed by paying a consultant a certain number of hours per week by Västernorrland.

The Finnish situation has also seen major developments. A formal question in parliament set the ball rolling. The starting point was the legal perspectives of external affairs already undertaken by the Uusima region. The positive answer given formed precedence. This was further underlined by a new law on the regional councils giving them the responsibility for regional development, including international contacts, 'formulated in a positive way' as one interviewee noted.[21]

The Danish regional offices were only accepted by Copenhagen after a process of discussion. These offices have become fully integrated into the city administration or the regional structure at home. But the Danish government was for a long time not very happy about having this competitor in external relations.[22]

The decisive impetus given by EU membership for the legal framework for external relations of sub-national entities is clear. However, it seems also that weaker forms of associations with the EU and the internal market may provide the necessary objectives to establish a regional office.

An Analysis of the Regional Offices

History and Context of the Regional Offices

The phenomenon of sub-national foreign representation is in itself not new. By 1882 Quebec had appointed a general agent to Paris on the grounds of developing business relations.[23] Representatives of the German *länder* took part in the negotiations leading to the Treaty of Rome in 1957. And in the same year the German *länder* established a representative, *Länderbeobachter*, in Brussels.[24]

The first regional offices were those of Birmingham and Strathclyde from 1984.[25] The first federal regions to establish offices were in 1985 when Schleswig-Holstein and Hamburg set up the Hanse office. Commissioner Haferkamp finished his period as Commissioner on 5 January 1985 and ten days later he established the 'Hanse office',

21 Association of Finnish local authorities, 7 June 1996. Also Helsinki EU Office, 30 May 1996.

22 Cf. the views of Marianne Jelved, Minister for Economic Affairs, e.g. in interviews with *Børsen*, April-May 1996.

23 Soldatos, 1990, p. 34 – citing L. Beaudoin (1977), 'Origines et developpement du role international du Gouvernement du Quebec' in P. Painchaud (ed.), *Le Canada et le Quebec sur la scene internationale*, Quebec.

24 Zumschlange, op.cit., pp. 222-223.

25 John, op.cit., p. 2.

giving it a highly political focus from the start. This culminated in a process of discontent with the system of a common representative for the *länder*.[26] Hooghe, Keating and Gren all identify the Single European Act as a pivotal moment for the new regionalist trend in Europe. Ratified in 1987 it set the timetable for the creation of the 1992 Common Market and to the domestication of influential sectors of policy. A linked process was the 1988 reform of the Structural Funds, of maybe even larger importance for the funding-focused offices. In this period the number of offices has grown: 15 offices in 1988, 54 in 1993, around 130 in 1996, and now in 2003 totalling 185.[27] However, this number is rising; at least three new Norwegian offices are being established in 2003, and there are still only very few from the upcoming member states. One can safely expect a new boost in numbers.

While these offices are competing for funding, they also have common interests. This caused a network to develop – adding a new dimension, enabling networks for the third level to take part in the decision-shaping. It seems that the first office to focus on the potential network of regional representatives was the *Scotland Europa* office, stating this as an objective in late 1994. The rationale was often 'partner searches' for finding partners for EU programmes, especially in the R&D field. In 1995 this moved beyond the reception circuit with more formal networks of regional representatives, like the Stavanger-Aalborg interregional working group with eight regional representatives in the field of education and training.

The European context has been called 'The Brussels Minestrone'.[28] For most regional offices this consists first and foremost of the EU institutions, with the main focus on the Commission. In addition this soup consists of the other regional offices, regional organizations and networks, as well as the Brussels mix of various interest groups, European and international companies, journalists, lobbyists and consultants.

Why Establish in Brussels?

Examining the motivation for the Nordic countries in coming to Brussels, we should be able to find part of the answer to whether or not the regional offices are part of the new regionalism and the nationalist regionalism of today's Europe. We have asked the regional offices not only why they were established, but also why they are still in Brussels, continuing to spend money. In asking this we found that the priorities grouped somewhat differently than what earlier research has pointed to:

- Funding for projects;
- Providing information to home region;

---

26 Måns Mårtensson, former Sydsam representative, interview 7 June 1996. Søren Z. von Dosenrode, Zumschlange, p. 227.

27 According to our definition and the above-mentioned list of the Niederösterreich regional offices, dated 21 February 2003.

28 Charles Woods, Chief Executive of *Scotland Europa*, 15 May 1996.

- Political lobbying;
- All other objectives.

These all contribute to overall regional development. However, the regional offices stress the various factors differently, as well as giving them varying content. It seems that for the Nordic offices, the first two are taking up most of their time.

Project Funding

The first of the three major reasons follows from foreign policy domestication. The EU has been given competence to treat a number of issues on a European level, rather than leaving it solely to the individual member states. Subsidiarity is still the underlying principle, matters should be dealt with at the lowest possible level. A number of issues are not limited to state borders and need to be handled on a European level. The EU uses various programmes as instruments for approaching this, thus fund-raising for projects in these sectors is possible for the regional offices, and they all list this very high. It is important to note that for the Nordic offices the funds in question are not the Structural Funds as these are negotiated between the EU, the member state and the region back home. These regional offices focus on the plethora of funding schemes for interregional co-operation in various European aspects of sectors as diverse as education, spatial planning, environment, culture, tourism, social challenges, etc. However, most of the offices emphasised that they give priority to specific sectors, listing up to eight sectors. The director of the Stockholm office said it most strongly: 'we do not work with anything other than our six priority areas'. Many of the regional offices will include one or more 'softer' sectors like culture or basic education, some of them strategically approaching potential partner regions with such fields first, before continuing with various aspects of more substantial regional development.

The regional offices have several functions when it comes to project funding: information during the regular home visits and newsletters, discussing ideas, providing relevant documentation, identifying partner regions, and most importantly, conducting a 'pre-check' on the Commission or the deciding bodies. Some regional offices also fill in the application forms, but as the South Sweden office points out, in order for it to be their own project, the project participants need to do this 'marathon' themselves: the regional office only being supporting. Otherwise the regional representative would only be able to work on very few projects per year, as an expensive consultant for the region.

The Danish regional offices have been well-known for getting the most out of the various EU funds. Unofficial studies have shown that Danish actors, e.g. in Phare and Tacis, obtain contracts for four to five times Denmark's part of the budget. Ringkøbing said that as an office for a smaller region, they were able to design projects according to the criteria in the Commission call for proposals. This is the more pragmatic way of looking at the EU funds, and this is very often how one has to act to win smaller projects as well as major Phare or Tacis contracts.[29] However, this rather short-term profit perspective is contrasted by the larger regional and more political offices like the Hanse office (Hamburg and Schleswig-Holstein) or *Scotland Europa*, both trying to build lasting relationships choosing strategic partner regions: around the Baltic Sea, or in the Nordic countries, respectively.

Providing Information to the Home Region

The second set of reasons, sending information back home, is very important in the first phase of a region's European activity. Gren holds that broadening the perspective of the regional administration to Europe is the most important task of all.[30] For a new regional office it is thus important to visit the region very often, possibly every four weeks, e.g. East Sweden, South of Denmark, and West Sweden during their first year. The importance of having a constant flow of delegations from the region to Brussels was underlined by most offices. A variant was Aalborg's attempt at saving money and organising 'EU Courses' at home. Mid Sweden stressed that EU courses should be both sector-specific as well as about the EU in general, though many offices have become tired of this latter one, preferring courses on education programmes for educationalists, environmental protection for those interested, etc. Sydsam, the South of Sweden office, had an interesting variant: inviting EU officials to the region for three or four conferences. This was certainly much cheaper and the Danish EU officials especially were very interested in a paid flight, combined with a weekend at home.

What information are we talking about? This could be programme information, connected to the preceding task of assisting in securing EU funds. This might be a colleague telling you about a not yet published programme, a programme you missed in the Official Journal (OJ) or the underlying criteria which cannot be written in the work programme for political reasons. Information can also be related to the Common Market and EEA, e.g. examples of public procurement or the answer to why the German customs official seems not to respect the EEA. It can be of major importance to have information before everybody else; information is power. Quite often it is of importance to interpret the information from the specific perspective of the region one is representing.

How to obtain information? Most Swedish offices rank their sources as follows: co-located regional colleagues, European Commission, other regional offices, various EU publications, other EU institutions – and then lastly the Swedish Permanent Representation.[31] The amazing lack of communication from the Representation is also

29 Ringkøbing, Spring 1996. International consulting companies organize their EU projects similarly: a Euro-unit putting together a multi-national team from their different European offices in order to specifically target each project.

30 Jörgen Gren, discussion 8 June 1996.

31 According to a survey by the Swedish Permanent Representation, June 1996.

experienced by the Vaasa office, the criticism being similar to the one towards the Norwegian delegation during the membership negotiations. This is very much a Nordic tradition, quite destructive in a European context, where most information is free flowing through, for example the UK Representation from Council meetings.[32] In the European context this represents an important handicap to the development of the Nordic regions and interests, increasing the importance of experienced representatives with a well-developed network of their own, including the representations of other member states.

Having *stagiaires*/trainees from the home region may also be seen as one way of approaching this objective. This can be an official from the regional authority on a specific project (Copenhagen), a student (Aalborg) or an unemployed person (Helsinki). However, many offices judge that for several months a new person is more a nuisance than a help, if s/he is not working on a specific project brought from home.

The rationale behind the weight given to this task of relaying information home is the inefficiency at the national level, i.e. information being delayed when going from EU to the capitals for distribution to the regions.[33] This is related to the questionable performance by the national representations of the 'new' Nordic countries, being the official national representation to the EU. Early, targeted information as well as their own perspective on the information, is emphasised by most of the offices.

Political Lobbying

The third task that regional offices mention is political lobbying, also known as upstream lobbying. The target is most often the European Commission; the decisive Council is often better lobbied from home. Also the Committee of the Regions, the European Parliament and the Economic and Social Committee can be interesting to lobby in specific cases.

Several examples can be found, though few among the Nordic regions: Highlands and Islands Regional Council of Scotland came to Brussels to lobby for status as an objective 1-region, defined as having less than 75 per cent of the EU GNP-average and thus receiving substantially more Structural Funds. They achieved this in 1994 after having won the Commission's acceptance for redefining the borders in which to calculate the GNP. Niedersachsen extended the geographic scope of the KONVER programme for transformation of former military camps, originally intended only for the former East German states.

A few Nordic examples can also be found: Sydsam has taken part in work defining borders across water as valid Interreg borders, and this lobbying succeeded in the

32 Several interviewees gave this example, explaining the UK rationale as a need to ensure that UK companies get the tender documents when their competitors get them, leaked from their representations many months before publication in the Official Journal. The interviewees noted that the Nordic model in such cases should adapt and become open.

33 One example being the tourism call May 1995, reaching the Norwegian regions two days before the deadline; Oslo had had it for a month.

Interreg IIc-programme. The Nordic regional offices have also been instrumental when fighting over Structural Funds. One can also find numerous smaller-scale examples, like the Stavanger office's successful lobbying for COMENIUS to open up for pre-school applications. However, such lobbying seems not to be one of the main concerns of the Nordic regional offices. This might be caused by still being rather new on the European scene, not yet part of the old networks. Or it could be contributed to the Nordic dislike for even the term 'lobbying'. This is the type of political lobbying Keating is referring to when he is not particularly enthusiastic about the functioning of the regional offices. When questioning the concrete benefits he says that 'the Commission is always happy to talk to the regions, thus extending its own information sources; it is rarely able to respond to specific demands, given the rules about funding and programmes'. However, even 'rarely' may prove a very profitable target to the region. He does however acknowledge the importance of the creation of networks of influence around the Commission, exchanging information, planting ideas and gradually developing policy.

However, Keating is also referring here to the less tough manner of political lobbying: bringing the region's concerns and problems to the attention of the Commission. This is being done to a certain extent by the Nordic regional offices. The Stavanger region, the oil capital of Norway has regularly invited key officials from the EU Directorate-General for Energy (DGXVII) to the region, presenting the attractions of the region, as well as their views on energy policy. For West Sweden the Gothenburg harbour is very important, but a commission in Stockholm was changing the framework for maritime transport in Sweden to the detriment of Gothenburg. Seen from West Sweden this is a good example of what Soldatos calls a 'federal error'. So what did the region do? It mobilized. Stena Line, one of the major interests, had a meeting with Transport Commissioner Kinnock, organized by the West Sweden office. As a follow-up, West Sweden organized a major conference for raising the profile of Gothenburg as the north European infrastructural centre, especially concerning short-sea shipping. The message reached several EU officials, including Commissioner Kinnock, who came to give a speech. More importantly, however, his advisor was present for the whole conference. The objectives of the conference were obviously increasing the profile – as well as mentioning two of the harbour innovations for which they were applying for EU funding.

Other Nordic regions could benefit from using similar strategies as Stavanger or Gothenburg. Also other Nordic regions have learned this way of lobbying since the regional offices were first established, but it seems clear that the Nordic regions are still being nicer, and possibly more naïve, than their neighbours to the south.

Other Objectives

Our aim is to identify all the objectives of establishing and upholding a Brussels office. A further six objectives were identified, in addition to the main three discussed above. Marketing was mentioned by several of the offices. This was, however, most often seen as an indirect result of the office. Merely by being present in the European capital, the region can be more easily seen by various actors. Both foreign investors and tourists are of course welcome; however the approach for attracting them is very often either through generally increasing the profile of the region[34] or through promoting the region in interregional co-operation projects, thus inviting other European regions to work with the region, instead of with the neighbouring region – if present or not in Brussels. To this extent there is a competition among the regional offices. Most of the offices have brochures for inward investment, but this target group is hardly ever given priority by the regional offices.

Two related objectives are Dosenrode's cultural presence and Gren's objective of trying to get European institutions to the region. Cultural presence and representation as one of the tasks of the regional office is often true for the larger and wealthier regions, e.g. the German *länder*. But one may question the function of the receptions. At German regional receptions one notes that typically 60-90 per cent are Germans; at the opening of the Helsinki office in June 1996, a similar percentage were speaking Finnish. In October 1995 the Ringkøbing office had a vernissage for an EU-funded project for painters of many countries; except for a short resume in English all the lengthy speeches were in Danish. Typically some regional dignitary is present at these occasions, giving a speech on how interesting and fantastic the region is, not very much tuned to the atmosphere of the 'New Regionalism' prevalent among most regional offices, especially the smaller ones, e.g. the Nordic or the English. It seems that this kind of cultural presence, corresponding to Keating's 'nationalist' regionalism, can to a certain extent be said to be undertaken more for the home region than for fulfilling a function other than providing an easy-going cocktail-atmosphere for those present. It also has to be mentioned that regional offices are typically invited to such events two to four evenings per week.

Gren's objective of localization of EU institutions is a somewhat far-fetched objective. Mid Sweden can boast of having one of seven EU Regional Energy Agencies and a Business Innovation Centre (BIC). This is very good, but we are still talking small-scale European offices, not institutions. Locating various types of smaller EU-funded centres to the home region is of course interesting, and in these cases it is then a question of knowing before the neighbouring regions that the EU want to set up such an office. But it is true to say, more important EU agencies or institutions also have to be located somewhere, such as for example the European Monetary Institute (Frankfurt) or the European Environment Agency (Copenhagen). The regional offices may also play a role in locating this, or for deciding the location of the European Council Summits. The Birmingham office had a decisive role in localizing the Summit to Birmingham in 1992.

34 The best example is the Tuscany regional office (consortium) established in Brussels in February 1996, organising several major 'soft' events in Brussels such as an exhibition of Etrusque culture, a sculptural park and a concert. General profile-raising is also one of the objectives for the Scottish office, and they undertake this by taking part in the ongoing Brussels debate on current topics – e.g. by publishing a series of discussion papers. None of the Nordic regions seem to have capacity for this sort of action as of today.

Soldatos points to the effect of imitation, and this may lead to what Keating mentions as 'the rise of urban politicians as cities seek to project themselves on the national and international stage'.[35] The feeling of 'Be there or be square' can be said to have a certain effect as all the Nordic regional offices are frequently visited by regions which have not yet set up their own office, asking how to lobby, practicalities, success stories and sometimes for possible co-operation.

'Assymmetry of federal units' is given by Soldatos as a possible cause for para-diplomacy. In the Nordics this seems not to be of major importance; both the Danes and the Finns emphasized that the whole nation-state is so small and coherent, and the regional differences that exist are only minor, regional traditions. The capital region may feel that they have a certain duty to be present in Brussels. This was the case for the Helsinki office which had its official opening in the summer of 1996, nearly one year after it was first set up. The immature start was due to political reasons: the capital wanted to accept its self-imposed duty to establish a regional representation. It should be noted that all the Nordic capital cities have had their own ways of approaching the world of regional offices; suddenly they are not together with their main ally, the nation-state. Stockholm had an incredibly expensive 'tourist office' even though this perception would be strongly contested by them. Even now, several years after moving from their flashy Grand Place location, Stockholm is still mentioned by interviewees as the most flamboyant example of misunderstanding the nature of the regional offices. Based on interviews and views of other interviewees, for a long time after establishing their regional office Copenhagen seemed to be totally unaware of the advantages of the network of regional offices. They rather wanted to do it fully on their own – even when located in the Hanse office, one of the best information channels in the regional world in Brussels.[36] In the case of Oslo; following a report in 1992 they decided that a regional office was of no interest. A number of interests have pushed for it ever since, and at the time of writing it is about to be opened in September 2003.

Interregional co-operation is in itself also a major objective, often stressed by the Stavanger European Office, relying on the EEA. The partnerships created and the experiences they bring are maybe more important than the amount of Euro brought home to the region. To a certain extent this might be a necessary perspective to adopt when not a member, even though the EEA ensures participation in a majority of EU co-operation programmes. Together with the automatic adoption of EU directives this provides the answer to the most frequently asked question of why a non-member region would want to have a regional office in Brussels.

---

35 Michael Keating, 1995, pp. 13-14.

36 Schleswig-Holstein and Hamburg invite their co-located regional offices to Wednesday meetings, sharing all available information – but the Copenhagen office was seldom seen there or in the rest of the blooming environment of the Hanse office.

Different Types of Regional Offices? – Practical Aspects

This leads us to the question if there are different types of regional offices. As already mentioned in the introductory remarks, it seems that there is a difference in focus; some regional offices are more pragmatically oriented towards funding and information, while others seem to be more politically oriented, either by lobbying or by representing the home region. This possible functional typology seems to distinguish most Nordic offices, including the Danish offices, as well as many smaller UK offices – from the larger offices of federal or regionalized states. The size and budget thus seems to have an impact on the tasks and focus of the office. Thus it also becomes interesting to look into different practical arrangements. However, both the Sydsam office and the Copenhagen office emphasise the political dimension. This can possibly be partly explained by the specific reason for coming to Brussels – and their location in Brussels. South of Sweden was invited to establish in the Hanse office as part of the latter's Baltic Sea initiative. Thus Sydsam is present on favourable economic terms, and is also given a political framework right from the start. The Hanse office has also invited Copenhagen, Vaasa and more recently South of Denmark on these terms, based on the existing regional partnerships around the Baltic Sea.

The main alternative to a regional office is having some sort of Euro-unit in the home region, travelling to Brussels when needed and actively taking part in various European networks, possibly also providing regional information on the Internet. This has often been the first step to opening some sort of regional office. Most smaller regions would like to start with part-time representation in Brussels. Regional representatives often wear two or more very different hats. A number of creative solutions have been found, such as being a regional representative and a journalist, or an official for some organization or institution, or a consultant, company executive, lawyer, housewife, retired, student or an alternant member of the ECOSOC committee, for instance. Some represent a region only on specific occasions; most have a specified number of hours per week or percentage of their week devoted to the region. Questions like this, as well as home organization, communication to home, profile and localities, etc. are most important, though such deliberations do not belong here.[37]

The interlinked topics of budget and personnel are very basic practical aspects. The budget for an independent office varies considerably between €100,000 and €750,000 for the Nordic offices, Stockholm representing the latter figure, more than double of any other Nordic regional office.[38] Most often the salary to one or more carefully selected persons will be a substantial part of this, the other costs amounting to an absolute minimum of €50,000 per year if one has such favourable conditions as the Nordic regions being hosted by the Hanse office, or if buying part-time services from a consultant or other organization. The Finnish regions of Oulo and Northern

37 A closer look at this belongs in a consultancy study, and not here. This was, to a certain extent, developed in the original MA-thesis (Lein-Mathisen, 1996).

38 They are changing location in 1997, leaving Grand Place. This will affect the budget.

Ostrobothnia became affiliate members of *Scotland Europa*. Starting at €30,000 annually, this included a newsletter and service visits from the region.

The question of personnel is maybe the most decisive for a regional office as everything relies on personal contacts. Generally it can be said that two generations are present in the regional offices: the younger generation in their late 20s or early 30s – and the older in their 50s. Larger regions with a need for heavy political lobbying typically choose a senior politician or businessman as representative. In some cases this has proved very wrong, as this is 'NOT a next-to-retirement post', but rather a 'specific vocation in its own right'.[39] Also senior executives would rather choose a younger person for the regional office.[40] As one of the 'owners' of the East Sweden office argued as follows, after choosing a young person: the representative has to be a trained generalist opening doors for the heavy-weighters that have to come from home in any case.[41]

South of Denmark set up their regional office in the autumn of 1995, not giving priority to any specific sectors but rather including a little bit of everything from the start; the representative had Brussels experience but not from a regional office. The East Sweden office headhunted the second-in-command at the West Sweden office and her two-and-a-half years of experience and contacts; she started working directly in seven carefully selected sectors. A thorough strategy plan determines how soon the office can become effective, and most regional offices start developing such a plan, seen both from the perspective of the region and of the possibilities of a regional office – preferably with the help of consultants with experience of a regional office.

Future Nordic Regional Lobbying

Trends Among the Current Regional Offices

A number of trends can be found in the interview material, both from the 1995-96 period and from 2002-03.

A first trend is that of reconsidering the cost of the 'Euro-chic' effect. After the 1995-96 rush, many regions were looking at costs and benefits. Setting up a regional office in Brussels was an important step forward for the regions of the Nordic countries in the EU or the EEA, maybe without a full study on costs and benefit, rather imitating neighbouring regions – an example of 'Euro-chic'.[42] One indicator of this can be that none of the Nordic offices made a list of evaluation criteria to use when considering renewing the presence after the first period. Of those interviewed in

39 Måns Mårtensson, 7 June 1996.

40 Mr Levin, senior researcher at the Swedish Permanent Representation, 2 July 1996. Mr Lücke, Director of the Hanse office, 16 July 1996.

41 Roland Johansson, Director Linköping's municipality, 3 June 1996.

42 John, op.cit., p. 1 – referring to the British Audit Commission report *A Rough Guide to Europe: Local Authorities and the EC*, 1991.

1995-96, only *Scotland Europa* and the Nottingham Brussels Office had planned this review in advance, with qualitative and quantitative targets set for continuous self-evaluation.

A second trend is moving competencies home. This is a question of finding a viable organizational form. This does not mean it is less interesting to be present in Brussels, only that one should undertake a thorough study of costs and benefits for the individual region. Moving home could be seen as becoming more 'mature', more targeted in their actions, following a clear-cut strategy analysing the objectives to pursue. Stavanger moved project design competencies home in 1996. In 2002 East Sweden made a clear choice of having the representative significantly more at home, as the job in Brussels was well on track and the challenges of European co-ordination back home were greater. Even though the importance of the Structural Funds will decrease for the old member states after enlargement, it is not unlikely that the number of EU programmes could increase. Furthermore, the psychological importance of this 'interregional glue' may increase, especially when the Structural Funds will have to diminish as new member states are accepted.

A third trend is strategic choice of partner regions when setting up the regional office. Both Mid Sweden and the Top of Sweden have carefully chosen regions to co-operate with. Oslo and Østfold county of Norway have for some time been associated members of West Sweden. East Sweden used consultants to identify the Lancashire house as a suitable location, and this seems to have been successful. Though one example seems to have been using opposite criteria: Stockholm originally set up in expensive offices on the highly touristy Grand Place – two to three kilometers from the EU area.

A fourth trend is the concept of 'Euroregions' which we are likely to see more of. Øresund is trying to establish itself as a region and has to a certain extent successfully placed itself on the map. But the common branding is obviously and understandably still a problem as there are not one but two regional offices, neither called Øresund. A better example then is the Euroregion Tirol which has set up a common office, with one representative for each of the three regions – from both sides of the Italian-Austrian border. Across the channel we find three common offices: Essex-Picardie, Basse-Normandie and Hampshire-Dorset, and *Euroregion*: Brussels, Flanders, Kent, Wallonia, and Nord-Pas de Calais involving three countries. The oldest regional co-operation of this kind is *Euregio* between eastern Netherlands and western Germany, founded in 1958. This has later developed into the Association of European Border Regions (AEBR). However, the *Euregio* has a secretariat in Gronau, Germany, but none in Brussels.

Sometimes the Americans lead developmental processes. In 1995 nine US states were represented in Brussels, and a fifth trend is that already then they were much more selective when targeting potential regions – all the US regions taking part in a ULB study had made contacts with the 'Four Motors of Europe'.[43] Few Nordic and other regional representatives are acquainted with this term, much less taking account

43 PhD survey by Mike van Cutsem, CERIS, Universite Libre de Bruxelles, spring 1996.

of it, for example the Aalborg office moving to the same building as Rhone-Alpes, without being aware of this network.

As mentioned in the introduction, we can also see a sixth trend of increased formal representation. As the regional offices are only unofficial representations, some regions also experience a need for formal representation through the national permanent representations. The Austrian *länder* have their own representative in the Austrian permanent representation, which is also the case for Germany, Belgium, Italy – and the Netherlands, though with a slight variation. Other member states have also considered this type of solution, including Sweden.[44]

When most of the Danish regional offices were established early/mid 1990s they chose to establish at the same location. However, interregional co-operation is all about cross-border co-operation, and over time this common location was seen more as a liability than an asset. Co-locating with regional offices from other countries provides almost instant access to European partners as well as indirect access to networks based on other nationalities – the Hanse office being the best example. As mentioned, Aalborg was the first to leave the Danish 'ghetto'. However, the new West Norway office has chosen to be located on the premises of the Norwegian national representations, as opposed to with their UK partner region.

Whether it should be called a separate trend is uncertain. It is, however, quite clear that the B7 regional office is quite special. It represents the seven largest islands in the Baltic Sea, from five different countries. Such cross-border regions represent a quintessentially European trend; they represent the essence of the interregional co-operation that the EU is promoting. Østfold of Norway was an affiliate member of West Sweden. Øresund could be mentioned. The Mid Scandinavia office covers both Norway and Sweden.

Linköping and Norrköping were always enemies and are now setting up a common Brussels office in order to compete with the stronger regions of Stockholm, South-Sweden and West Sweden. Establishing a common office further enhances the 'we-feeling' in the region, especially for the high-level groups coming to Brussels. This is however only sound and fruitful patriotism, not nationalist regionalism, patriotism that furthers economic development. As several Nordic interviewees pointed out: the differences among us are so small, and even more so within our countries, why should we be nationalist on behalf of our region!

Yet another trend is that not only regions of member states, especially new ones, open up offices; regions of countries with association agreements of various kinds are coming as well. The Stavanger office opened in September 1993, during the membership negotiations. French Polynesia has its own office, the Dutch overseas territories have their own representative in the Dutch mission. The Channel Islands are represented through the UK Representation, having a special, independent agreement with the EU. The Swiss cantons have their representation, and western Turkey has been looking at the possibility of opening an office. Kaliningrad was an early bird

44 Wolfgang Burtscher, Austrian Permanent Representation, 16 July 1996. Compare also Tage Levin, op.cit., and Wilfried Swenden, op.cit.

with a person in the Aalborg office. Examples are known where various forms of such regional representation have made an important political impact in negotiations with the EU. For the 2004 enlargement the only surprising thing is that not more regions have established regional offices before enlargement.

Future European Development for the Nordic Regions

Looking at the individual Nordic countries, it is not unlikely that we will see new Norwegian regional offices establishing. Regions realize that the negative outcome of the 1994 referendum still left them in the EEA-agreement, the closest link with the EU existing today. As we have seen, a number of different types of presence in Brussels is possible, and the Norwegian regions can be expected to try out different models in the months and years to come. During the winter of 1995-96 two attempts were made to set up the second Norwegian regional office: one county was in discussions with a Norwegian partner in Brussels. Another region asked the Norwegian Export Council to be their representative.[45] Yet another region had an MA thesis done for them on the question of setting up a regional office.[46]

The typical Swedish regional office has a large number of individual municipalities as members, cf. Sydsam and West Sweden with 60-70 members. Quite remarkably, in 1991 there was already an agreement to work for a common representation for the four northernmost *län*, if Sweden should become an EU member, though this was hard to carry through, as differences are large. In any case, the enthusiasm is impressive: during the spring of 1996 several small northern municipalities visited Brussels to discover for themselves the possibilities of setting up an office; also Jämtland *län* has been using a consultancy for various services until in 1997 they set up together with Mid Sweden at the *Scotland Europa* office. It seems that the tendency to have large offices will remain strong in Sweden,[47] though several representatives have pointed out that these larger offices have problems with reaching the individual municipality.

The Finnish regions were more hesitant than the Swedish following accession in 1995. Several regions tried minimum solutions before setting up proper offices. Oulo and Northern Ostrobothnia as affiliate members of *Scotland Europa* have already been mentioned. Satakunta seconded senior officials to the Brussels office of their twin region Bremen during their first period. Similarly, the Vaasa office started in the Hanse office and developed into the larger West Finland Alliance. Even Helsinki had such a period, opening prematurely in summer 1995; even after the official opening in June 1996 it was not clear who should take up the post. Another three Finnish regions were also in Brussels on longer temporary stays.

---

45 Knut Revling, Norwegian Export Council, 7 June 1996.

46 On which this chapter is based.

47 SydSam, 16 July 1996, and Levin, op.cit.

Concluding Remarks

As we have seen, more and more Nordic regions have established a regional office in Brussels. In 2002-2003 even the regions of the EEA-member Norway have followed suit. Charlie Jeffery has drawn up the distinction between the German offices, as a 'statement of virility' of the *länder*, and the more modest and pragmatic UK offices. The Nordic regional offices are clearly of the British type; they are focusing on funding and information, rather than on policy-making and influencing decisions. Among the Nordic offices in existence in 1996, only the South Sweden office confirmed that they wanted to play an active part in the strong regionalist trend. However, this is only one side of the story, when comparing with the federal *länder* of Germany.

When applying the concept of new regionalism to the Nordic regional offices, we find that this corresponds rather well with the empirical situation: horizontal functionality and links between regions, regions interacting directly on the global arena, as well as taking part in European integration on their own. At the same time, the Nordic nation-states are becoming transformed as foreign policy is being domesticated. This is not only true for the EU members, but also for the EEA members Norway and Iceland as most *acquis* is implemented also by them. Therefore, the answer must be 'yes' to the question of whether or not the Nordic regions are part of the new European regionalism. This is not a nationalist regionalism, but rather a 'new regionalism' based on interdependence in a system of multi-level governance.

Following their membership referenda of 1994, the Nordic regions are slowly beginning to realise that they are in a completely new situation. They are more closely linked with the rest of Europe than ever before; a multi-layered interdependence where they will have to take on more responsibility. And this is true regardless of Norway's 'No' to full membership in 1994 or Sweden's €-'No' in 2003. Having a regional office in Brussels is therefore more than the latest in 'Euro-chic' among the last round of new member states. It is rather a first substantial move towards taking an active part in the developing multi-level decision-shaping process in the new Europe.

Bibliography

Oral Sources

Representatives from the following: Swedish EU representation, Icelandic mission to the EU, South of Denmark EU office, Austrian Permanent Representation, CEMR, DG XVI-Sweden unit, Swedish COR member, Basque delegation, Stavanger European Office, Linköpings municipality, Vaasa EU office, Norwegian mission to the EU, Sydsam, Stockholm Meeting Point, Mid Sweden, East Sweden, Linköping international office, Copenhagen EU office, Essex regional office, Aalborg EU office, West Sweden, Alto Adige office, Norwegian Export Council-Brussels, Finnish Association of Local and Regional authorities, Helsinki EU office, Patronat Catalan, LKAB EU office, International Secretariat of Swedish Federation of County Councils (Brussels and Stockholm), East

Sussex, French Polynesia, *Scotland Europa*, Dom-Tom, ULB/CERIS, Nottingham, Saarland, Hanse office, COR, AER.

Written Sources

Bocklet, Reinhold (1996), 'A Reorientation of the European Agricultural Policy', speech delivered 23 January 1996 by the Minister of State at the representation of the Free state of Bavaria to the European Union.

COAST presentation package, conference 22 May 1996.

Fallik, Alain (ed.) (1995), *The European Public Affairs Directory – The Comprehensive Guide to Opinion-formers in the Capital of Europe*, Brussels: Landmarks.

'Friends of Flanders 2002 VZW' – Invitation for concert and reception 7 June 1996 sent to the regional offices ultimo May.

Jones, Tim (1996), 'Cities Forge Lobbying Links', p. 20 in 'Survey: Regions', European Voice, 23 to 29 November 1996, pp. 13-20.

Klau, Thomas (1996), 'Europe Enters the Age of Regions', European Voice, 30 May to 5 June 1996.

Stavanger Aftenblad (1996), 'Flamsk nasjonalisme med eksplosiv kraft', 29 May 1996, p. 12.

Academic Literature

Andersen, Tron Lande (1995), *Nettverks-samarbeid – et regionalpolitisk virkemiddel i EU*, NIBR-notat 1995:107, KS-forskning

Craven, Greg (1993), 'Federal Constitutions and External Relations' in Hacking, Brian (ed.), *Foreign Relations and Federal States.*

Dosenrode, Søren Z. von (1995), 'Going NUTS: amter, delstater og kantoner i Europa' in *Nordisk Administrativt Tidsskrift* 2/1995, vol. 76.

Duchacek, Ivo D. (1990), 'Perforated Sovereignties: Towards a Typology of New Actors in International Relations', in Michelmann, Hans J. and Soldatos, Panayotis (eds), *Federalism and International Relations – the Role of Subnational Units*, Oxford.

European Commission (1994), *Competitiveness and Cohesion: Trends in the Regions – Fifth Periodic Report on the Social and Economic Situation and Development of the Regions in the Community*, Brussels. CX-85-94-147-EN-C.

Farsund, Arild, Meissner, Rudolf and Nødland, Svein Ingve (1995), *Regionalt samarbeid over landegrenser i Europa – norske fylkeskommuners alliansebygging for næringsutvikling*, RF-95/234, Stavanger: RF.

Gren, Jörgen (1992), *Place-marketing in Europe – A Manual*, unpublished MA thesis, Institut d'etudes politiques, Grenoble.

Gren, Jörgen (1993), *Regional Lobbying in the European Community – A Manual*, unpublished MPhil thesis, Cambridge.

Hacking, Brian (1993), 'Introduction' in Hacking, Brian (ed.), *Foreign Relations and Federal States*.

Hooghe, Liesbet (1995), 'Subnational Mobilisation in the European Union' in *West European Politics*, vol. 18, no. 3, July 1995, London: Frank Cass, pp. 175-198.

Jeffery, Charlie (1997): 'Regional Information Offices in Brussels and Multi-Level Governance in the EU: A UK-German Comparison' in Jeffery, Charlie, *The Regional Dimension of the European Union - Towards a Third Level in Europe*, London: Frank Cass.

John, Peter (1995), *A Base in Brussels – a Good Investment for Local Authorities?*, Special Report no. 2, Local Government International Bureau.

Keating, Michael (1995), 'Europeanism and Regionalism' in B. Jones and M. Keating (eds), *The EU and the Regions*, Oxford: Clarendon Press.

Keating, Michael (1996), 'The Invention of Regions, Political Restructuring and Territorial Government in Western Europe', ECPR conference, Oslo.

Lein-Mathisen, Jørn (1996), *Regional Lobbying: The Nordic Regions Approaching Europe*, unpublished MA thesis, CERIS, Universite Libre de Bruxelles.

Levin, Tage (1996), *Bättre kontakt mellan EU-arbetet och den regionala nivån – Förslag till förbättrad information mellan Sveriges EU-representaion och länsstyrelserna*, Bryssel juli 1996, for the Swedish government, final draft.

Soldatos, Panayotis (1990), 'An Explanatory Framework for the Study of Federated States as Foreign Policy Actors', in Michelmann, Hans J. and Soldatos, Panayotis (eds), *Federalism and International Relations – the Role of Subnational Units*, Oxford.

Veggeland, Noralv and Hedegaard, Lars (1994), *Det sterke Norden i et regionalisert Europa*, Oslo and Copenhagen. This is based on one of the three studies undertaken as part of the Europe 2000 report by the European Commission 1991.

Zumschlange, Konrad (1989), 'Berichte und Kritik – Die Informationsbüros der Bundesländer in Brüssel' in *Die Verwaltung*, vol. 22, no. 2/1989, Berlin: Duncker&Humblot.

Chapter 7

Regional Perspectives on Integration in the Baltic Sea Region

Andreas P. Cornett

Introduction

Location and integration as well as adaptation and co-operation are the key issues to be addressed in an assessment of the future position of the Baltic Rim in the European system. The purpose of this chapter is to address the influence of the changes in the European economic landscape in the aftermath of the break up of the Iron Curtain, and the new dynamics of the process of European integration since 1989. Integration is probably the single most important social force in the process of transition of the Baltic Sea Region (BSR). The success of the various aspects of the process of integration will have decisive influence on the regional networking system within the region and between the Baltic Rim area and the European and global systems.

Regional integration has altered the spatial dimensions of regional activities, and this chapter will discuss regional integration frameworks' impact on the regional development and potentials of the Baltic Sea Region.

Among the topics discussed are issues like regional impacts of changes in the regional production system, impacts on regions from international trade and the ongoing development of the regional structure with regard to economic, political and organizational aspects. In particular, the issue of regionalization is of crucial importance in the Baltic States and Poland with regard to the adaptation to the European Regional Policy. Recently Poland has altered the regional system creating larger regional units. With regard to the Baltic States the issue is less relevant due to the size of the countries, but can become more important in the longer run when regional disparities increase within the countries due to more diversified economic performance. In particular, centre-periphery disparities are expected to become more salient in future, if the current tendency of concentrated economic development in the metropolitan regions continues.

In this perspective the sub-regional development has to be seen in the context of the overall integration of the BSR into the European economic system. The next section of this chapter briefly discusses the concepts of regional integration as a theoretical anchor for the analysis of integration and transition of the regional system of the Baltic Rim, before embarking on an investigation of the real world processes in the third section. The final section provides an assessment of the BSR in an overall European perspective.

Spatial Integration – A Comprehensive Concept for the Study of Regional Transition?

Regional integration has been an important factor in the political development of Europe since the Second World War, and has altered the spatial dimensions of regional activities. After the break up of the Iron Curtain the process of integration changed in scope and intensity, in particular in the Baltic Sea Region, and became a major force in the process of transition of the former command economies and the reintegration into the western market-based economic system.

This section provides a tentative outline of concepts based on regional integration for the analysis of the process of reintegration of the Baltic Rim region into the mainstream economic and political system in Europe, the European Union and the market-based economies of the world as a whole.

The theoretical fundamental of the processes of regional integration can be found in economic and political theory of integration, but as stated above, this is in particular the case in this process, which has to be seen in a spatial perspective as well. Theoretically, the first two approaches are distinctly based in economics, in particular concept from the field of international economics and trade theory, and various branches of political science. The economic concepts of regional integration were originally introduced by Jacob Viner (1950) in his analysis of Customs Unions, but the concepts have been expanded in scope and depth to cover most aspects of regional economic co-operation.

There are several reasons to extend the analysis beyond the traditional economic and political aspects of integration, when dealing with processes of transition and reintegration simultaneously. The relationship between macroeconomic integration and the necessity of providing instruments to cover specific areas or sectors from significant adverse effects of this process is obvious. In particular the political approaches to integration are useful when focusing on the need for restructuring of the existing EU policies to meet the challenges of the enlargements with former CMEA countries.

Theories of Political Integration

Traditionally, four approaches to political integration are distinguished: the federalist approach, the transaction or pluralistic approach, and the functionalist and the neofunctionalist approaches, the 'theory of Western European integration'. The different schools indicate that no common consensus with regard to a definition exists. Some focus on the process of forming a regional body, whereas others emphasise the stage of integration. In a review of the state-of-the-art of political integration theory after the first 'honeymoon' of political integration and the first major drawbacks in real world integration as well as theory-building, Charles Pentland (1973) made the attempt to formulate what he called a common denominator of political integration:

> All it seems possible to say is that international political integration is a process whereby a group of people, organized initially in two or more independent nation-states, come to constitute a political whole which can in some sense be described as a community (Pentland, 1973, p. 21).

Based on Lindberg and Scheingold's models of system change (1970, pp. 134-139), and the challenges to political integration theory in general (Chryssochoou 1997, p. 1) the following preliminary conclusions seem possible:

- The virtuous circle in this process can result in a system transformation but with a possible outcome which at the best will be reinforced by forward linkage (or in a Haas' terminology, spill over) mechanisms. The alternative after the system transformation is 'output failure' if the EU is not able to follow up on the fundamental transformation initiated by the reintegration of the East and Central European Countries.
- The experiences of the first years of the transition process indicate that the risk of negative outcomes (output failure or spill back) is real. Particulary, in the fields of economic restructuring (within the EU, as well as in the accession countries) and external (with regard to economic assistance and the implementation of preferential treatment in the area of trade and other forms of economic exchange) the risk is evident.
- In the field of political integration, the record at present seems to be less ambiguous. The decisive test will come when East-West negotiations will change character from more or less traditional intergovernmental frameworks (led by the presidential country of the EU) to become an integrated part of the EU decision-making with majority voting etc. This will stress the still unsolved institutional issues only superficially dealt with in the Intergovernmental Conference (IGC) of Amsterdam, and is another reminder of one of the crucial shortcomings of the concepts of regional integration, and the lack of an operational approach towards integration (Cornett, 1999, pp. 258f.).

The result is that it seems useful to distinguish between several forms of international co-operation and integration depending on scope (range of co-operation) and institutional capacity (procedures and intensity of mutual decision-making) of the framework under consideration. The distinction was originally introduced by Lindberg and Scheingold (1970, p. 99f.). Recently, a similar argument has been forwarded in a textbook on European Economic Integration by Jacques Pelkmans (2001, p. 23):

The European Community has developed in essentially three ways:

- deepening (of its economic liberalization, common regulation and politics and of the commitments and prohibitions of the member states);
- widening (of the scope of its economic and other powers);
- enlargement (of membership).

With regard to the reintegration issue, the main conclusion is that the ambivalence between the scope and institutional capacity dimension of integration will persist after a geographical enlargement. Additionally, the problem of regional imbalance within the European system will become more topical, not only from an economic, but also from a political point of view. The importance of the latter becomes manifest in the final stage of the enlargement process with the East and Central European countries both internally in the EU, here in particular in the EU summit in Nice 2000 (the Economist 2000), and with regard to the new member states in the final negotiations at the Copenhagen summit last December (Der Spiegel, 2002, p. 51).

The two classical problem areas stipulated in 1970 will persist. Whether the history of internal structural problems will repeat itself or not, only time will prove. The reaction in the 1970s was to extend scope at the price of serious shortcomings in decision-making and institutional capacities. This will not necessarily be supranational in a neofunctionalistic sense, but rather of intergovernmental or confederal (Sæter, 1971) style, combined with the institutional structures developed in the EU system.[1] The crucial argument with respect to the choice between a federalistic and a confederalistic approach to co-operation is that the national government still has the control over the most important areas of politics, and that unanimity is still required if joint policy has to be made.[2]

In an enlargement perspective the most important impact is that for every enlargement, the decision-making structure becomes more complicated and the risk of being unable to produce necessary decisions increases (spillback or output failure in Lindberg and Scheingold's terminology).

The role of Greece with regard to the EU's policy toward Turkey, and to some extent Cyprus, illuminates this point. Enlargement with new members without institutional reforms becomes a risky business, if the general principle of equal treatment and equal rights on obligations for all members is maintained. In policy areas governed by the principle of veto according to the 1966 Luxembourg accord the EU will be unable to act if issues are at stake considered to be of national

---

1 For a graphical illustration of two variants of the sketched transnational political system see figure 2 p. 535 in Chryssochoou (1997).

2 'Applied to the present Union, the term "confederal" refers to the structure of the larger management system, suggesting that not only has the role of the member nation-states remained effective, but also that their governments have found ways of strengthening their position domestically, regionally and internationally' (Chryssochoou 1997, p. 524). This is still a central issue in the ongoing work for a draft of a European constitution in the European Convent.

interest. In particular latent ethnical cleavages in East and Central Europe can become a major challenge to the EU's political and economic ability to act.

Economic Integration

At the first glance problems look less complicated with regard to economic issues and economic integration. Traditionally, regional economic integration takes place between relatively similar countries regarding economic development or political traditions and institutional frameworks. As long as we are dealing with economic integration between competing countries we are in the mainstream of economic integration, which is usually considered to be the area where the chance for economic gains is highest. Since the main benefits come from economies of scale, specialization and economies of scope, the classical trade-related advantages (trade creation) come on the lower level of integration according to table 7.1.

The taxonomy of economic integration in table 7.1 coincides with the institutional commitment or capacity concept discussed in the previous section. The tighter the economic co-operation, the more important a joint system of policy-making is.[3]

Economic integration in the Baltic Rim has in many respects been a complicated task due to the fact that we are dealing with an area which a few years ago was covered by three major – and two fundamentally different – trade blocks. The regional arrangements were very different: the ambitious EU framework, the more limited scope of the European Free Trade Area (EFTA), and the fundamentally different state-trade framework of the Council of Mutual Economic Assistance (CMEA).

3 The concept of an economic and monetary union and the European Political Union were originally considered to be two pillars of the Maastricht Treaty of the European Union.

Table 7.1 Stages of economic integration

Stage	*Definition*	*Comments*
Free Trade Area	No tariffs and quotas within group	Only negative integration, removal of barriers Framework according to GATT/WTO art. 24
Customs Union	Common tariffs (and quotas) Suppressing discrimination for CU-members in product markets	Only negative integration, removal of barriers Framework according to GATT/WTO art. 24
Common Market	No restrictions on factor movements No invisible barriers for trade	No positive integration
Common Market (extended)	Service sector included, all invisible barriers removed (i.e. harmonization of technical standards)	EU internal market programme Elements of positive integration in specific sector policies
Economic and Monetary Union	A Common Market with some degree of harmonization of economic policy Common Currency and Monetary system	Euro / European Central Bank Convergence criteria (i.e. inflation and budget targets) Elements of positive integration
Complete economic integration	Unification of monetary, fiscal, social and countercyclical policies Supra-national authority where decisions are binding for the member-states	Centralized economic policy-making, supra-national institutions with joint decision-making

Source: Here based on Pelkmans (2001, p. 8), Robson (1987) and Hansen *et al.* (1992, p. 4). Originally the typology was elaborated by B. Balassa in the early 1960s.

The records of the three are mixed, but not necessarily with the EU as the best performing unit according to the aims originally set up in the various agreements. Brada and Mendez (1985) compared various types of economic integration systems, including the three mentioned. In their study, based on the examination of their ability to promote inter-member trade, one result was that the environmental factor of inter-member distance was the most important individual factor, an important finding in a regional network perspective. Regarding the effectiveness of their integration policy, the study showed a relatively poor record for the highly institutionalized EC. The latter can partly be explained by the period of investigation, the early seventies, when most trade effects from the implementation of the Customs Union were achieved. Regarding their comparison of the CMEA with the western approaches the most interesting conclusion is:

> Thus the combined effect of central planning and of integration policy in CMEA causes that integration grouping to under-fulfil its potential by about the same amount as the EEC. Consequently it does not seem that CMEA integration policies or the system of

> central planning appear to be significantly greater barriers to promoting inter-member trade than do politics adopted among integrating market economies (Brada and Mendez, 1985, p. 555).

The first crucial issues regarding these roads to integration are how the structural shortcomings are solved and how the process of transition can avoid serious social and political conflicts without huge transfer payments. This requires an appropriate set-up both in the accession-countries and in the EU. The problems with the reforms of the Common Agricultural Policy and the Structural Funds illuminate this problem both in an EU enlargement perspective and an internal accession perspective.

A central issue in the discussions of the role of regional economic integration with regard to the formation of an international trade regime is whether regionalization has to be considered competitive or complementary to global solutions. This issue is also relevant in a reintegration perspective since close agreements with or membership of the EU requires acceptance of the *acquis communautaire*, the total of legal rules and customs developed through 40 years of co-operation, represented in the accession process by the so-called 31 chapters. In particular with respect to competition and trade policy the direct economic impacts will be significant from the beginning in the East and Central European countries. In a longer perspective of integration similar effects will arise in the field of environmental policy, industrial policy and labour market regulations, when adaptation to the Common Market level of integration takes place.

Table 7.1 does not only indicate an increasing level of economic integration, but also a growing need for policy co-ordination. In particular, the intermediate steps of integration are unstable in an economic sense, since traditional instruments of economic policy are not available on the national scene, and a joint policy-making system with supra-national power is not established on a Community level.

Spatial Integration

Usually, there is a strong correlation between geographic adjacency and strong economic ties. In economic theory this has not always been a part of mainstream economic thinking and analysis (Tichy, 1998).

Regional integration is in many respects an ambivalent notion varying from a very general concept that describes co-operation between nations or regions, to very specific social theories of human or organizational behaviour. Spatial integration is not a commonly used phrase, but rather a kind of summarizing description of a comprehensive notion dealing with an overall assessment of regional changes. Spatial integration includes features like:

- The development of specific geographical defined systems of production, such as industrial district, cluster of industries, or systems of innovation;
- A system of urban networks defined according to specific functional links;

- The availability of a relevant regional infrastructure linking the analyzed area together;
- Last but not least, the intensity of intra-regional flows relative to the outside flows can be considered to be the 'conditio sine qua non' when we talk about a spatial integrated area.

In particular the last condition is restrictive. In this notion the concept of spatial integration has to be understood as the most far-reaching concept of integration. The spatial concept is not merely a consequence of the physical environment, but also the result of economic and political integration.

In a continental or regional perspective we have strong evidence that political and economic integration is 'powered' by spatial proximity and adjacency, but at the same time, political and economic integration reinforce the other aspect of spatial integration, accessibility.

Figure 7.1 provides a brief summary of this approach focusing on the main factors leading toward spatial integration and the impact of this process on the future development through a feedback mechanism reinforcing accessibility. The final result could be a kind of 'network based' (spatial) theory of integration (Gidlund 1990, pp. 145ff). The next section will address the role of integration in the process of transition of the former state-trade economies in the BSR.

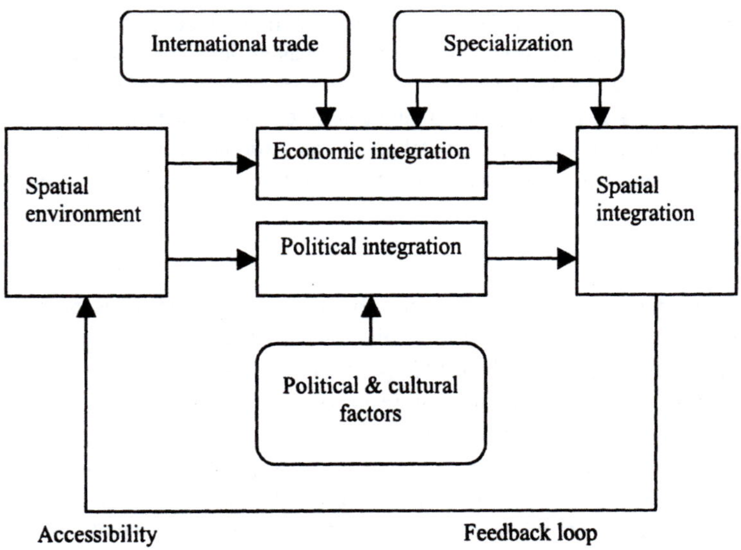

Figure 7.1 A revised concept of integration

Source: Cornett 2002a.

A Framework for Transition?

Regarding the reintegration of the former state-trade economies into the western dominated market economic system, the nature of the issue of complementarity and competitiveness is more complex. Historically, most of the countries are familiar with the principles of the market, and at least some of the mechanisms used in the CMEA were similar to western concepts of integration. The traditional principles of integration in the former CMEA were at least to some extent based on the exploitation of scale economies in competitive sectors of the involved countries, according to common plans within the framework of the socialistic division of labour (see Robson, 1987, pp. 215-232).

The crucial issues for the emerging market economies are that strategies reasonable in developed capitalistic countries in the 1960s and in a slightly modified version when launching the Single European Market Programme in the middle of the 1980s are not necessarily feasible for countries undergoing a process of total societal restructuring. First of all, strategies based on multilateral trade liberalization will not work in an environment of huge differences in economic performance and structure. The increasing competition from the established market economies will require protection of infant industries with potential harmful effects of developing a 'substandard' industrial base[4] to guarantee the development of a healthy industrial base. Experiences with the economic agreements between the EU and East and Central Europe in the first years of the accession process, proved the reluctance of the EU to grant preferential agreements in sectors within which the East European countries are potentially competitive, such as textiles, steel and agriculture (see European Economy, 1994).

From a principle and a conceptional point of view, the result of our discussions so far seems to be clear. In real world politics obstacles persist. With regard to practical policy-making, it can be questioned whether regional integration is an appropriate framework at all for countries which for a considerable period will rely on exports from sectors with relatively limited potential for scale economies, rather than on sectors with large potential for scale and scope economies.

The lessons of the 'ups' and 'downs' of West European integration are unambiguous. It seems unavoidable that economic and political integration has to go hand in hand, and the political part still seems to be the easiest to fulfil, i.e. 'the stability of institutions guaranteeing democracy, the rule of law, human rights and respect for and protection of minorities' (here quoted from EBRD, 2001, p. 27) of the Copenhagen principles from 1993. Only a co-ordinated policy in these two branches of international co-operation – both on the regional and global level – can lead to a successful and lasting result. The central bricks of these processes applied to the reintegration of East and Central Europe are summarized in figure 7.2.

4 Third World experiences with regional economic associations as a means of economic development have at best been mixed (Robson 1987, pp. 194ff). See also Brada and Mendez, 1985.

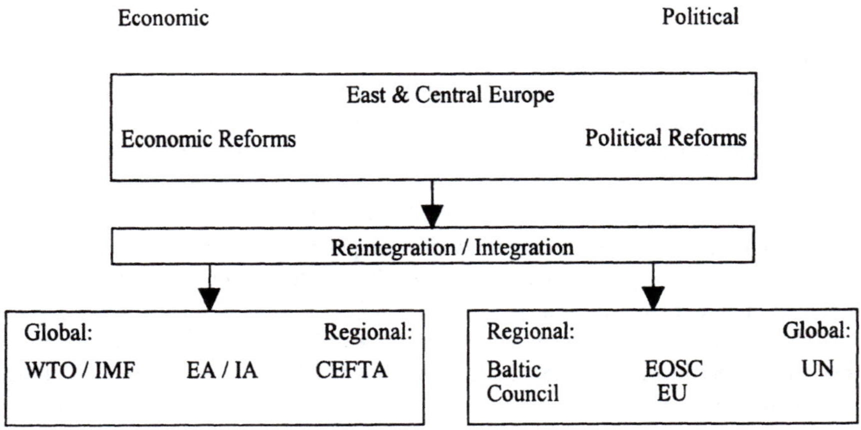

Figure 7.2 Political and economic aspects of integration and transition

Source: Adapted from Cornett and Iversen 1993.

Transition and Integration in the BSR

Twelve years of transition and reintegration in the BSR have resulted in huge changes in the economies of the countries, some expected, some unexpected at the beginning of the 1990s. Reviewing reports on transition and transformation (see EBRD, 1995 ff. or European Economy, 2001-C4) no unequivocal pattern for all transition economies emerges. Also, the BSR countries follow only to some extent the same pattern and timing. In particular in the first years Poland and a little later Estonia were front-runners. Nowadays, the three Baltic States in particular seem to be almost on the same level, at least according to the EU pre-accession evaluations, and the division into first six and second six group of accession countries has disappeared.

Analysing the process toward reintegration has at least two aspects, the internal domestic transformation and the external relationship toward the regional and global economic system. In practice these are closely interrelated. The focus of this chapter is mainly on the external aspects, but the institutional regime[5] of the economies is of crucial importance for economic growth and the size of income and production. They are important determinants for foreign economic relations, and are the crucial parameters for the estimation of future economic performance and the linkages to foreign markets. In the analysis of external linkages and the evaluation of the state of the reintegration process, trade and foreign direct

5 For an overview, see the country assessments in the Transition report 2001, EBRD 2001.

investment figures play an important role.[6] After the breakup of the Iron Curtain, FDI became an obvious means in the process of reintegration and the emerging new division of labour and specialization in the region. From a structural point of view, the region consists of countries with the gravity point of economic activities within the region like the Baltic States and three of the four Nordic countries. The three largest countries of the BSR have only a minor part of their population and economic activity located in the region. For obvious reasons trade in the Baltic Rim region is dominated by Germany. The small open market economies in the Baltic Rim account for the largest per capita trade in the region. The transition economies in the Baltic Rim contribute only a relatively small share of trade in the area. Before embarking on an economic assessment of the transition process and the regional impacts, a brief assessment of the institutional impacts of the process is presented in the next section.

Institutional Change and Realignment

The components of the process of transformation and institutional realignment in the BSR transition economies is almost finalized, at least on the international scene, see figure 7.2 above. All four Central and East European Countries (CEECs) will become members of the EU in 2004, and the three Baltic States were among the seven new members of NATO, approved at the Prague summit in November 2002 (Spiegel-online, 2002). Economic and institutional adaptation to the EU system is on track, and the last controversial (economic) issues were solved at the Copenhagen summit in December 2002.

This does not necessarily mean that all problems are solved with regard to institutional change and realignment. According to the EBRD comprehensive index for liberalization and institutional performance and the functioning of democracy and institutional development the four CEECs are among the best-performing countries, but huge differences persist with regard to specific indicators.[7]

6 Usually, trade is the first step in a process of building up economic relations between distinct markets. In this perspective, FDI can be considered a process toward closer integration. In some cases, the opposite may take place, i.e. the investment in the automobile industry in Latin America in the 1960s due to trade protectionism. Similar mechanisms were at work in the 1970s and 1980s when joint ventures between CMEA countries and western market economies became popular. In this case shortages of foreign exchange of the state-trade economies and the perceived market potential of western industry powered this process. See also Cornett, 2001.

7 For details see EBRD, 2001 pp. 17ff. Generally, the early starting countries perform best. This can also explain the rather modest score of Russia, in particular on the democracy index. In any case, this type of combined index has to be taken only as a very rough indication in a comparative perspective. A survey of each country with regard to the reform process and specific issues like financial institutions, social and enterprise reforms or privatization can be found in the country-section of the annually published transition report of the European Bank for Reconstruction and Development (EBRD).

The Baltic States and Poland are democracies based on parliamentarism. Since 1989/1991 all countries have proved that democracy is real through various changes in government. In most countries we have seen alterations between former communist parties or other left-wing groups and more traditional conservative parties. The Baltic States have one-chamber systems similar to the Nordic countries; Poland is ruled by a two-chamber system. In all four countries, the prime minister is elected by the parliament. A prime minister is politically more important than a president, who has mainly honourific responsibilities. Since 1993, Russia also has a two-chamber system, ruled by democratic principles. The main difference between Russia and the four other countries is that Russia has a very strong presidency with a directly elected president and that Russia is a federation of Russia, 21 other republics and 11 autonomous regions.[8]

On the local and regional level Poland and in particular the Baltic States have undergone several organizational changes with regard to the geographic division of local and regional government. In Poland the reduction of the number of counties in the late 1990s from more than 40 to 16 provinces (*wojwodztwa*) is the most important change in the spatial organization of the country.

Obviously changes and fluctuations in the spatial organization of society were more intensive in the new Baltic States after 1991, both with regard to the functional division of responsibilities and geography.[9] Estonia has a single-tier system of local government with a considerable level of autonomy for the 247 municipalities (year 2000). The country is divided into 15 regions (*maakond*) with appointed governors and no elected representative councils. Their objective is mainly co-ordination of state functions, including regional policy and planning.

Latvia is the only Baltic state with a two-tier local government system similar to what can be found in the Scandinavian countries. The most interesting aspect of the Latvian system compared with other transition countries and the Nordic countries is that Latvia like some German *Länder*, distinguishes between rural (26 districts or *rajons*)[10] and town regions (seven cities or *lielpilsetas*). The latter has both town and district functions. In 2000 the remaining part of the country was divided into 400 rural and 70 urban municipalities. The division of functions between the branches of government is to some extent overlapping. Districts and municipalities often take care of similar tasks, just on a larger scale. The function of district administration includes planning and local economic development.

Like Estonia, Lithuania dismantled the two-tier system of local government in the mid-1990s. The ten new districts or counties (*apskritis*) are local branches of

---

8 Information based on Spiegel Almanach 2000 and Spiegel Jahrbuch 2002 (www.spiegel.de).

9 This section is mainly based on Nordregio 2000, pp. 17-24.

10 In 1999 the government of Latvia decided to reduce the number of districts to nine before 2004, Nordregio, 2000, p. 19.

central government, and they serve like their Estonian and Latvian counterparts as co-ordination and control units with regard to the activities of the 56 new municipalities.

The financial base of the decentralized government is weak in all Baltic states. The most important own sources of revenue are personal income taxes, which due to a narrow tax base are rather limited. For this reason transfers of payments from the central government are crucial for local and regional authorities' ability to maintain their functions. A precondition for real decentralization is sufficient own financial resources, and a sustainable tax base. The latter depends on economic growth and development as well as a balanced distribution of wealth between the centre regions and the periphery.

Economic Transition and Linkages in the BSR

The process of catching up on the income level in the EU requires not only political and economic reforms, but also excessive economic growth to reduce the gap.[11]

Table 7.2 shows that Poland has been ahead of the other transition economies in the BSR in the mid-1990s. With regard to the Baltic States the picture is mixed, but the most recent numbers (and forecasts) indicate a relatively high growth performance. A comparison with the old market makes the saliency of the catch-up problem evident, since the excess growth compared to the traditional market economies in the region seems to be rather modest.

As mentioned above, trade is usually the first type of link between independent economic units, and therefore it is also often the most sensitive indicator of changes in the economic environment. The redirection of foreign trade was also a first and most significant change after the dissolution of the CMEA in 1991. Historically, trade flows in the Baltic Rim have suffered from the artificial economic borders between economies in the area. This does not mean that the region historically – at least not for the last hundred years – has constituted a functional internal coherent region. In the 1970s and 1980s the region belonged to three different economic associations, the market based EU, EFTA, and the CMEA, the latter being based on non-market principles. The economic border between the two former did not have major importance for trade flows for most groups of commodities.

11 For a detailed analysis of this problem, see Agenda 2000 'Reinforcing the Pre-Accession Strategy' and the specific country-studies in European Commission 1997 and European Economy 1997.

Table 7.2 Economic growth in the Baltic States and Poland

	Annual change in GDP at constant prices							
	1995	1996	1997	1998	1999	2000	2001E	2002F
Estonia	2.9	3.9	10.6	4.7	-1.1	6.9	5.3	4.7
Latvia	-0.8	3.3	8.6	3.9	0.1	6.6	7.9	4.5
Lithuania	3.0	4.7	7.3	5.1	-4.1	3.9	4.5	3.5
Poland	6.9	6.1	6.9	4.8	4.1	4.0	1.5	1.9
CEEC-10	5.2	3.9	3.5	2.3	2.2	3.7	3.1	3.1

Note: E: estimates, F: forecast.

CEEC-10: Bulgaria, Czech Republic, Estonia, Hungary, Latvia, Lithuania, Poland, Romania, Slovakia and Slovenia.

Source: 1995: European Economy 1998 C-2 1996-1999: European Economy C-4, 2000- : European Economy 2001-2. For CEEC-10 1997 and 1998 European Economy 1999-C4.

The division between market and non-market based trading frameworks was much more important, and the redirection of trade flows took place mainly with regard to trade between the countries belonging to the former Eastern bloc, the Nordic countries, and Germany. Table 7.3 illuminates this process based on intra-regional trade-flows for the BSR. The most important trend is that the Baltic Rim region is the dominant foreign trade partner for the smaller economies only. Considering the nature and the size of the German economy, the importance of the Baltic Rim as a geographical region diminishes further. With regard to future trends of trade, the three Baltic States will probably move toward a trade pattern more similar to the Nordic countries, and find their historical place in the regional trading system (Laaser and Schrader, 1992). The reorientation of trade, visible in table 7.3, has to be interpreted carefully due to the significant decrease of the foreign trade volume immediately after the breakup of the CMEA. With regard to Poland, a broader European orientation seems likely. In an integrative perspective, the development of linkages beyond trade is of special interest as an indicator of a stable and lasting relation.

Table 7.3 Share of intra-regional trade as percentage of total trade of Baltic Rim countries since 1988

	1988	1992	1996	2000
Denmark	39.8	48.7	42.5	40.9
Estonia	...	92.0	68.8	55.1
Finland	51.3	41.7	35.2	49.3
Germany (FRG)	13.5	8.6	9.3	9.6
GDR	24.6	...	...	...
Latvia	...	61.8	48.8	45.9
Lithuania	...	57.8	46.1	33.3
Norway	35.2	35.9	36.9	65.6
Poland	46.7	47.4	48.2	29.7
Russia	34.1	18.9	21.5	75.2
Sweden	37.5	35.5	32.2	39.4
Baltic Rim	26.5	17.9	18.9	19.9

Note: Figures based on exports to Baltic Rim countries as percentage of total exports. All figures are based on reported imports from receiving countries. Danish exports to Sweden 1992 are based on Danish exports. For 1992 some figures are missing for former state-trade countries. 1998 figures based on export to GDR and SU. Figures for GDR trade with Germany and SU 1988 are based on German sources and converted to US-$ based on annual average exchange rate at Frankfurt (ultimo 1987 and 1988). 2000 figures affected by unexplainable fluctuation in Russian and to some extent Norwegian trade, probably due to growing German energy import. 2001 figures are on the same level (IMF 2002).
Source: IMF 1995, 1998 and 2001. Statistisches Bundesamt 1991.

Foreign direct investment can be the result of barriers to trade (i.e. the case of the automobile industry's investments in Brazil or Mexico in the 1960s or many joint ventures with state-trade countries before 1990), or they can be the result of an integrative process beginning with trade and ending up in the creation of an integrated system of production. Since the BSR is in a process of fast removal of trading barriers, foreign direct investment is used as an indicator of more formalized international integration of the economic systems.[12] Table 7.4 summarizes the FDI inflow to the transition economies in the BSR. In particular, Estonia has received a considerable amount compared to the size of the population. Also Latvia has received over 1,000 US-$ per capita. The figures for Poland and Lithuania are significantly lower per capita, but not measured by absolute figures. In particular net inflow to Lithuania has increased in the late 1990s. Poland and Russia, the two transition economies not fully a part of the BSR are of course the largest net receivers of FDI, with Poland as the largest target.

12 For an assessment of firm behaviour concerning intra-regional FDI, see Snickars and Bourennane (2000).

Table 7.4 Foreign direct investment (net inflow in millions of US-$)

Year	Poland	Estonia	Latvia	Lithuania	Russia
1992	284	80	n.a.	n.a	n.a.
1995	1,134	199	245	72	1,663
1996	2,741	111	379	152	1,665
1997	3,041	130	515	328	4,036
1998	4,966	574	303	921	1,734
1999	6,348	222	331	478	746
2000(E)	9,299	324	398	375	-346
2001(P)	7,000	350	300	450	2,000
Cumulative inflow 1989-2000	29,052	2,008	2,498	2,387	9,998
Cumulative inflow 1989-2000 per capita US-$	751	1,400	1,056	646	69
% of GDP 2000	5.9	6.4	5.6	3.3	-0.1

Note: Net inflows as recorded in balance of payments. Gross inflows of FDI are in some cases considerably higher than net inflows on account of increasing intra-regional investment flows.
Source: IBRD 2001, Table A.3.9.

Considering internal flows of FDI the pattern is similar to trade, but the figures must be used very carefully due to lack of data, the methodological problems involved in the process of data collection, and the period of the flows. Nevertheless, the Baltic Rim economies' importance for FDI in the three Baltic States is evident. This can be considered to be at least a weak indication of increased participation in the regional system of divisions of production, due to the fact that most trade barriers have been removed or are in the process of becoming obsolete. In particular with regard to the regional dimension FDI seems to reinforce spatial concentration at least in the Baltic States.[13] Overall it is only possible to evaluate FDI patterns in a regional context based on national statistics for the smaller states in the region, i.e. the strong position of the German economy, and in particular of the non-Baltic Rim part, has to be taken into account. Based on GDP, the Baltic Rim part of Germany counts for only 8.3 per cent of the German GDP in 1991.[14] Similar problems can be found with regard to Poland and Russia.

Regional Convergence and Transition in the BSR

All countries have regional and economic disparities, and it is not always the absolute level of differences which matter politically. From a European

13 A study by Snickars and Bourenname (2000) of investment behaviour of Nordic companies in the Baltic State and Saint Petersburg showed a heavy concentration in the four major cities.

14 Another figure can illuminate the point. In 1996, export as a percentage of total turnover in the German manufacturing sector was 29.7 per cent. In the three Baltic Rim states the figures were: in Hamburg: 11.9 per cent, in Schleswig-Holstein 26.0 per cent and in Mecklenburg-Vorpommern 10.6 per cent (IdDW 1997, Table 4).

perspective, perceived disparities have been affected by real economic differences (i.e. differences in economic growth), statistical measures and of course the increasing number of countries in the EU. The last factor has been a decisive issue in the enlargement negotiations up to the Copenhagen summit, together with in particular the future of the Common Agricultural Policy. Without any doubt, one of the single most important factors affecting the statistical level of convergence – or the growth of regional disparities – has been the consecutive enlargement of the EU, see table 7.5 below. Regional disparities and regional coherence are complex concepts, and empirical measurements often depend on the indicators chosen. Nevertheless a slight trend toward convergence has been reported in several studies based on income per capita figures.[15]

Table 7.5 Variations in GDP per capita, current prices, lowest and highest country score (EU=100)

		1961	1973	1986	1995	'2000+'
EU-6	'highest'	152 (117)	142 (120)	125 (113)	173 (1[illegible]7)	184 (108)
	'lowest'	69	66	84	69	85
EU-9	'highest'		152(135)	132 (135)	182 (145)	178 (136)
	'lowest'		54	64	72	85
EU-12	'highest'			147 (149)	197 (152)	192 (1479
	'lowest'			32	48	50
EU-15	'highest'				195 (150)	190 (145)
	'lowest'				48	50
EU-27	'highest'					233 (178)
	'lowest'					7

Note: ( ) Figures without Luxembourg, 1986 without Denmark, '2000+': Calculation based on 1998 figures. Tentative estimations converted from national currencies according to average annual exchange rates for EURO/ECU. Figures for non EU-members converted from US-$.
Source: Here quoted from Cornett (2002b).

Long-run changes in the geographical distribution of economic activity are unavoidable in dynamic societies, and in particular in regions of regional economic

15 'The next approach is to check whether there has indeed been a reduction of disparities. In other words, to what extent regional wealth levels (measured as income per capita) have converged. There has recently been a revival of interest in the issue of convergence, ... All these studies find a long-term convergence of regional income levels, although they differ in their conclusions as to the speed of the process and the causal factors. In recent years the trends towards convergence, that is lower disparities, has levelled off' (Molle *et al.*, 1980; Molle and Boeckhout, 1995, CIC 1996). However, the aggregate figures hide important developments for individual countries. Particularly interesting is the case of Ireland. The growth of this country has been so substantial that it is no longer eligible for objective 1 status (its GDP/head is now higher than 75 per cent of the EU average) (Molle, 1999, p. 154).

integration. Some regions will gain, others will lose economic activity and employment. The purpose of this section is briefly to address the issue of regional diversion in a BSR context.

The figures in table 7.5 prove a tendency toward reduced disparities between the countries that have been members of the EU since the beginning or have entered the Community early (the 1973 enlargement). Reading table 7.5 horizontally, the level of disparities measured over time can be found for each group of EU-member states. If Luxembourg is omitted from the analysis, the gap in 1998 (2000+ scenario) is reduced to less than 25 per cent of the average for the original six EU members. Nevertheless, reduced disparities – measured by GDP per capita – on the national level do not necessarily mean a more equal development if the analysis is made on a more disaggregated level,[16] but is still a useful indicator of the overall development.

Table 7.6 Regional disparities in BSR countries 2000 (GDP per cap. PPS)

	National average		Richest BSR region		Poorest BSR region	
	EU-15 100	EU-25 100	Name	Index EU-15	Name	Index EU-15
Germany	106.4	117.3	Hamburg	181.5	MVP	69.4
Denmark	118.6	130.7	...	...	...	...
Finland	104.0	114.6	Uusimaa	143.2	Väli-Soumi	74.5
Sweden	106.6	117.5	Stockholm	147.0	Norra Mellan	91.0
Poland	38.9	42.8	Pomorskie	39.1	Wamin-sko Maz.	29.0
Lithuania	35.7 (29)	39.3	Vilnius	(35)	Taurage	(22)
Latvia	30.9 (26)	34.0	Riga	(37)	Latgale	(16)
Estonia	40.1 (31)	44.2	Põhja-Eesti	(51)	Kesk-Eesti	(22)
Russia	...	...	...	...	...	...

Note: Germany: Schleswig Holstein, Hamburg, Mecklenburg Vorpommern (MVP). Poland: Pomorskie Waminsko Maz. Kujawsko-Pomorskie Figures for Estonia, Lithuania and Latvia: (1996).

Source: European Commission 2003a, Table 12. Nordregio 2000, p. 37, 62f.

16 See e.g. Dunford (1994), Molle (1999), Armstrong (1995).

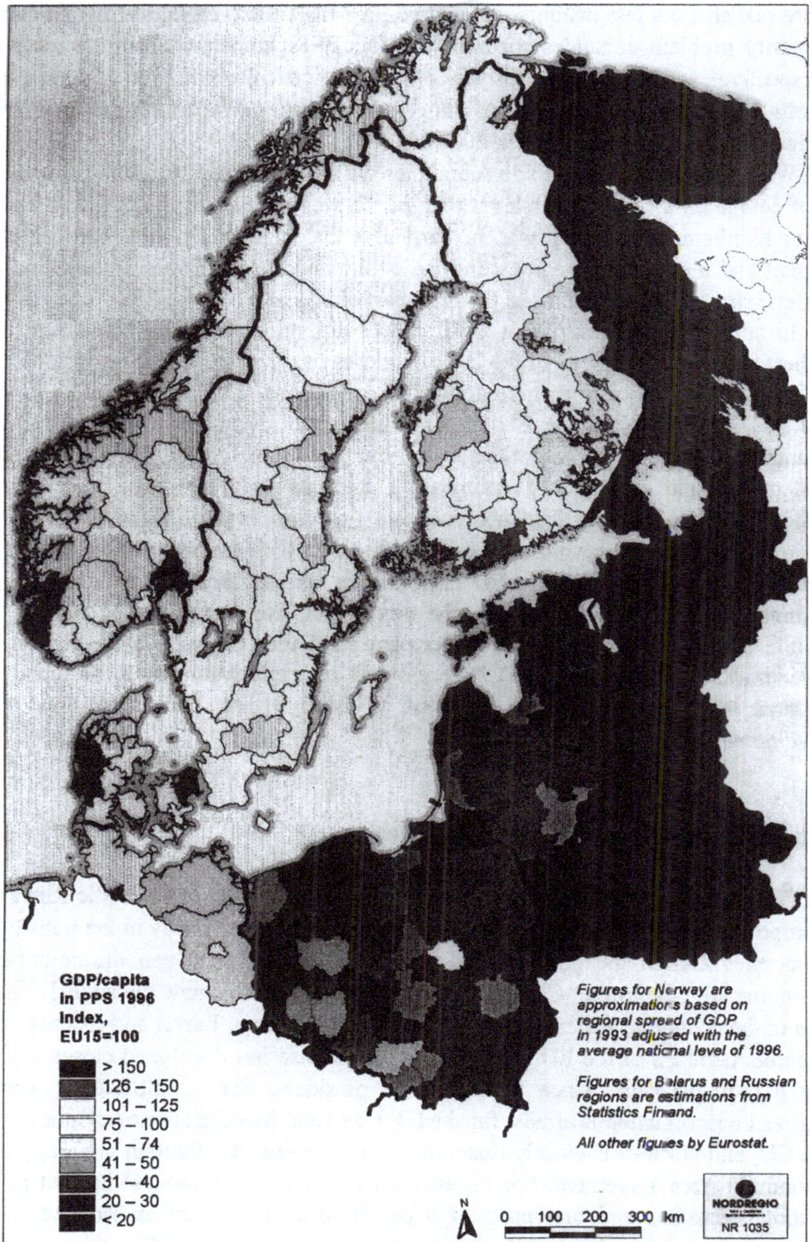

Figure 7.3 Regional disparities in the BSR
Source: Nordregio (www.nordregio.se).

A careful inspection of the regional map of the BSR (see figure 7.3) paints a more realistic, but less unequivocal picture. In a BSR perspective, the main income disparity problem coincides with the old East-West division. From a structural perspective, we nevertheless also face huge regional problems in a geographic North-South perspective due to huge depopulation problems in Northern Scandinavia and Finland (Hanell, 2000).

Within the former state-trade economies we also find huge regional differences – of course on a much lower level than in the western part of the BSR. A report from Nordregio (2000) stresses in particular the huge differences between the capital and metropolitan regions and the countryside in the Baltic States. Similar patterns are found in Poland and the BSR part of Russia.

In table 7.6 the intra-regional differences are summarized by comparing the richest and poorest regions in the BSR countries based on NUTS II regions of the EU regional classification where applicable, or national data corresponding to the EU NUTS III level of the EU regional classification system. Within all BSR countries huge regional disparities exist, but due to differences in the regional system and the principle of delimitation this can only be taken as a rough indication of the problem. The most interesting measure is probably to compare the poorest region with the national average rather than with the best performing area, often a rather narrow defined metropolitan region heavily depending on commuting from suburbs outside the city limits. No unambiguous pattern is visible. The lowest score is found in Germany and Latvia (65 vs. 62), the highest in Sweden (85) and Lithuania (76). It seems that the explanation has to be found in patterns of urbanization and regional division rather than transition and development.

The BSR in the European Regional System

More than ten years after the start of the process of transition in the Baltic Rim and Europe as a whole, huge changes have taken place, both internally in the transition economies and in the political and economic relations between the countries. Economically, the former CMEA has disappeared: the EU is now the unchallenged hub in the economic system of the BSR. Poland, Lithuania, Latvia and Estonia will become members of the EU in 2004, and Russia also has developed closer ties to the EU, in particular since Putin became president. For the BSR as a whole regional consolidation is almost finished. Finland and Sweden are now members of the EU, and Norway is closely linked to the internal market through the European Economic Area agreement. For the transition countries this process has not been without obstacles and drawbacks. No paved road leads from an isolated non-market based economic system to a position as a fully-fledged member of the western market based economic system. The purpose of this chapter is to assess the development in the BSR, to identify some of the trends of the past thirteen years. Main trends identified in the last decade are:

- Overall, the analysis of the pattern of trade – and to some extent also the changes in the composition of the traded commodities – confirm the tendency toward an adaptation of the patterns found in the EU as a whole or between the old market economies in the western part of the Baltic Rim;
- One important tendency we have seen is that trade patterns and economic links in the BSR are undergoing a significant change, especially for the transition economies converting toward West European patterns;
- The second result is that this conversion takes place at a slower pace and at a lower level than expected in the early 1990s. A closer look at the nature of this trade proves that huge differences persist, but that there are signs of levelling the disparities;
- For the transition economies in the BSR (i.e. Latvia, Estonia, Lithuania and Poland) the analysis of intra-industry trade indicates that they have embarked on a catch-up process with regard to an adaptation to the European market based system of production. They are still far behind the old market economies with regard to volume and intensity of participation in the international division of production (Cornett, 2002c);
- With regard to spatial organization, the regional and municipality structure has been altered in Poland and the Baltic States both with regard to geography and distribution of functions and authority.

It is still not possible to sketch a comprehensive picture of the development in the BSR since 1989; the path of development followed in the many transition economies has been too different. In particular, the speed and timing of transformation has been different. Nevertheless the direction seems to be the same, and with regard to adaptation to the EU chapters the previously slower countries have caught up. Out of the 31 chapters in the accession process, the Baltic countries and Poland had fulfilled between 19 (Estonia) and 16 (Latvia) at the end of 2001 (EBRD, 2001, p. 27). Also, after the conclusion of the accession negotiations full integration is – similar to previous enlargements – not yet reached in all areas due to a whole range of transitional agreements. Poland has transitional agreements in 13 out of the 31 chapters, Latvia and Lithuania in 11 and Estonia in 10 chapters (European Commission, 2003b). With regard to economic development in the BSR and in particular the transition economies, important features are that the potentials for trade were often overestimated in the first years of transition. Intra-industry trade analysis of the transition economies in general and the BSR region in particular supported these findings with regard to an emerging new system of specialization, at least in some sectors. A tendency toward adaptation and integration of the transition economies since the early 1990s is identified, but the latest figures point toward a slow down in the speed of the process, and the level of intra-industry trade is still much lower than between the old BSR market economies or the EU as a whole (see Cornett, 2002b).

Overall, this means that an analysis of a subsystem based on a concept of integration seems to be fruitful and can contribute to the understanding of the problems and potentials of the Baltic Sea Region system. With regard to the question of whether regional specialization can be a substitute for global specialization, the answer is ambiguous.

A tentative conclusion is that the processes are complementary rather than mutually exclusive. Further research of the linkages and pattern of co-operation between sectors of the economy and countries is needed, as well as in-depth investigations of the impacts on the emerging new systems of production on the regional and firm level. Nevertheless, this brief review indicates a potential for regional solutions in the BSR within the European economic system.

Bibliography

Armstrong, Harvey W. (1995), 'Convergence Among Regions in the European Union 1950-1990', in *Papers in Regional Science*, Vol. 74, Number 2, pp. 143-152.

Brada, J.C. and Méndez J.A. (1985), 'Economic Integration among Developed, Developing and Centrally Planned Economies: A Comparative Analysis' in *The Review of Economics and Statistics*, Vol LXVII No. 4, 1985, pp. 549-556.

Chryssochoou, Dimitris N. (1997), 'New Challenges to the Study of European Integration: Implications for Theory Building' in *Journal of Common Market Studies*, Vol. 35, No. 4 December 1997, pp. 521-42.

Cornett, Andreas P. (1999), 'The Problem of Transition and Reintegration of East and Central Europe – Conceptual Remarks and Empirical Problems', in M. M. Fischer and P. Nijkamp (eds) (1999), *Spatial Dynamics of European Integration Regional and Policy Issues at the Turn of the Century*, Springer-Verlag Berlin/Heidelberg 1999, pp. 255-279.

Cornett, Andreas P. (2001), 'Regional Economic Integration in the Baltic Rim: Towards a European Region after Ten Years of Transition?' in J. Bröcker and H. Herrmann (eds) *Spatial Change and Interregional Flows in the Integrating Europe – Essays in Honor of Karin Peschel*, Contributions to Economics, Physica Verlag, Heidelberg/New York 2001, pp. 13-27.

Cornett, Andreas P. (2002a), 'Spatial Development: Regional and Global Specialization', in C. Bengs (ed.), *Facing ESPON*, Nordregio R2002:1, Stockholm, pp. 51-73.

Cornett, Andreas P. (2002b), 'Regional Cohesion in an Enlarged European Union – an Analysis of Inter regional Specialization and Integration', in J.R. Cuadrado Roura and M. Parellada (eds), *The European Monetary Union and Regional Convergence, Facts Prospects and Politics*, Advances in Spatial Science, Springer Verlag, Heidelberg/New York, 2002, pp. 147-164.

Cornett, Andreas P. (2002c), 'From Trade Integration to the Integration of the Production System – a Case Study of the Impact of Economic Transition on Trade and Specialization in the Baltic Rim', in *Uddevalla Symposium 2001 Regional Economics in Transition*, research reports 02:01, University of Trollhättan/Uddevalla, 2002, pp. 201-215.

Cornett, Andreas P. and Iversen, S. P. (1993). 'Commercial Relations in the Baltic Rim Region in an Integration/Network Perspective', in L. Lundqvist and L. O. Persson (eds)

(1993), *Visions and Strategies in European Integration. A North European Perspective*, Springer-Verlag, Berlin 1993, pp. 107-130.

Dunford, Mike (1994), 'Winners and Losers: The New Map of Economic Inequality in the European Union', in *European Urban and Regional Studies 1994* Vol. 1, No. 2, pp. 95-114.

EBRD (19995ff), *Transition Report*, London.

Economist, news magazine, London.

European Commission (1997b), 'Communication of the Commission Doc 97/7: Reinforcing the Pre-accession Strategy', Agenda 2000, Volume I. (http://europa.eu.int/comm/dg1a/agenda2000/en/rpas.htm).

European Commission (2003a), 'Communication from the Commission – Second progress report on economic and social cohesion', Brussels, 30 January 2003 COM(2003) 34 final.

European Commission (2003b), 'Report on the Results on the Negotiations on Accession of Cyprus, Malta, Hungary, Poland, the Slovak Republic, Latvia, Estonia, Lithuania, the Czech Republic and Slovenia to the European Union', prepared by the Commission's departments (http://www.europa.int/comm/enlargement/negotiations/index.htm).

European Economy (1994), 'The Economic Interpenetration between the European Union and Eastern Europe', *Reports and Studies*, No 6, 1994, Luxembourg.

European Economy (1997), 'The Challenge for the EU of Eastern Enlargement', Reports and Studies No. 5, 1997, Luxembourg.

European Economy (1998ff): 'Supplement C Economic Reform Monitor', Luxembourg.

Gidlund, Janerik (1990), 'Den oförklarede integrationen – statsventenskapen inför Europas omvandling' in Karlquist, Anders, red. (1990), *Nätverk Teorier och begrepp i samällsvetenskaben*, Gidlunds Bokförlag, Värnamo, pp. 119-151.

Hanell, Thomas (2000), 'Troubling Demographic Trends in the Baltic Sea Region', in North, Vol. 11 No 2/3 2000, pp. 5-11.

Hansen, J. D. *et al.* (1992), *An Economic Analysis of the EC*, McGraw-Hill, London.

IdDW (Institut der Deutschen Wirtschaft) (1997), 'Zahlen zur wirtschaftlichen Entwicklung der Bundesrepublik Deutschland 1997', Köln.

IMF (1995ff), *Direction of Trade Statistics Yearbook*, Washington.

Laaser, C.-F. and Schrader, K. (1992), 'Zur Reintegration der baltischen Staaten in die Weltwirtschaft', in *Die Weltwirtschaft*, Heft 2, 1992, Kiel, pp. 189-211.

Lindberg, Leon N. and Scheingold, Stuart A. (1970), *Europe's Would-Be Polity. Patterns of Change in the European Community*, Prentice-Hall Englewood Cliffs New Jersey.

Molle, Willem (1999), 'The Dynamics of Economic Integration and the Cohesion in the EU: Experience from the Past and Challenges for the Future', in M. M. Fischer and P. Nijkamp (eds) (1999), *Spatial Dynamics of European Integration Regional and Policy Issues at the Turn of the Century*, Springer-Verlag Berlin/Heidelberg 1999, pp. 145-162.

Molle, Willem with Boeckhout, Sjaak (1995), 'Economic Disparity under Conditions of Integration – A Long Term View of the European Case', in *Papers in Regional Science*, Vol. 74, No. 2, pp. 105-123.

Nordregio (2000), 'Regions of the Baltic States', *Nordregio Report 2000:2*, Stockholm – Tallin.

Pelkmans, Jacques (2001), *European Integration Methods and Economic Analysis*, second edition, Financial Times-Prentice Hall, Harlow, Essex.

Pentland, Charles (1973), *International Theory and European Integration*, Faber and Faber London.

Robson, Peter (1987), *The Economics of International Integration*, Allen and Unwin, (third ed.), London 1987.

Snickars, Folke and Bourennane, Malika (2000), 'Industrial Networking in the Baltic Sea Region', *a study carried out as a part of the Interreg IIC project Urban Systems and Urban Networking in the Baltic Sea Region*, Danish Forest and Landscape Research Institute, Hørsholm, Denmark.

Der Spiegel, news magazine, Hamburg.

Spiegel Almanach (1999), 'Weltjahrbuch 2000', Spiegel Buchverlag, Hamburg 1999.

Spiegel online (2002) (www.spiegel.de).

Statistisches Bundesamt (1991), *Statistisches Jahrbuch 1991 für das vereinte Deutschland*, Metzler Poeschel Wiesbaden 1991.

Sæter, Martin (1971), *Det politiske Europa*, Universitetsforlaget Oslo-Bergen Thromsø.

Tichy, Gunther (1998), 'Geography Lost and Found in Economics (?)' *Keynote presentation at 38th European Congress-1998*, Vienna, Austria, 28 August-1 September 1998, CD-Rom proceedings, Vienna 1998.

Viner, Jacob (1950), *The Customs Union Issue*, New York/London.

Chapter 8

Constructing a Transnational Mobility Region – On the Øresund Region and Its Role in the New European Union Spatial Policy

Ole B. Jensen and Tim Richardson

We have, so to speak, gone from an approach aimed at reducing disparities to one of supporting growth opportunities in each of the regions (Bendt Bendtsen Minister for the Economy and Industry of Denmark, Inforegio, 2002).

Introduction

In November 2002, international delegates gathered in Copenhagen to discuss 'European Cities in a Global Era – Urban Identities and Regional Development'. At the conference, workshops explored the experience of a number of cross-border spatial co-operation projects supported by the EU's Interreg programme. These included the Baltic Palette Region project, the North West Europe Region project on New Urban landscapes, the Metrex Transnational European Network, the CADSES region, the Basque Eurocity Bayonne-San Sebastian, and the Øresund Region. The European Commission representative Rudolf Niessler framed these cases as reflecting a major shift in the EU's intervention in space, from the early construction of national borders as problems, to their reconstruction as windows of opportunity.

This chapter analyses the role of the Øresund Region in the new spatial policy of the European Union.[1] The main argument develops around an understanding of the interplay between new representations of space, institutions and practices of

1 For an elaborated exploration of this policy field, see Richardson and Jensen, 2000, Jensen and Richardson, 2001, forthcoming. Also please note that as we explore the rationales of policies within planning and spatial development, we use the terms 'space'/'spatial' and their connotations to the physical and material environment. In political science the words 'territory'/'territorial' seem to us to cover only part of the spatial, as they connote only the political dimensions of the organisation of physical space.

European spatial planning and their potential contribution to European political integration. Our analysis of the new spatial policy visions and arenas of implementation explores how constructions of the Øresund Region contain a rationale of increasing spatial mobility at a transnational scale – a 'Europe of Flows' in Maarten Hajer's terminology (Hajer, 2000).

By excavating the rationale of a 'Europe of Flows' it is shown how important the spatial policies dealing with physical mobility are to the question of European integration. This is for example the case with 'hard infrastructures' (e.g. the Trans-European Transport Network, TEN-T) and its 'missing links' (e.g. the Øresund fixed link between Sweden and Denmark). However, this view of mobility is also reproduced in the new spatial visions of European integration (e.g. the European Spatial Development Perspective, CEC, 1999) and their regional arenas of institutionalization (e.g. the Interreg programme, CEC, 1996). Thus a new layer of spatialized policy thinking and practice is added to the already declared aims of the European internal market, with its reliance on increasing mobility. The chapter identifies the Øresund Region as being the showcase of both TEN-T and the ESDP in terms of its potential to become a 'Global Economic Integration Zone' within the EU spatial policy discourse, or in our terms a 'Transnational Mobility Region'.

The structure of the chapter is as follows. First, we shall look into the Øresund Region as a 'transnational laboratory' for the making of European space. Then we focus on the role of the Øresund Region as an example of a Transnational Mobility Region, emphasizing the region's role within a bigger picture of a seamless European territory. This takes us into the question of the region as a locus of struggle, as diverging political interests and stakeholders meet in this new transnational arena. From here the focus is on the potential of the new spatial scale of cross-border institution building, transgressing national boundaries, to contribute to European integration. We look into two ways of branding the territorial identity of the region, namely as 'Medicon Valley' and as a 'Human Capital'. The chapter closes with some reflections on the significance of this new context for policy development to European integration at the regional level in general, and on the meaning of such a development for the Nordic regions in particular.

The Øresund Region as a Transnational Laboratory

Conceptually one can operate with (at least) five different notions of the term 'Europeanization'. It can either be seen as changes in the external territorial boundaries of the EU (e.g. in the form of enlargement); as the development of institutions of governance at the European level; as top-down penetration of national and sub-national systems of governance; as exporting European forms of governance beyond the European territory; and finally as a political project aiming at a unified and politically stronger Europe (Olsen, 2001, p. 3). Accordingly we are dealing with a complex amalgam of Europeanization in this chapter, even though we predominantly see the construction of an EU-endorsed transnational mobility region to express the 'political project aiming at a unified and politically stronger Europe'.

There is thus a new source of influence of EU spatial policy on planning activities in member states, focusing on the implementation (or 'application') of the European Spatial Development Perspective (ESDP) in cross-border regions. Unpacking the complexity of 'Europeanization' points towards an examination of both the standard view of trickle down (e.g. Interreg), and the opposing view of the 'open house' opportunity in the case of the Øresund Region. In our view this metaphor of 'open house' (coined by Tangkjær, 2000, p. 170) is a useful story-telling device for the general policy situation marked by the 'recovery' of the regions. The notion of 'open house' carries the meaning of a relatively open institutional field within which stakeholders and institutional players can choose to make their entrance. The new spatial policy discourses working at different scales expresses the overlapping of these different notions of Europeanization. Challenges of implementing the new spatial policy discourse leads to the question of how planning agencies in member states, from national to regional levels, and other actors, take these policy discourses into their own practices. EU intervention, principally through the Interreg programme, adds crucially to this picture by enabling the formation of new networks and institutions of transnational planning in a contested policy environment. This form of intervention can be understood as the application of an informal policy (the ESDP) with the use of a formal intervention (Interreg) which makes the way for a 'silent development' of an EU spatial policy (Graute, 2002). Issues of transparency and democracy in these new modes of transnational planning activity and institution building explain why bridges and mobility should interest a policy science audience. Furthermore, we would argue that the incremental and network-organised character of these new transnational planning activities further brings down barriers of both institutional and cultural differences, nurturing yet another phase of European integration.

Twentieth century Europe has been described as 'a factory of borders' (O'Dowd, 2001, p. 95), leading to 'trans-frontier regionalism' (O'Dowd, 2001, p. 100) a phenomenon which is manifested in the Interreg programme.

The notion of transnational cross-border regions as 'experimental laboratories' (Maskell and Törnqvist, 1999, p. 12; O'Dowd, 2001, p. 101) and 'integration laboratories' (Tangkjær, 2000, p. 187) have become more widespread in the last few years. This adds to the notion of the European territory as one of many actual changes of which the outcome is far from certain. The use of words such as 'experiment', 'risk' and 'vision' are thus making their way into the vocabulary of official policy documents as well as in the minds of developers and policy makers.

The Nordic case of the Øresund Region is a very practical example of a new kind of transnational territorial development between Denmark/Sweden and the towns and cities it embraces. This development, stimulated by a new fixed link between the two countries is one of the many cross-border regions materializing across the EU. The region, comprising the national capital of Denmark, has for some time been looked upon as the most competitive urban region that the Danish state could support in the global game. Thus we find the Øresund Region as one of the high priorities in the Danish national planning reports from 1992, 1997 and 2002. According to the 1997 national planning report, a balanced Danish urban system could be obtained by means of a five-string strategy, focusing among other things, on the Øresund Region as an international urban region (Minister of Environment and Energy, 1997, pp. 55-58). However the Øresund also reflects the EU spatial policy discourse since the national planning report of 1997 explicitly adopts the basic rationales of the ESDP (Jensen, 1999).

The region itself includes some 3.5 million inhabitants and covers an area of 21,000 sq.km. The Øresund Region comprises Zealand, Lolland-Falster and Bornholm on the Danish side and Skåne, the southernmost part of Sweden.[2] Its core competencies are listed to be: provisions, research, medico, biotechnology, tourism, environmental industry, design and distribution. The most notable dimension of the Øresund Region is probably the 16 km-long bridge opened in July 2000. This fixed link for road and rail is part of the bigger transnational infrastructure project of the TEN-T and the project as such is said to have effects on 'the spatial structure of Europe as a whole' (Williams, 1996, p. 176). The growing expectation of increasing flows of cars and trains across the bridge, epitomized by an expected 16 per cent rise in traffic on the bridge and 222,000 more cars across the bridge in the first half of 2002 clearly illustrates the very tangible practices of European integration as this new transnational mobility region increasingly integrates.

Hands Across the Border: Contested Mobility Futures

In this section, we explore the spatial reconstitution of the Øresund, and the possibilities for its future development, by placing it in the context of European spatial policy. The creation of a transnational metropolitan region such as the Øresund Region within, and with the help of, the EU can be said to depend on both material conditions of economic, institutional and physical resources as well as on fantasy and imagination (Berg and Löfgren, 2000, p. 19). Or in our analytical vocabulary: a discourse fusing material practices and symbolic meanings in order to bring forward a particular policy development embedded in a certain configuration of power-rationality (Jensen and Richardson, forthcoming).

The future of the Øresund Region is framed in the ESDP as a core element in a possible 'global economic integration zone', proposed as a counterpart to the traditional European growth pole of the 'blue banana'.[3] Although pointing to some problems in achieving such a powerful spatial role – including disintegrative forces

---

2 Information on the Øresund Region is based on this web site: http://www.oeresundsbron.com/press/index.php?code=1.

3 The 'blue banana' is the iconic metaphor for the industrial/urban core that runs from south-east England through the Benelux countries toward Catalonia.

such as high costs for crossing the fixed link; unco-ordinated nation-state bureaucratic rules; and the lack of an overall political follow-up on the commitment to make the Øresund Region a global player – Mathiessen and Andersson express a certain optimism concerning the future prospects of the region (Mathiessen and Andersson, 2002). They highlight the region's welcoming of the ESDP, whose combined rationale of a polycentric urban development and global economic integration zones creates a powerful spatial logic for the strengthening of the Øresund Region (Mathiessen and Andersson, 2002, p. 82).

Contextualizing the Øresund Region within the new transnational European space also means locating it within the TEN-T, and mapping its relations to other important and highly prioritized links that may materialize in the future. One such link is the Fehmarn Belt link between Denmark and Germany. In the 2001 European Commission White Paper on Transport it is argued that the physical link between Denmark and Germany should become one of the 'priority TEN-T' projects, and this is linked to the future development of the Baltic Sea Region:

> Fehmarn Belt: The bridge/tunnel crossing the natural barrier of the Fehmarn Belt between Germany and Denmark is a key link which will complete the north–south route connecting Central Europe and the Nordic countries and allow the development of trade between them. This project on the route including the recently opened Øresund fixed link aims to cross the 19 km-wide belt. Completion of this project, which is still at the preliminary study stage, should contribute to the development of the Baltic Sea region (CEC, 2001, p. 55).

The future spatial development of the Øresund Region is also being refashioned in response to the expectations in the wake of EU enlargement. Seen in this perspective, enlargement will reposition the Øresund Region thus changing its relative position within the European geography from one of periphery to one of centrality:

> At the beginning of the 1990s, the Øresund Region was located at the periphery of the European Communities. Now, at the end of the 1990s, the situation of the region has changed. It is still, formally, a Danish-Swedish border region, but in the European Union, it is also a region that transcends boundaries, a laboratory for a trans-national city construction and a model for European integration (City of Copenhagen and City of Malmo, 1999, p. 16).

The linkage of the two nation-states by the fixed link is a very explicit example of the 'politics of mobility', which is also a very strong underlying rationale from the TEN-T to the ESDP (Jensen and Richardson, 2001; Richardson and Jensen, 2000). The fixed link across the Danish-Swedish border also exemplifies how this process is not only coined around a notion of mobility as such, but rather in terms of a new configuration of links and networks between cities. This can be seen by the very fact that the bridge is not built where the distance is the shortest (the usual 'rational' argument in terms of diminishing the 'friction of distance'). Rather it is built where the major urban agglomeration is found. Thus showing the new logic of transnational governance as one that operates with territorial entities other than the nation-state. In other words a process of 'transnational metropolisation' (Löfgren, 2000, p. 29), in which we find embedded a particular view of EU territory and its relation to the urban places (nodes) and the infrastructures connecting them (flows):

> This metropolitanism is immanent in much thinking in Europe since the introduction of the now famous 'Blue Banana' (Linde-Laursen, 2000, p. 155).

In the centre of such a process the mobility rationale behind the Øresund Region comes out very strongly in key metaphors contextualising the region; speed, mobility, flexible and mobile subjects and the bridge as concrete artifact and symbolic connection (Löfgren, 2000, p. 27). Such an interpretation goes along fine with the notion of the region as a place with 'exciting possibilities':

> Where else in the world can you choose to spend the evening in an outdoor café in your hometown and be in a world city thirty minutes later? Without a doubt, the Øresund bridge has created new, exciting possibilities (Malmo City, 2002).

This is an explicit example of the cultural grammar of seeing mobility and speed as progressive forces and distinctive for an (upwards) moving metropolis. The fixed link is thus part of the 'positive narrative of globalization and European integration' (Löfgren, 2000, p. 38) as well as the vision of the region can be understood as an explicit quest for increased speed, interaction and movement:

> In the Øresund vision there is not only a cult of speed but a cult of flow … The bridge and the transformed transport infrastructure of motorways, railroads, and airports are part of a vision of *zero friction* (Löfgren, 2000, pp. 46-47), italics in original).

Linking to the tension between a 'Europe of Places' versus a 'Europe of Flows' (Hajer, 2000), the Øresund Region embodies 'a tension between everyday life of local settings and the larger abstracted space of the transnational' (O'Dell, 2000, p. 232). This tension bears witness to one of the crucial dilemmas that the European Union faces when it applies this new transnational regionalism in its attempt to fuel the political integration process. Here the functionality of, for example, the Øresund bridge does not stand alone, but rather relates to more visionary forces who envisage the making of a genuine 'identity region', even though such identity work will take time:

> It took generations to build national identities and establish complex national innovation systems favouring growth and prosperity, including at a regional level. It will take years of hard work to amalgamate two countries' distinctive innovation systems into one, even when most formal barriers have been eroded. It will take even longer for a common

> cross-border regional identity to form. Only then will the full potential of cross-border synergy begin to materialise (Maskell and Törnqvist, 1999, p. 11).

How such strategies of nested visions and functional/symbolic attachments to regions coincide with the Union's notions of 'European identity' and European democracy is a critical issue:

> While the EU has encouraged a more consensual and negotiated approach to state borders, border policy continues to be relatively undemocratic with consequences for the EU as a transnational polity (O'Dowd, 2001, p. 96).

Furthermore, it is also an issue to see whether the Øresund Region is a particularly Nordic region, or something with a more European and transnational quality. Precisely this leverage in interpretation and the questions of different spatial scales point towards the issue of seeing the Øresund Region as a locus of struggle and contestation, which will be the next theme to follow from here.

The Øresund Region as a Locus of Struggle

The Øresund Region is the locus of a series of struggles: between environment and industrial growth; between Danish and Swedish communities now linked in the new region; and between local, transnational and European scales of interest. The Øresund fixed link itself has functioned as an iconic statement of the inherent mobility struggle for both industrialists (e.g. The European Round Table of Industrialists, ERT) and environmentalists (e.g. A SEED) in Europe:

> A SEED started campaigning against the TEN-T proposals in 1992, concerned both about the environmental impact of road building, and about the globalizing impact of the programme: 'Our position was clear: we were against new motorways, and the TEN-T plans were shaped by and for industrial giants like Volvo, Philips and Fiat (ERT members). All these roads would be used to shift goods back and forward through the regions of Europe and strengthen the grip of TNCs on markets everywhere' (environmental lobbyist, pers. comm.).

The origins of the A SEED position can be traced back to campaigns against infrastructure projects in member states that had European dimensions:

> Swedish environmental groups (like Miljoforbundet) campaigning against the Øresund bridge which was part of TEN-T. The campaign against the Øresund bridge all the time hammered on the fact that the bridge was not built for people in Denmark or Sweden but for long distance transport of goods from and to the Internal Market. (environmental lobbyist) ... Alongside this was the work of Belgian NGOs that had been monitoring the activities of the European Round Table of Industrialists in promoting TEN-T. Awareness of the motives behind the infrastructure 'boost' was there all the time. But A SEED's central message was 'No more roads', and arguing linkages between the 12,000

> km of new roads proposed in the TEN-T with environmental impacts of transport. Those involved in the A SEED campaign were surprised at the lack of involvement by other NGOs: 'During the first years of campaigning (mainly through information distribution, action days, letter writing, etc.) we were amazed that the big NGOs kept so quiet and did not do anything against TEN-T' (environmental lobbyist, pers. comm.).

Targeting the roads bias of the emerging trans-European network, and the powerful role of the infrastructure lobby in the decision-making process, campaigns focused on major planned infrastructure projects filling key 'missing links' in environmentally sensitive areas. Critical transnational projects such as the Øresund link between Sweden and Denmark, and the Somport Tunnel, linking France and Spain across the Pyrenees, were targeted. This was done because the powerful infrastructure lobby promoted the fixed link across Øresund as a critical 'missing link' of iconic status.

However, the pro-Øresund Region stakeholders see the region in a slightly different light. Thus we will now listen to the voice of the managing director and CEO of the A/S Øresundsforbindelse that is the main contractor for the bridge. Here the CEO is targeting what he finds to be the 'dishonest methods' of the environmentalists:

> The effects of the Øresund link on the environment has been the principal concern for those who have opposed building the bridge. It's my feeling that critics have employed dishonest methods. When it comes right down to it, their opposition is founded on a political concept about what sort of a society we want: one based on economic growth, or one based on stagnation? ... Seen from an international perspective, the matter is absurd. I have just returned from a trip to South-East Asia and the rape of nature I witnessed there makes the Øresund issue tame by comparison (Henning Hummelmose, managing director and CEO of A/S Øresundsforbindelse in the SAS Journal 'Scanorama', July /August 1995).

As can clearly be detected, the Øresund Region is the locus of a struggle between different powers and interests, and their accompanying knowledge forms. The themes and issues at stake are not confined however to the question of the environment alone, but reach deeper into the normative and political interests in the new power geometry of transformed territorialities and spatial practices. Thus, the CEO relates to the question of the changing power balance between the nation-state, the regions and the supra-national level and argues for a new 'spatial fix' (Harvey, 2001) or space-power configuration based on a strategy of strong urban agglomeration growth and concentration as opposed to the welfare state rationale of equal growth and redistribution:

> The general philosophy among politicians has long been to equalise economic growth and try to distribute it throughout the country. I think this has been wrong. No one profits by holding the strong region in check; on the contrary. If strong regions are permitted to grow, the cake to be divided will be that much bigger and growth in one region often offers various spin-off developments in others ... The development in

> Europe shows unequivocally that national states and traditional boundaries are becoming less significant. Instead it's the regions that are growing stronger, demanding self-determination and guarding their individuality. I don't think Øresund will be any exception (Henning Hummelmose, managing director and CEO of A/S Øresundsforbindelse in the SAS Journal 'Scanorama', July /August 1995).

Interestingly, the CEO statements appeared in 'speakers corner' of the Scandinavian Airlines journal 'Scanorama' (which must be considered to be the voice of yet another pro-region player in the field). The CEO's assessment clearly should be seen as a position-statement. Nevertheless it strikes a chord with the analysis pointing at the changed position of both cities and nation-states within the European Union. A policy development in which the European cities are re-positioned at multi-level dimensions (Le Galès, 2002, pp. 5 and 75).

The divergence of interests and rationales behind the stakeholders in the Øresund Region can also be traced back in time to the historical conditions of the cities within the region. The Swedish City of Malmö has for example 'suffered' from being defined as peripheral within Swedish territory:

> Swedish and Danish political and economic actors have, however, different geographical visions about the future of the Sound. The Danish establishment has, as a primary goal, the enlargement of Copenhagen's hinterland (as a hexagonal hinterland in the central place theory) and at the same time wish to enhance Copenhagen's position in Northern Europe (with Hamburg and Berlin as main competitors). In Sweden, regional actors (in Scania) see this as an opportunity to take advantage of the Scania's close proximity to Copenhagen and the (eu)ropean heartland. The possibility to strengthen Scania's provincial position in Sweden has also been of significance. Since the 17th century, Scania has felt itself unjustly treated by central powers in Stockholm. The central actors in Sweden hope that the bridge will provide a way for Malmö in particular to emerge from its structural stagnation and revitalise the economy (Ek, 1998, p. 11).

Moreover we would argue that the physical infrastructure of the fixed link will act as a potential symbolic signifier for the attempt to construct not only a transnational mobility region, but also in due time to the construction of a new transnational regional identity. The notion of a Europe of strong cross-border city regions provides new territorial referents for social agents living on each side of the bridge, reshaping their understanding of their lived and perceived spaces. Obviously, the everyday life of people in the region has not yet come to such a state of practice and mind. However, if one speaks with people for example in Copenhagen about the practical importance and the symbolic meaning of the bridge, one clearly senses that it has turned into a combined practical and symbolic landmark. In an interview made for a research project on Transportation and Urban

Planning[4] conducted at Aalborg University we thus find the voice of people whose everyday practice relates to the bridge one way or the other:

> I have crossed it [the Bridge]. And even very fast because that seemed fun to do so. But otherwise I really find that bridge misplaced. To be honest. I can't understand why at all ... And it may be that in one hundred years time people will pilgrim across it because things take time ... But I cannot understand why people suddenly ... why people are puzzled by the facts that the Swedes are not crawling the place and we don't ... why should we? (Copenhagen resident interviewed in 2001).

Clearly this statement does not call for over-optimism about the prospects for the speedy construction of a new transnational identity. However, it seems to be a rather widespread way of perceiving the bridge and the region amongst 'ordinary people' on the Danish side of the nation-state border. At the end of the day, the bridge evidently serves more than functional needs, as argued here by the City Director of Planning in Copenhagen:

> The bridge is needed more as a symbol than for speeding up transportation flows (Newman and Thornley, 1996, p. 238).

Needless to say, the 'Nordic experiment' does not stand alone in the context of European examples of transnational border crossings. In the next section we will look into this broader fund of examples in order to put the Øresund Region in a perspective.

European Experiences of Organizing Across Borders

The challenge of cross-border organization to make possible transnational spatial intervention is significant. The Øresund reflects a positive adoption of the EU agenda, which has not been universal. From case studies published in 1998 on cross-border co-operations in Kent-Nord-Pas de Calais (France and UK) and Euroregio Maas-Rhine (Holland, Belgium and Germany) Brown reaches the conclusion that certain limitations in terms of different national regimes of regulation, disagreement about economic development themes, implementation and status of cross-border plans and a lack of co-ordination between public regulation and planning function lead to only a partial success evaluation of the

---

4 The research program Transportation and Urban Planning was financed by the now abolished Danish Transportation Council, with additional funding from Aalborg University. The research started in 1998 and was completed in 2003. The citation quoted here is from the Greater Copenhagen research project on the relationship between the urban structure of the city and everyday life transportation (see this web site for more information: http://transurb.plan.auc.dk/).

Europeanization of spatial planning as we find it in the guise of the ESDP and its trickling down:

> Under the rationale for the development of a European spatial planning policy discussed at the beginning [the ESDP], emphasis was placed on the general role of spatial planning in the integration process, as well as the specific contribution that spatial planning is deemed to be able to make towards integrating borders. However, although consideration of the issue in a theoretical context suggested that the benefits ought to be considerable, findings from two different border regions highlighted the limitations of spatial planning in the cross-border context (Brown, 1998, p. 13).

Elsewhere, Tewdwr-Jones and Williams (2001), in their analysis of the Europeanization of planning in England, conclude with comments on the 'dismissive' attitudes within British planning towards European policies. They point to an isolationist view which prohibits the actors the 'capacity for thinking in terms of EU space and spatial relations' (Tewdwr-Jones and Williams, 2001, p. 162).

However evidence from other cross-border co-operations in the EU does suggest that there is a growing practice of 'open-house' Europeanization within spatial planning across Europe. Thus Schulz (1999) concludes that in the case of the Saar-Lor-Lux-Region co-operation between Germany, France and Luxembourg:

> The projects are generally well accepted by the local population and reinforce the transborder regional identity of the people. Their contribution to the reduction of the inner borders of the European Union seems exemplary. By establishing networks between local authorities, the common motivation and the financial support are used to take advantage of synergy effects and to strengthen the position of these areas in their national and European frameworks. They are the basis for a bottom-up integration as an alternative to the top-down forces executed by European Directives, the Common Market or the Monetary Union (Schulz, 1999, p. 240).

This rather up-beat conclusion of the new regional transborder activities as bottom-up antidotes to centralized European bureaucracy and the 'democratic deficit' can, however, be contested as one looks more closely at how similar local and regional stakeholders are playing compared to the stakeholders at the EU level. What seems to be inescapable, however, is the notion of the transnational level and its increasing significance in the Europeanization of spatial planning.

Our case study of the Øresund is helpfully contextualized in this respect by Böhme's research, which finds a strong correspondence between spatial agendas in the Nordic countries and the ESDP (Böhme, 2002, pp. 214-233). However, from Böhme's analysis we can establish that Sweden, unlike Denmark, has entered transnational spatial planning exercises with a national planning system not very well equipped for this kind of work, suggesting a likely imbalance in the institutional arrangements of the Øresund Region, and the corresponding engagement in spatial planning. Böhme concludes that the corporatist decision-making, the widespread reliance on network governance, and the influence of the policy discourse as an informal frame of mind makes links to the ESDP very evident as an expression of European integration by means of network governance within the Nordic countries (Böhme, 2002, pp. 230-231). As such this can be seen as indicative of verifying the hypothesis stipulating that the Øresund Region is a distinct Nordic endeavour within the field of European political integration.

Here, then, we discuss how the need to establish an institutional framework to support the new Øresund Region was addressed. The Øresund committee is the political body responsible for co-operation in the region. It has members from Swedish and Danish counties and municipalities in the region. Amongst other activities the committee administers the Interreg programmes.[5] The Committee administered EU's Interreg fund with approximately 100 mill. Danish kroner in the regional fund period 1994-1999. The new budget for the IR IIIA Øresund Region is 460 m. Danish kroner for the 2000-2006 period. The Interreg programme has been widely acknowledged as being influential in engaging political actors in Europe's cities and regions (Boye, 2000), allowing the European Commission to become a 'major actor in cross-border regions' (O'Dowd, 2001, p. 102). The Øresund Region was related to the EU Interreg IIA programme from 1994-99 and is now linked to Interreg IIIA for the structural fund period 2000-2006. This actualizes the question about the relations between EU and regional interests in the establishment of the region.

The Øresund Region presents radically useful lessons for cross-border co-operation as there have been proposals for a directly elected council with tax-raising powers (CEMR, 2002, p. 1). The mentioned proposal of a directly elected council was probably more of a provocative suggestion made by the Lord Mayor of Copenhagen in the press. However, the following public debate about this issue showed that people at least started to think transnationally about the issue of metropolitan governance in this region, and that the issue raised by the Lord Mayor may serve as a catalyst for similar future debates.

It is, furthermore, interesting to note that the Øresund Chamber of Commerce, representing business interests in the Danish and Swedish halves of the Øresund Region, feels that progress on institutional integration has failed to keep up with the material construction of the bridge. Here we see market stakeholders demanding new transnational regulatory frames and regimes. Specifically, they call for a new 'transnational authority with powers to cut through a raft of legal and

---

5 The EU Structural Funds Interreg programme was originally developed in order to break down the barriers made by the nation-states to community actions at a regional level. The first programme, the Interreg I was targeted at border regional co-operation. The Interreg II was then expanded towards cross-border co-operations between regions without common borders. Within the Interreg II programme the strand of IIA, which was the funding programme of the Øresund Region, is now being continued in the Interreg IIIA programme.

practical differences between the two sides. Otherwise there is a risk that the dynamics created by the new bridge will be replaced by stagnation and inertia' (Øresund Chamber of Commerce, 2002). Bent Larsen, Chairman of the Øresund Chamber of Commerce commented:

> We can only take note that the positive effects of the new bridge have yet to materialize. The dynamics of the integration process are coming to a halt (Øresund Chamber of Commerce, 2002).

The key obstacles identified by the Øresund Chamber of Commerce include differential tax regulations, lack of a common currency, and the toll fees on the Øresund Bridge.

On the level of regional mobility, though, we do find new practices in attempts to facilitate transnational flows within the region. As one example of this development the Swedish and Danish transport authorities have already harmonized transport taxes across the Øresund Region.

In the following sections, we examine how the new cross-border institutions are beginning to market and 'brand' their 'product'.

Branding Territorial Identity I: 'Medicon Valley'

The Øresund Region is often pictured as 'Medicon Valley' thus giving associations to one of the most iconic mega-regions of global competitiveness: Silicon Valley. This kind of place promotion practice can obviously be criticized both in terms of being yet another copy of the US knowledge intensive region and also in questioning who really decides and wants this type of regional development? Having said that, it is worth noticing that the notion is furthermore based on a strong regional competency within the field of medical research and business (Clausen, 2000, p. 54). Moreover the branding of 'Medicon Valley' incorporates all the five dimensions of an alleged successful strategy for global competitive regions (metaphorically richness, geographical positioning, existing local competencies, legitimizing analogies and supportive regional agents) (Boye, 2000, pp. 215-216). As always, though, there is scope for a more cautious interpretation:

> Only within fields where a region processes a strong and distinct scientific base do R&D intensive firms stand a chance of sustained growth and competitiveness. It may therefore be questioned whether it would be reasonable to expect that the Øresund Region could become a European Silicon Valley or a Boston in the 21st Century (Maskell and Törnqvist, 1999, p. 56).

Furthermore, by giving the region a name, and by reproducing the name over and over again – in statements, in written texts, at meetings, etc. – the presence of the region becomes acknowledged (Berg, 2000, p. 77). Here we find a strong parallel to the way that EU spatial policy discourse frames the cities in terms of global competition and regional knowledge-based industries, reflecting an important shift in the thinking around regional development in Europe in the 1990s:

> This is a shift of emphasis from immediate support for the lagging and less successful to an acceptance that successful cities and regions hold lessons for all, and will also benefit, eventually, more peripheral areas. The propositions of the new regionalism have a clear affinity with the changing direction of thinking in the European Commission (Herrschel and Newman, 2002, p. 61).

This 'new regionalism' is part of a wider general transformation from traditional Keynesian-style and welfare-oriented policies towards more city-focused and network-based growth strategies (Herrschel and Newman, 2002, p. 75). A process within the European Union in which the nation-state borders have become increasingly less visible as locus for territorial identities (Herrschel and Newman, 2002, p. 107), is especially the case in cross-border regions such as the Øresund Region.

The 'Medicon Valley' brand is articulated with reference to the successful US role model as well as to the region's endogenous potential. However, we can find even more complex notions of branding the region as in the case of 'The Human Capital' to which we will now turn.

Branding Territorial Identity II: 'The Human Capital'

In the vast number of place marketing publications being spread out as part of the naming and branding of the Øresund Region the creativity of self-labelling seems endless. Thus it has now become official policy to brand the region under the label 'The Human Capital' (Øresund Network AB, 2002). This is explicitly an attempt to add a more 'soft' dimension to a project that often seems to be solely about hard infrastructure and co-ol business. This is certainly also a contribution to the identity construction in the region – a work in progress that is supposed to identify a particular 'Øresund Way of Life'(Øresund Network AB, 2002):

> Balance and harmony are keywords for life in the Øresund Region. The people of the Øresund live in one of Northern Europe's fastest growing business areas, while the good life awaits them right on their doorstep ... According to an American survey based on 160 countries, Denmark is the best country in the world to live in. Sweden is not far behind in fourth place. The social systems are well developed and take good care of the sick and the old. Crime is limited and unemployment is low. Interest in taking care of the environment is expressed in the unspoilt countryside and in urban development ... Accessibility characterizes the Øresund Region. The tailor-made road and rail network blurs the borders and puts the entire region within reach ... The quality of working life and leisure activities makes the Øresund Region peerless (Øresund Network AB, 2002, p. 9).

On the one hand we thus find the branding of the region by means of traditional tourist and place marketing techniques highlighting the particular attributes of the region – here not least capitalizing on the widespread goodwill of the Scandinavian welfare state. On the other hand, we find a place promotion and branding strategy potentially threatening to overlook or even neglect the particular Nordic dimension by using these 'universal' notions of knowledge intensive cities in global competition

Furthermore, the Øresund Region has been described as a new 'transnational metropolis' and as a model for the 'new Europe without borders' (Berg and Löfgren, 2000). Some see this as a reaction to the processes of globalization, or even as a kind of 'regional panic' in which stakeholders and government bodies are busy transforming themselves into competitive global players (Berg and Löfgren, 2000, p. 8). However, as we saw before, making such a new transnational metropolis is not an expression of concerted consensus. What we find in the case of the Øresund Region is a loosely defined institutional and territorial arena for those players who want in on the global game, or in other words:

> The only thing that actually unites many of the actors is that they agree upon working under the label 'the Øresund Region' and that they often share a specific optimistic rhetoric we call *Ørespeak* (Berg and Löfgren, 2000, p. 12, italics in original).

This corresponds to our analysis of the development behind the emergence of the spatial policy discourse in the European Union in general and in the case of the ESDP in particular as it can be understood as an arena for power struggles over meaning (Richardson and Jensen, 2000). In many other ways the Øresund Region seems to fit the picture of such a new territorial policy discourse.

Constructing a Transnational Mobility Region – Final Remarks

In this chapter we have analysed one case of cross-border co-operation as an example of the transgression of the nation-state borders in a general attempt to further European integration processes.

The institutional arrangements for the region are characterized by their informal and ad hoc nature, reflecting the situation in many other institutions of European spatial policy:

> The authority structure in the Øresund Region can thus be perceived as a black hole which has exercised its gravity on all kinds of political organizations and made various actors and agents rush in to fill it (Berg, 2000, p. 63).

This kind of 'open house' strategy (Tangkjær, 2000, p. 170) challenges the more rigid notion of top-down versus bottom-up strategy as it is an illustration of the multiple scales and levels of institutions that all go together in forming a particular place such as the Øresund Region. Needless to say such a place still has to be comprehended by means of its relations to other places and flows as is the point in the 'relational approach' to regional development (Allen *et al.*, 1998).

The 'open house'-strategy suggests that the stakeholders, agents and policy-makers playing on this field are engaged in a game characterized by a high degree of uncertainty and with an explicit experimental status. But also that this new European transnational urban mega-region is open to anyone interested in playing the game of global interurban competition at a transnational level. However, the Øresund Region seen as an 'open house'-strategy represents a very selective openness thus running the risk of sidestepping democratic processes (Berg *et al.*, 2000, p. 280). The formation of transnational regions as new territorial units and the projected spatial planning according to the principles of the ESDP are genuine innovations in the EU toolbox of political integration. It is the bringing together of regional policy proper and spatial planning which adds a new quality to the prospective transnational regions (Jørgensen and Nielsen, 1998, p. 314).

What these new forms of governance crossing the nation-state boundaries may mean is obviously difficult to predict let alone to explain. Here we modestly offer a crude topology of hypothesis that calls for further research. Roughly we can identify (at least) four types of hypothesis suggesting why there is a new regionalism in the wake of European integration:

- Economic and social cohesion in order for the EU not to 'break apart' – the reactive top-down argument;
- Challenging the nation-state borders as a strategy for further political integration – the proactive bottom-up argument – global competitiveness – the external argument;
- Creating new nested identities and territorial loyalties – the project identity argument.

These four tentative dimensions as to why there is a new regionalism on the verge in the EU, and what that could mean links to the five dimensions of Europeanization presented at the beginning of this chapter, even though the political project aiming at a unified and politically stronger Europe (Olsen, 2001, p. 3) still seems to be at the centre of the activities.

Thus the Europeanization of spatial planning as it is firmly expressed in the cross-border lessons of the last decade goes to show how mixed rationales and different outcomes of the policy process merge at various spatial scales and with the inputs form various stakeholders. At the end of the day, though, the Europeanization of spatial planning seems to be emptied for the participation of civil society representatives, NGOs and other voices that (potentially at least) could contest the whole democratic legitimacy of those new spatial practices:

> Cross-border secretariats consisting of administrative and technical personnel may be set up to propose or implement particular objects ... Their importance, however, illustrates the bias towards bureaucracy and technocracy in trans-frontier regions. Electoral

> constituencies do not span borders, limiting democratic involvement of elected representatives in cross-border networks. Instead, cross-border regions involve a series of flexible strategic alliances between loyal political, administrative and business elites. To this extent they are fora for limited forms of participatory democracy (O'Dowd, 2001, p. 104).

Despite the rather critical edge to O'Dowd's analysis it is recognized that the new EU supported breed of trans-frontier regionalism potentially could help underpin 'a form of European multiculturalism which favours free choice of identity, multiple affiliations and dynamic group formation' (O'Dowd, 2001, p. 106). Whether such progressive outcomes are to be expected is not easy to say, however we would remain sceptics when it comes to that dimension. So far we would recognize the Europeanization of spatial planning as a predominantly interesting example of how policy fields make themselves into institutions:

> ... the ESDP ... represents above all how European spatial planning has made itself an institution by itself, in spite of the original shortcomings in the Treaties. More than its 'policy aims', its development process and the related 'informal' constitution of a European Council of Ministers for Spatial Planning is one of the greatest demonstrations of how the concrete needs of a community can trigger institutional changes in practice and, with the possibility of giving real shape to Europe's 'economic and social cohesion' (one of the fundamental principles after the Single Act), show how deep the aspirations of the European Community to become a Union are (Rivolin, 2002, p. 12).

The Europeanization of spatial planning as manifested in the Øresund Region has become a vehicle for a reconfiguration of European integration. Furthermore, this is re-contextualized within diverse practical settings across the new scales and arenas of spatial planning.

Such re-contextualization can be read as an expression of the 'domestic politics of transnationalty'.[6] By this we refer to the situation where the Øresund Region is used as a flag of convenience to divert investments and resources to the capital (in the Danish case) as opposed to the traditional rationale of equal development in Danish regional policy. This is particularly the case when the issue is the construction of the Øresund bridge, where the northern part of the country has argued that such a mega-project detracts investments from the more peripheral regions in Denmark. Furthermore, the investment in the transnational infrastructure can be read as an up-scaling of the spatial agendas coined around the notion of territorial cohesion within the nation-state's territory. In a similar way, we would argue that the Swedish dimension of the Øresund Region also carries an element of 'domestic politics of transnationalty' as the main city of Scania, Malmö, seems to have found use of the region building in its own struggle for regional autonomy vis-à-vis the Swedish capital of Stockholm. Such a development adds another layer

6 The authors wish to thank Henrik Halkier for drawing our attention to this dimension of the case, and for coming up with the concept of 'domestic politics of transnationality'.

to the complex discussion of the Europeanization of the Nordic regions as it fuels a 'politics of scale' at the transnational level which may be seen as an expression of drawing together the Nordic regions under the flag of the European Union as opposed to a situation where Nordic co-operation was coined exclusively around the interaction between the autonomous nation-states.

This takes us to our final point namely that of seeing these new transnational planning and branding exercises as an ambivalent discourse. By this we mean that, on the one hand, we find a branding of the region by means of traditional tourist and place marketing techniques highlighting the particular attributes of the region – here not least capitalizing on the widespread goodwill of the Scandinavian welfare state. On the other hand, we find a place promotion and branding strategy potentially threatening to overlook or even neglect the particular Nordic dimension by using these 'universal' notions of knowledge intensive cities in global competition. In other words, a de-contextual and homogeneous urban growth strategy on a par with countless other contemporary urban growth strategies.

Finally, we return to Rudolf Niessler's comments at the Copenhagen conference mentioned at the start of this chapter (and its striking accordance with the introductory quote from the Danish Minister for Economy and Industry). Niessler argues that, with Interreg becoming the dominant instrument in the deepening of the European integration process, we are on the verge of leaving behind the context of cohesion policy. The future of European intervention seems likely to be increasingly shaped by the positive framings associated with the new windows of competitive opportunity, rather than by the more 'negative' need to deal with the weaker regions.

Bibliography

Allen, J., Massey, D. and Cochrane, A. (1998), *Rethinking the Region*, London: Routledge.

Berg, P. O. (2000), 'Dreaming up a Region? Strategic Management as Invocation', in P. O. Berg, A. Linde-Laursen and O. Löfgren (eds), *Invoking a Transnational Metropolis. The Making of the Øresund Region*, Lund: Studentlitteratur.

Berg, P. O., Linde-Laursen, A. and Löfgren, O. (eds) (2000), *Invoking a Transnational Metropolis. The Making of the Øresund Region*, Lund: Studentlitteratur.

Berg, P. O. and Löfgren, O. (2000), 'Studying the Birth of a Transnational Region', in P. O. Berg, A. Linde-Laursen and O. Löfgren (eds), *Invoking a Transnational Metropolis. The Making of the Øresund Region*, Lund: Studentlitteratur.

Böhme, K. (2002), 'Nordic Echoes of European Spatial Planning', *Nordregio*, Stockholm.

Boye, P. (2000), 'Competing with Concepts. The Conception of an Industrial Platform', in P. O. Berg, A. Linde-Laursen and O. Löfgren (eds), *Invoking a Transnational Metropolis. The Making of the Øresund Region*, Lund: Studentlitteratur.

Brown, C. (1998), 'Planning for an Integrated Europe: Lessons from the Border Regions', Aveiro: The XII AESOP Congress: Planning, Professionals and Public Expectations, 22-25 July, 1998.

CEC, C. f. t. E. C. (2001), 'White Paper. European Transport Policy for 2010: Time to Decide. COM (2001) 0370', Luxembourg: Office for Official Publications of the European Communities.

CEMR, C. o. E. M. a. R. (2002), 'CEMR Initial View on Urban Development': Council of European Municipalities and Regions, European Section of IULA.

City of Copenhagen and City of Malmoe (1999), *Our New Region*, Copenhagen and Malmoe: City of Copenhagen and City of Malmoe.

Clausen, O. B. (2000), *Øresundsregionen*, Frederikshavn: DAFOLO.

Ek, R. (1998), 'The Öresund Region as a Geograpichal Vision', *paper for Nordic Doctoral Course, Urban and Regional Change in Europe: Economic and Political Restructuring in Contemporary Europe*, University of Oslo.

Graute, U. (2002), 'Kooperation in der Europäischen Raumentwicklung [Co-operation in European Spatial Development Policy]'. *IÖR Chriften*. Band 37, Dresden: IÖR.

Hajer, M. (2000), 'Transnational networks as transnational policy discourse: some observations on the politics of spatial development in Europe', in W. Salet and A. Faludi (eds), *The revival of strategic spatial planning*, Amsterdam: The Royal Netherlands Academy of Arts and Sciences, pp. 135-142.

Harvey, D. (2001), *Spaces of Capital: Towards a Critical Geography*, Edinburgh: Edinburgh University Press.

Herrschel, T. and Newman, P. (2002), *Governance of Europe's City Regions. Planning, Policy and Politics*, London: Routledge.

Jensen, O. B. (1999), 'At ville noget med rummet – diskurs & rationalitet i Danmarks og den Europæiske Unions planlægning af byernes rumlige udvikling [Re-thinking the Urban Systems – Discourse and Rationality in Danish and European Union Spatial Planning]' *Institut for Samfundsudvikling & Planlægning*, Aalborg: Aalborg.

Jensen, O. B. and Richardson, T. (2001), 'Nested Visions: New Rationalities of Space in European Spatial Planning', *Regional Studies* 35(8): 703-717.

Jensen, O. B. and Richardson, T. (forthcoming), *Making European Space: Mobility, Power and Territorial Identity*, London: Routledge.

Jørgensen, I. and Nielsen, J. (1998), 'Spatial Development and Planning between "High" and "Low" Politics: Interreg IIC in the Baltic Sea Region', in B. Lindström (ed) *The NEBI Yearbook 1998: North European and Baltic Sea Integration*, Berlin: Springer-Verlag.

Le Galès (2002), *European Cities. Social Conflicts and Governance*, Oxford: Oxford University Press.

Linde-Laursen, A. (2000), 'Bordering Improvisations. Centuries of Identity Politics', in P. O. Berg, A. Linde-Laursen and O. Löfgren (eds), *Invoking a Transnational Metropolis. The Making of the Øresund Region*, Lund: Studentlitteratur.

Löfgren, O. (2000), 'Moving Metaphors', in P. O. Berg, A. Linde-Laursen and O. Löfgren (eds), *Invoking a Transnational Metropolis. The Making of the Øresund Region*, Lund: Studentlitteratur.

Malmo City (2002), 'Malmo.com: living and projects', Vol. 2002.

Maskell, P. and Törnqvist, G. (1999) *Building a Cross-Border Learning Region. Emergence of the North European Øresund Region*, Copenhagen: Copenhagen Business School Press.

Mathiessen, C. W. and Andersson, Å. E. (2002), 'Øresundsområdet: Det regionale udviklingsprojekt – status og forslag [The Øresund Area: The Regional development project – status and proposals]', Malmö: South Swedish Chamber of Industry and Commerce.

Minister of Environment and Energy (1997), 'Denmark and European Spatial Planning Policy, National Planning Report for Denmark', Copenhagen: Minister for Environment and Energy.

Newman, P. and Thornley, A. (1996), *Urban Planning in Europe. International Competition, National Systems and Planning Projects*, London: Routledge.

O'Dell, T. (2000), 'Traversing the Transnational', in P. O. Berg, A. Linde-Laursen and O. Löfgren (eds), *Invoking a Transnational Metropolis. The Making of the Øresund Region*, Lund: Studentlitteratur.

O'Dowd, L. (2001), 'State Borders, Border Regions and the Construction of European Identity', in M. Kohli and M. Novak (eds), *Will Europe Work? Integration, Employment and Social Order*, London: Routledge.

Olsen, J. P. (2001), 'The Many Faces of Europeanization': ARENA Working Papers.

Øresund Chamber of Commerce (2002), 'Renewed call for Øresund integration', Vol. 2002: Øresund Identity Network.

Øresund Network AB (2002), 'The Øresund Region', Malmö: Øresund Network AB.

Richardson, T. and Jensen, O. B. (2000), 'Discourses of Mobility and Polycentric Development: a Contested View of European Spatial Planning', *European Planning Studies* 8(4): 503-520.

Rivolin, U. J. (2002), 'Shaping European Spatial Planning: How Italy's Experience Can Contribute' *XVI AESOP Congress*, Volos, Greece.

Schulz, C. (1999), 'City-networking and Bottom-up Development by Transborder Co-operation: The Influence of Local Authorities in the Saar-Lor-Lux-Region', in H. Knippenberg and J. Markusse (eds), *Nationalising and Denationalising European Border Regions 1800-2000*, Dordrecht: Kluwer Academic Publishers.

Tangkjær, C. (2000), 'Øresund as an Open House strategy by invitation', in P. O. Berg, A. Linde-Laursen and O. Löfgren (eds), *Invoking a Transnational Metropolis. The Making of the Øresund Region*, Lund: Studentlitteratur.

Tewdwr-Jones, M. and Williams, R. H. (2001), *The European Dimension of British Planning*, London: Routledge.

Williams, R. H. (1996), *European Union, Spatial Policy and Planning*, London: Paul Chapman Publishing.

Chapter 9

Denmark of the Regions? Europeanization, Multi-level Governance and Danish Regional Policy Strategies

Henrik Halkier

Since the beginning of the 1990s, Danish regional policy has changed dramatically. As of January 1991, all central government incentive schemes were terminated, and since then the main components of spatial economic policy have been a host of sub-national initiatives and the European Structural Funds. Denmark would in other words seem to be an extreme example of more general European trends well-known in the literature (Albrechts and Swyngedouw, 1989; Stöhr, 1989; Anderson, 1990; Martin and Townroe, 1992; Borras Alomar, 1994; Hooghe, 1996; Keating, 1997; Bachtler, 1997; Tömmel, 1998), namely the shift away from national schemes towards regional and supra-national initiatives, and an enhanced position of sub-national government based on increased involvement in European matters as envisaged in the 'Europe of the Regions' slogan.

The aim of this chapter is to examine the transformation of regional policy in Denmark from the perspective of political decentralization and Europeanization in order to establish to what extent recent changes have increased the capacity of Danish regions to pursue their own agendas with regard to economic development, and explore the organizational strategies pursued by various tiers of government in this process of rapid and profound policy change.

The text is divided into three parts. The following section provides a brief outline of the analytical framework, based primarily on contributions from traditions within policy analysis, network theory and the new institutionalism. The main body of the text examines the changing face of spatial economic policy in Denmark, dealing in turn with the development of policies and initiatives emanating from the national, European and regional levels respectively, and assessing their implications for the relative influence of the different levels of government involved. Finally, the origins of what can be shown to be a considerable degree of decentralization are discussed, especially with regard to the possible role of the European and other tiers of government in the process.

The Analytical Approach

The relationship between different tiers of government has been studied from a variety of spatial perspectives, and thus it will be possible to draw upon inspiration from a range of existing, and not entirely unrelated, bodies of literature. On the *European level* Gary Marks and other proponents of the 'multi-level governance' approach have argued that 'decision-making competencies are shared by actors at different levels rather than monopolized by state executives' (Marks *et al.*, 1996, p. 346; cf Marks, 1996b), and that it is therefore necessary to adopt an 'actor-centred' approach that specifies the role of particular individuals and institutions in the decision-making process. On the *national level* parallel arguments can be found in the 'Power-Dependence' approach developed by Rob Rhodes (1988) as an alternative way of understanding the relationship between central government on the one hand and sub-central public bodies on the other. Rhodes stressed the mutual dependency of different tiers of government based on their respective control of resources that are of importance to the development and implementation of public policy, and like Marks in his polemic against the state-centric approach, he refused to give priority to one particular type of resources – constitutional or legal authority – at the expense of for example informational or organizational sources of influence. Finally, the steady growth in studies focusing on *policy networks* has also led to the recognition that 'policy-making includes a large number of public and private actors' exchanging 'information, expertise, trust and other policy resources' (Jordan and Schubert, 1992, pp11f; cf van Waarden, 1992; Hanf and O'Toole, 1992; Rhodes and Marsh, 1992), and although the approach was originally developed to deal with policy sectors within national polities, it can clearly also be applied to policy networks with an international dimension such as for example the European Structural Funds (e.g. Conzelmann, 1995; Heinelt and Smith, 1996; Cameron and Danson, 2000; Östhol, Svensson and Halkier, 2002).

The analytical approaches of these three traditions clearly move along parallel lines, focusing on institutions and their mutual resource dependencies in a historical context. Working along these lines a general analytical framework can be developed around the proposition that regional policy is essentially about attempting to change patterns of behaviour amongst private actors in pursuance of public priorities with regard to spatial development. From this perspective three types of actors and their interaction become central:

- As a form of public policy, regional policy will have *political sponsors* from whom the political authority to institute options and incentives for private firms is derived;
- The *implementing organization* may or may not be identical with the administrative arm of the political sponsors and interacts directly with firms and other private actors by instituting the options and incentives entailed in a particular form of regional policy;

- The *targeted private actors* are important in the sense that spatial economic objectives are to be achieved by making individual firms and other private actors behave in ways they would not otherwise have done, and while policy instruments entailing options and incentives are employed by the implementing organization in order to bring about the changes desired, the outcome still depends on a response from private actors that may or may not be forthcoming.

Figure 9.1 Actors, inter-organizational relations and environments of regional policy

It follows from this that two types of inter-organizational relations are at the centre of any form of regional policy: the relationship between the political sponsors and the implementing organization on the one hand, and the relationship between the implementing organization and the private actors target by policy measures on the other. But these actors and their interaction are set within the context of broader inter-organizational relations and institutional features, and the economic and political environments which influence the positions and strategies of the three central sets of actors should therefore also be taken into account, especially in a situation where several forms of regional policy sponsored by different tiers of government coexist. While each of these individual policies can be studied as a set of inter-organizational relations as summarized in Figure 9.1, the entire field of regional development must be seen as a number of more or less parallel policies interacting because sponsorships overlap, implementing organizations are involved in more than one policy programme and the same firms are targeted by several public initiatives.

This general approach can be translated into a very detailed conceptual framework for detailed studies of particular organizations or policies (Halkier, 2000; 2003), but as the present chapter focuses on a more limited range of issues, a simplified version has been adopted which treats each tier of government as a single entity and focuses on their key organizational features and relations. For each tier of government three dimensions are seen as crucial (cf Table 9.1), namely the resources at its disposal, the assumptions on which it operates, and the strategies pursued in relation to its environment. *Resources* are the means by which organizations maintain themselves and influence their surroundings, either by employing them as policy instruments vis-à-vis private actors or as means of linking up with other organizations to achieve specific goals, and the text distinguishes between four basic resources: authority, information, finance and organization (Hood, 1983; Windhoff-Héritier, 1987; cf Halkier, 2000). The way particular phenomena are interpreted and the basic values espoused may have important bearings on the strategies adopted (Andersen and KjΦr, 1996; Halkier, 2003), and from the perspective of regional policy key *assumptions* will relate to the nature of 'the regional problem', namely the inter-regional inequalities perceived to be significant, and the underlying values that transform inter-regional inequalities into a social problem warranting public intervention. Finally the *strategies* are an obvious object of study, both as operational strategies which entail particular goals and policy instruments in relation to the private firms targeted and as positioning strategies vis-à-vis other organizations or tiers of government. All three dimensions clearly have implications for inter-organizational relations and the development of policies: resource dependencies between organizations will make some courses of action more feasible or attractive than others, and assumptions and strategies may be more or less compatible.

Table 9.1 Organizations and policy-making – an analytical framework

Levels of analysis	*Dimensions*	*Sub-dimension*
Organizational	Domain	Territory Function
	Strategies	Policies Positioning
	Resources	Authority Finance Information Organization
Inter-organizational	Bargaining	
	Exchange	
Multi-organizational	Integration	

Source: Adapted from Halkier and Damborg 1997.

All in all the conceptual framework summarized in Table 9.1 should thus be able to differentiate between different regional development strategies and capture key aspects of the relationship between different tiers of government in the process of policy-making, and thus on the basis of this it should be possible to illuminate the relationship between decentralization and Europeanization with regard to regional policy in Denmark.

Regional Policy and the Danish Regions

Given the high level of inter-tier collaboration in the field of regional policy, the picture drawn is bound to be a complex one, and in the following, the analysis is organized according to the tier of government from which a particular programme originates, i.e. a combination of spatial coverage and political institutions. In practice this means that programmes initiated by central government applying only to Denmark will be discussed under the heading of national policies, the supranational Structural Funds of the EU are discussed under the heading of European policies although they are implemented through specific national and regional programmes, and initiatives for particular localities developed by regional authorities, i.e. the 14 directly elected county councils and their associated bodies, are covered under the heading of regionally-based policies. For each of these three levels, the analysis begins with an outline of the development of policies from the 1970s to the present, followed by an assessment of the changing strategies and resource dependencies with regard to this particular set of programmes and initiatives.

National Policies

Regional policy in Western Europe started out as national-level measures to promote economic development in 'problem regions', primarily through financial incentives to private firms. Especially from the 1980s onwards central government regional schemes have become more and more targeted in terms of designated localities and eligible projects, and in combination with increasingly discretionary award procedures this has led to significant real-term reductions in central government expenditure on regional policy in Western Europe (Bachtler, 1997; Yuill et al., 1999, pp. 3-25). While this basic plot can also be found in the Danish version of the story, it comes with a radical twist.

In Denmark overall responsibility for regional policy rests with national authorities, and from the late 1950s till the early 1980s the proclaimed objective of regional policy was to promote equality between different parts of the country with regard to economic welfare, especially between the urban centres and the rural peripheries. From the mid-1980s, the assumptions underpinning national regional policy did, however, change when the case was primarily put in economic terms, i.e. mobilization of indigenous regional resources in support of the general attempt to improve the international competitiveness of Danish firms (Bogason, 1982; Gaardmand, 1988; Bogason and Jensen, 1991; Erhvervsministeriet, 1995; Regeringen, 2001; Knudsen, 2002). Direct subsidies to individual firms were the mainstay of central government regional policy from 1958 till 1990, and the administration of the grant schemes was firmly centralized and did not involve input from the regional level. The first decade saw a gradual introduction of an array of schemes targeting primarily individual firms (soft loans, investment grants) but also local authorities (soft loans for construction of industrial property). From 1967, support was restricted to designated problem areas, and since the beginning of the 1980s spatial coverage has been gradually reduced, partly because of pressure from the European Commission, and currently designated areas comprise only around 17 per cent of the total population (Direktoratet for

Egnsudvikling, 1980-87; Industri- og Handelsstyrelsen, 1988-91; Erhvervsfremmestyrelsen, 1992-96, 1999; Bogason, 1982; Gaardmand, 1988; Industriministeriet, 1990).

As can be seen from Figure 9.2, the dominant trend in central government expenditure on regional policy would appear to have been one of decline at least since the late 1970s, but until the mid-1980s accounting conventions artificially inflated the figures, and thus in expenditure terms the turning point must be located much later, i.e. around the year 1988 (Yuill *et al.*, 1992, Table 5.3). Figure 9.2 also shows that national-level regional subsidy schemes were supported by both sub-national and European means. While the involvement of local authorities was limited to co-funding certain infrastructure projects, the financial contribution from the European level was more sizeable. Some of the latter was simply counted as a general reimbursement of Danish government expenditure, but most of it was used to establish a soft-loan programme parallel to the existing national one.

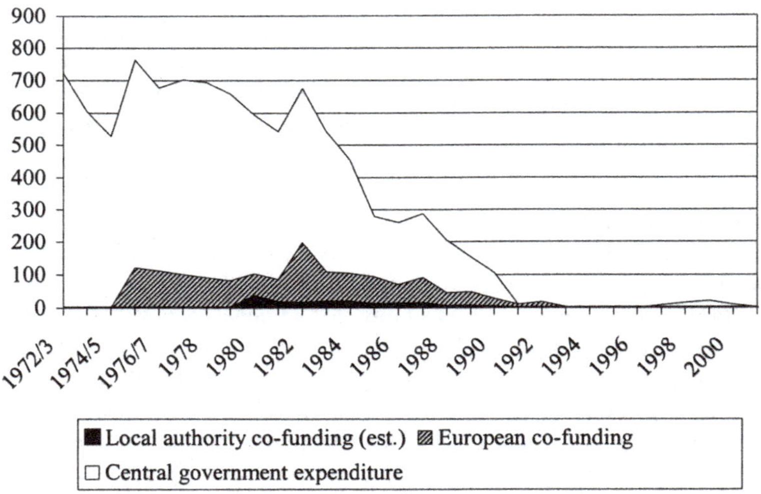

Figure 9.2 National policy programmes expenditure by source. Mill. DKK, 1995 prices (1981-88 figures are commitments, 1989-95 figures expenditure)

Source: Direktoratet for Egnsudvikling 1981-87, Industri- & Handelsstyrelsen 1988, Finansministeriet 1989-2001.

The circumstances leading to the termination of all regional subsidy schemes operated from the national level by the end of 1990 are in need of further inquiry (Halkier, 1998), but it is already clear that in addition to short-term factors like party-political manoeuvring in connection with the yearly budget negotiations in late 1989, underlying long-term causes must also have been present: from an economic perspective a significant decrease in the traditional polarization between core and periphery on a range of key indicators and the emergence of a much more complex regional historical 'mosaic' (Illeris, 1989; Huggins, 1996; Maskell, 1998), and from a political perspective a generally waning support for financial subsidies to individual firms as a policy instrument, and perhaps also the availability of alternative – European – sources of funding for regional development. The outcome was, however, that from 1991 onwards the role of central government in regional development was very different from what it used to be. The Danish Agency for Trade and Industry (DATI) continued to produce a national map of Assisted Areas, and its approval by the European Commission allowed central government to give financial support to individual firms in problem regions when providing matching funding in connection with Structural Fund programmes (Yuill *et al.*, 1999, pp. 203-5; Erhvervsfremmestyrelsen, 1996 and 1999) But the most important generic task of central government now was to ensure that disadvantaged regions also had access to business and technological services (Erhvervsministeriet, 1995). On the one hand the existing network of regionally based Technology Information Centres (TICs), sponsored by central government but co-funded by sub-national actors, entailed a deconcentrated delivery of national business services that did not give preferential treatment to particular localities. On the other hand, a flexible system of 'fire-fighting' operated from 1996 to 2002 in the form of the so-called Notification Pool which provided funding for new regional initiatives in for example temporary advisory services in localities threatened by major industrial closures (Arbejdsministeriet, 1997; Erhvervs- og Boligstyrelsen, 2003).

Table 9.2 National policies for regional development in Denmark: resources and levels of government

Input	*Authority*	*Finance*	*Information*	*Organization*
European	Increasing influence on designated areas and grant levels	Some co-funding from mid-1980s until early 1990s		
National	Redistribution latent since 1991 Consensus changing	Self-financing, from 1991 mainly potential	Statistical surveys maintained	DATI maintained Deconcentrated TIC network becomes central
Regional		Limited co-funding	Notification Pool project design	

On the basis of the above analysis it is clear that the nature and role of national-level regional programmes changed profoundly from the 1970s to the present. Firstly, the *raison d'être* of regional policy changed from addressing inter-regional inequalities to boosting the contribution of every region to national economic competitiveness. Secondly, national-level strategies shifted away from redistributive programmes of financial incentives to a deconcentrated form of industrial policy. And thirdly, the pattern of resource dependencies also changed, albeit in a perhaps less dramatic fashion. As illustrated by Table 9.2, summing up the changing input of resources from the three levels of government implicated in national programmes, it is of course immediately evident that the abolishing of traditional grant schemes in the early 1990s affected the situation profoundly. In the original set-up national policies were a largely self-contained entity, financed and administered by central government, and given the generally relatively low level of expenditure on national-level regional programmes compared to other European countries (Yuill *et al.*, 1992), it would be reasonable to assume that the continuation of national programmes cannot have been contingent on co-funding from other tiers of government, and that European regulations would have had a limited direct impact on its operation. With the introduction of the new approach central government abandoned its role as redistributor of private economic activity between the regions and, apart from a minor fire-fighting role in connection with major industrial closures, adopted a position in which its direct role with regard to regional development was limited to ensuring that national business development programmes were made available in every region, weak as well as strong ones. As the limited sub-national co-funding for the TICs is hardly a financial prerequisite but probably a token of sub-national political commitment, the extent to which nationally sponsored organizations depended on resources from other tiers of government in other words remained limited. In a comparative context the Danish case can be seen as an example of the broader Western European trend of shifting regional policy away from the national level, albeit the radical and sudden nature of change seems to be a feature not replicated elsewhere.

European Policies

Regional policy acquired a new dimension with the establishment of the European Regional Development Fund (ERDF), and although it is clear that the operation of the Structural Funds differs between the member states of the EU (Conzelmann, 1995; Heinelt, 1996; Bachtler and Taylor, 1997), the basic features of the development of its operation in Denmark do of course reflect the general direction in which these European programmes have moved, with the changes introduced by the 1988 reforms as a major watershed (Staeck, 1996; Wishlade, 1996).

From 1975 until 1988 regional policy on the European level was essentially a mechanism for redistribution between the member states, operating through a system of national quotas employed either as an outright reimbursement of expenditure on national policy programmes or as co-funding of major improvements of the regional and local infrastructure. In Denmark the Structural Funds came to play a significant role only from the mid-1980s, because in the early years most of the European funds for regional development had been spent on

Greenland (Erhvervsministeriet, 1995), and only after the Arctic dependency left the EU in 1985 did substantial sums become available for development projects in the continental parts of the kingdom. The Danish expenditure pattern was in line with that in other relatively prosperous member states, and only gradually did more innovative types of projects begin to emerge, for example more advanced forms of infrastructure such as sector-based industrial parks or comprehensive regionally-based development programmes such as NordTek in North Jutland (Direktoratet for Egnsudvikling, 1980-87). Prior to the 1988 reform regional actors were given the opportunity to indicate their preferences with regard to applications from their own area, but the final decision rested with the central government agency responsible also for national subsidy schemes (Direktoratet for Egnsudvikling, 1984). All in all this certainly suggests that the ERDF began its operation in Denmark as an extension to national policies rather than as a separate programme with a distinct identity.

The origins of the 1988 reform have been associated with European high politics (Hooghe, 1996; Hooghe and Keating, 1994), and in the following the development of the Structural Funds will therefore be treated as a change in the external environment to which Danish actors respond. The reform changed the functioning of the Structural Funds by introducing a multi-year programme-based approach to regional policy and adopting partnership between the Commission, national government and sub-national actors as a basic principle. Under the new rules Denmark was allocated two Objective 2 programmes, targeting areas of industrial decline in North Jutland and Storstrøm respectively, and one Objective 5b programme covering rural areas on a number of small and medium-sized islands, but also benefited from some of the spatially targeted Community Initiatives, notably Interreg and Pesca. In the second round of programming, starting in 1994, the designated areas were expanded significantly and came to cover 15.3 per cent of the Danish population while the budget allocation of European monies nearly doubled (Yuill *et al.*, 1992, p. 64; 1996, p. 78), and the level of expenditure on European regional programmes in Denmark ended up surpassing that of the then abandoned national programmes by a significant margin.[1] Also the profile of Structural Funds projects gradually changed: in the latest programming periods starting in 2000 support for so-called 'knowledge projects' – supporting capacity-building in firms with regard to for instance research or marketing – was planned at 32 per cent, while infrastructure projects and investment subsidies account for only 24 per cent and 12 per cent respectively of budgeted public expenditure, a trend that continued in subsequent European

1 Already in the period 1991-93, i.e. before the increase in funding from 1994 onwards, the average aggregate annual expenditure on European Objective 2 and 5b programmes was more than 50 per cent above the average level of expenditure on national regional policy in the years 1988-90 (calculated on the basis of Industri- og Handelsstyrelsen (1988) and Finansministeriet (1989-93)).

programmes in Denmark (Erhvervsministeriet, 1995; Halkier, 1997; Damborg *et al.*, 1999; Erhvervsfremmestyrelsen, 2000).

The introduction of the partnership principle has often been heralded as a measure that advanced the role of regional actors in the policy process (Hooghe and Keating, 1994; Bullmann, 1996; Keating and Loughlin, 1997), but as the role of a particular tier of government may well differ in the various phases of the policy process (Heinelt, 1996; Marks, 1996a), a more detailed analysis capable of distinguishing between planning and implementation is needed (Halkier, 1997; Damborg, 1998; Halkier, 2000). In the planning stages of Structural Funds programmes the role of central government is primarily concerned with negotiating area designations and the proposed development strategies with the Commission, ensuring that strategic priorities are in accordance with basic principles of national policy, especially the current preference for framework measures. The partnership principle is also evident in the way in which ERDF programmes are funded, with sizeable contributions from both central government and sub-national public bodies. Although the structure of co-funding varies between different types of projects, making national or regional/local co-funding a precondition for approval of Structural Funds programmes deliberately creates a mutual resource dependency between the three tiers of government involved. The lead in the actual programme formulation is to be found at the sub-national level with regional government organizing a process of consultation with local government and private sector 'social partners', developing new policy initiatives and producing the draft version of the development programme for the region. Also in the implementation phase the role of central government has gradually become a limited one: although central government provides matching funding for subsidies to individual firms and undertakes a formal appraisal of applications especially with regard to issues of legality, the crucial early and substantive stages of project evaluation in which the economic, technical and organizational prospects of an application are assessed are now firmly situated on the regional level in a process where regional government, the elected county councils and their administrative apparatus, plays a pivotal role.

Table 9.3 European policies for regional development in Denmark: resources and levels of government

Input	*Authority*	*Finance*	*Information*	*Organization*
European	Establish ground rules Increasing influence on objectives and strategies	Part-financing	European statistics	DG XVI
National	National procedures Negotiate with Commission Define strategic principles Decreasing role in approval of individual projects	Co-funding of subsidies to firms from 1988	National statistics	DATI
Regional	Increasingly since 1988: * strategic planning * processing of applications * recommendation of projects	Co-funding of infrastructure and framework measures	Regional statistics Knowledge of firms	Regional programme administrations

On the basis of the above analysis it can be concluded that the Structural Funds programmes in Denmark represent an interesting combination of different regional policy strategies within a new organizational framework. In terms of assumptions and strategies the European programmes clearly maintain the notion that some disadvantaged regions should be given preferential treatment at the expense of more well-off localities, but at the same time the operational strategies have come to focus more and more on improving the competitiveness of indigenous firms rather than merely redistributing economic activity to problem regions by means of investment subsidies. With regard to resource dependencies, the 1988 reforms of the Structural Funds which introduced the new partnership-based approach certainly made a major difference in the case of Denmark, as illustrated by Table 9.3. While the European Commission and central government still establish the basic spatial and financial delimitation of Structural Funds activities, substantive issues are primarily dealt with by sub-national institutions, although the higher tiers maintain a general role with regard to process management, legality and basic policy principles. Two conclusions can be drawn on the basis of this. Firstly, that the European measures never constituted a self-contained programme of spatial economic policy, and that both before and after the 1988 reform it has depended upon national and regional levels of government for access to a wide range of resources. Secondly, the internal division of labour between the national and regional levels now places Denmark among the most decentralized countries in the EU with regard to Structural Funds programming compared to those reported in other member states (see Heinelt, 1996; Bachtler and Taylor, 1997), with central government deciding to rely on sub-national actors for both political authority and financial, informational and organizational resources in key parts of the policy process. All in all the Danish approach to administration of the Structural Funds can perhaps best be described as having evolved towards a state of 'controlled decentralization' within a multi-level governance setting which delivers policies that increasingly resemble a decentralized form of industrial policy – but only in designated areas.

Regionally-based Policies

The rise of the 'bottom-up' approach to regional development in Western Europe is well-documented (Alden and Boland (eds), 1996; Halkier, Danson and Damborg (eds), 1998; Danson, Halkier and Cameron (eds), 2000), but apart from the basic feature – *development organizations and policies which only operate in one particular region* – regionally-based initiatives in economic development have been characterized by a high degree of diversity with regard to political sponsorship, development strategies, policy instruments and organizational patterns. The Danish case presents a profile that combines well-known elements in a distinct manner.

Also the field of sub-national development policies must be analysed in terms of 'before' and 'after', although in Denmark the boundary between the two is not as clear-cut as was the case with national and European regional policies. Bottom-up initiatives in economic development began with the setting up of public-private partnerships in the form of Development Committees in the 1930s and 1950s, aimed at attracting firms from outside to locate in the area by means of promotion and advice, but from the mid-1980s local and regional government gradually became more active in economic development (Bogason, 1982; Industriministeriet, 1987a; Erhvervsministeriet, 1995). The result was a conspicuous increase in the level of sub-national initiatives, and from the early 1990s all regional and the majority of local governments were engaged in activities aiming to stimulate indigenous economic activity, promote employment within their area, and secure a higher level of taxable income. The new emphasis on indigenous growth in the 1980s also involved a notable shift with regard to policy instruments: more or less specialized advisory services came to dominate – supplying information on for example markets, technology and general management issues – supplemented by provision of various forms of technological and organizational infrastructure such as incubator units, test facilities and collective marketing efforts (Damborg and Halkier, 1998; Erhvervsministeriet, 1995; Industriministeriet, 1987a). Reliable statistics can only been obtained from 1994 onwards, but the level of expenditure has been relatively stable with a yearly average of around 200 mill. DKK in the period 1994-99 which certainly establishes the regional level as a major player in spatial economic policy (AmtsrΔdsforeningen and Kommunernes Landsforening, 2000). The extent to which co-funding of Structural Funds projects is included in this grand total is unclear, but the availability of funds from the European level has undoubtedly in many ways played a catalytic role by prompting sub-regional actors to engage in economic development activities (Halkier and Damborg, 2000).

The role of central government as a regulator of regional and local development initiatives has evolved gradually. While it was always crystal clear what sub-national government was *not* allowed to do, namely grant financial subsidies to individual firms, what they actually *could* do remained unclear until 1992 when a new parliamentary act designated collective business services – i.e. framework measures targeting all or a group of firms within its area – as the field in which regional and local authorities could engage (Lov 383, 20 May 1992). The other central plank in central government regulation has been attempts to bring about a higher degree of co-ordination amongst actors on the sub-national level. In most of the regions bottom-up development activities have involved a large number of relatively small organizations since the beginning of the 1990s, including both regional and local government organizations, a host of quangos and a wide range of public-private partnerships (Damborg and Halkier, 1998; Halkier and Damborg, 2000; Halkier and Flockhart, 2002). This complex institutional pattern would seem to have been brought about by a number of factors – political preference for collective framework measures, the uncertain legal position, a need to maintain a business-like image and a high public profile – but it has nonetheless given rise to concerns about duplication and waste of public resources. Central government has launched several schemes aiming to induce sub-national actors to co-ordinate their activities, first through the production of joint Regional Development Plans, then through the setting up of so-called Business Nodes as permanent fora for discussion between development bodies in a particular geographical area, and most recently through a series of inter-regional growth partnerships which have established an ad-hoc framework for intensified collaboration between public and private actors as well as national and sub-national authorities (PLS Consult, 1997; Halkier and Flockhart, 2002; Regeringen, 2003). The attempts by central government to promote co-ordination have relied exclusively on voluntary organizational measures backed by limited financial incentives, and the long-term impact of these schemes remains to be seen.

Table 9.4 Regionally-based policies for regional development: resources and levels of government

Input	*Authority*	*Finance*	*Information*	*Organization*
European		Co-funding of some initiatives		
National	Regulation of policy instruments Since early 1990s encouragement of co-operation	Limited co-funding for co-operation		DATI
Regional	Since late 1980s: * institution building * strategic priorities	Since late 1980s a large aggregate divided between many actors	Increasing knowledge of firms	Since late 1980s many small actors * regional/local * quangos * partnerships

On the basis of the above analysis it is clear that although the underlying assumption has remained the same – public intervention is needed to promote economic development in particular localities – strategies have gradually come to focus primarily on attempts to improve the competitiveness of indigenous firms. Also in terms of input of resources from the three levels of government implicated in regionally-based programmes for economic development, it is noticeable that the situation has changed profoundly since the end of the 1980s. From playing at best a marginal role through place promotion, bottom-up development has become a growth industry in its own right with a large number of actors involved and important links to actors on the national and European level, as illustrated by Table 9.4. On the one hand central government regulation has established the legal framework, and when the use of financial subsidies to individual firms has been ruled out, it is hardly surprising that sub-national development activities have been dominated by provision of advisory services and organizational infrastructure which can be tailored to suit the needs of individual localities. On the other hand funding from the European Structural Funds has undoubtedly acted as a catalyst for the development of a burgeoning bottom-up economic development scene by enlarging the financial scope for regional and local action. The degree of dependency created by this would, however, seem to be moderate because the Danish Structural Funds programmes rely on the generation and development of projects by sub-national actors, and European co-funding could in most cases be substituted by regional government if they decided to use their political authority to increase taxation or redirect financial resources towards this area of public policy. All in all sub-national actors would in other words now seem to have the capacity to pursue their own priorities with regard to spatial economic policy within the regulatory framework established by the national and European tiers of government, but the consequences for individual regions of this freedom will clearly depend on their economic and institutional strengths and weaknesses, and thus the growth of bottom-up regional policy may potentially contribute to the maintenance or aggravation of inter-regional disparities. From a comparative perspective the Danish case appears to be very different from that found in countries like Germany, Spain and the UK where bottom-up strategies are much more diverse, targeting both indigenous firms and potential inward investors, and where large multi-functional development agencies, sometimes sponsored by central government, operate on the regional level (Halkier, Danson and Damborg, 1998). Instead Denmark belongs to a group of countries which includes the Netherlands and Austria where the focus is near-exclusively on indigenous growth and competitiveness pursued by a network of small single-function development bodies – in effect a form of decentralized industrial policy.

Political Dynamics and Organizational Strategies

Having identified the three main developments in Danish regional policy as the withdrawal of central government from implementation, the greatly enlarged role of the European Structural Funds, and the widespread growth of sub-national initiatives in economic development, it is evident that the ways and means of spatial economic policy have changed profoundly at all levels of government in a short span of years. This may of course just be a coincidence, but it could also suggest that these developments have somehow been related, and it will therefore also be necessary to consider the political dynamics of other parts of the process and the inter-organizational strategies of the actors involved. However, while the rise to prominence of the Structural Funds in general and the partnership-based 1988 reforms in particular were decided on the European level, the implications of these changes in the external environment have still depended upon the way in which they were mediated through the interaction with national and sub-national actors, and in the following they will therefore be considered in the discussion of organizational strategies on the national and sub-national levels.

Starting in a true top-down fashion on the national level, the sudden abandonment of traditional central government programmes of regional policy was of course crucial in increasing the relative importance of regionally-based actors in spatial economic policy. Apparently the decision had very little to do with long-term strategic thinking or indeed Europeanization of regional policy: a deal struck by the then centre-right government with the far-right Progress Party during negotiations about the state budget for 1990 involved considerable cutbacks in various programmes of industrial support, and on the back of this the 1990 Business Promotion Act instigated a major restructuring of the whole policy area that did not include mainstream regional grants as a mandatory activity for central government (*Folketingstidende F* 1989-90 col. 5520-37, 10100-117, 10752-76). These circumstances suggest – not particularly surprising – that financial constraints and liberal ideology were important in bringing about change, but as both these phenomena to a greater or lesser extent had been around for most of the 1980s, other factors must be examined, too, especially because the new legislation had been in preparation for some time before the political deal about the 1990 budget was struck (*Børsen*, 20 December 1989; Bjørn Westh and Torben Nørkjær Hansen, personal interviews), suggesting the importance of underlying long-term causes.

Firstly, it is important to note that the administrative position of regional policy within central government had already been downgraded in 1988 as part of a major reorganization of central government's Department of Trade and Industry which incorporated the former Regional Development Directorate as a unit within DATI alongside other forms of business support (Direktoratet for Egnsudvikling, 1987, p. II). This reflected partly administrative considerations (Industriministeriet, 1987b; Ib Frederiksen and Torben Nørkjær Andersen, personal interviews), and partly the gradual blurring of the boundaries between the hitherto separate domains of regional policy and industrial policy in the 1980s where the increased emphasis on selectivity with regard to eligible sectors and types of projects took regional programmes closer to industrial intervention. Secondly, as we have seen new preferences with regard to policy instruments started to emerge from the mid-1980s, giving priority to framework measures over direct financial subsidies, and as the traditional regional schemes operated by means of grants, the case for maintaining these programmes was further weakened. And finally, the political case for maintaining a policy of spatial redistribution had been considerably weakened because on a range of key indicators the economic differences between the Danish regions had decreased significantly (Illeris, 1994; Industriministeriet, 1985). It is in other words evident that especially since the middle of the 1980s a number of developments on the national level gradually undermined the position of traditional regional policy schemes, and it is in this context that the impact of developments on the European level must be seen. The 1988 reform significantly enlarged the funding available in Denmark, and especially in the peripheral regions previously supported by central government programmes this is likely to have made the sudden death of the national policies less politically contentious.

All in all it can be concluded that the demise of traditional regional policies in Denmark is likely to have been caused by a combination of internal and external factors. On the one hand Denmark was the only member state in which the vastly increased role of the Structural Funds was accompanied by an outright discontinuation of all central government programmes for regional development, and this in itself indicates that internal, national factors must have been involved. On the other hand the 1980s had indeed witnessed a gradual process of transformation that pointed towards a downgrading of traditional grant-based regional subsidies, but the fact that less than 18 months passed between the 1988 revision of the Danish Regional Development Act and the 'fatal' budget agreement for 1990 strongly suggests that the emerging new consensus on ways and means in regional and industrial policy must have been pushed to the fore by a 'sudden impetus' from outside. On the basis of the above analysis, this would appear to have been a combination of a flourish of ideological liberalism cutting back funding for traditional business support programmes and the vastly increased financial opportunities of the Structural Funds now capable of providing a political 'cushion' for weaker regions.

Turning to the increased direct involvement of sub-national actors in economic development initiatives, this has been shown to stem partly from the rapid growth of regionally-based initiatives and partly from a new and prominent role in European policy programmes. With regard to the former, the recurring conflicts in the 1980s about what regional and local government were allowed to do with regard to economic development clearly demonstrates that the spread of bottom-up policies was very much driven by sub-national actors (Bogason and Jensen, 1991), but the timing also suggests that national and European developments will have played a role in making regional and local actors venture into this new area of activity. Firstly, in the 1980s a significant impetus behind the markedly increased level of activity would seem to be the decentralized administration of labour market policies in a period of high levels of unemployment and the dominance of a liberal discourse of economic management (Industriministeriet, 1987a; Jørgensen and Lind, 1988). Secondly, in the 1990s the termination of the regional support schemes of central government will have left a policy void in the peripheral regions that could be at least partly filled by sub-national actors. Thirdly, the availability of new European sources of finance will have facilitated bottom-up initiatives, both directly via decentralized partnership arrangements favoured by central government in Denmark, but probably also indirectly through a 'domino effect' where more wealthy localities outside the areas designated for Structural Funds support introduced economic development initiatives in order to avoid losing out in the inter-regional competition.

All in all the increased policy-making capacity of regional actors within a multi-level governance setting was not only of their own making, but also clearly aided by European developments and strategies on the national level. In Denmark central government has been a major force for decentralization with regard to spatial economic policy, albeit perhaps mainly as a side-effect in the process of pursuing other goals.

Conclusions and Perspectives

Having analysed the changing nature of spatial economic policy in Denmark, two substantial conclusions have been reached.

Firstly, it has been demonstrated that changes within the area of regional policy taking place in a short span of years around 1990 have not only led to an increased involvement of regional and other sub-national actors, but also vastly enhanced the capacity of these actors to pursue their own preferences with regard to spatial economic policy within a system of multi-level governance. Bottom-up activities still depend on external resources, primarily central government regulation and to some extent funding from European programmes, but given the relatively broad nature of both the former and the latter, targeting the needs of the individual locality should certainly be possible. Although the position of the economically weaker regions would still seem to be more precarious in terms of external financial dependencies, even their situation contrasts sharply with the policy regime dominant from the 1960s and throughout the 1980s in which centralized national schemes were the only form of spatial economic policy.

Secondly, the transition to a new policy regime of a less centralized nature has come about as a result of the interaction of the changing strategies of actors on three levels of government, both in terms of the nature of the policies implemented and with regard to the inter-organizational strategies pursued. Although sub-national actors have pushed hard to carve out a role for themselves in economic development and the presence of the Structural Funds can be seen as enabling, and in some cases catalytic, the intervention of national actors is clearly also required in order to account for the dramatic changes in spatial economic policy and the decentralized nature of the new institutional set-up surrounding the new policy paradigm. The 'Europe of the Regions' scenario – where national governments are being 'sandwiched' by concerted pressures from the European and sub-national levels – is in other words at best a very incomplete perspective on the process that resulted in a distinctly decentralized approach to regional policy in Denmark. Instead the analysis in this chapter would seem to lend support to the claim of Marks *et al.* (1996) that central government cannot *a priori* be assumed to pursue centralizing organizational strategies because alternative strategies involving for example decentralization may be even more attractive. Danish regional policy would appear to offer an excellent example of this, with responsibility for planning and implementation being decentralized and Europeanized at the same time in a process in which central government even sometimes took the lead, and thus the last decades would seem to be ones in which the various actors gradually assume more clearly-defined roles within a system of multi-level governance. In spite of this it is, however, uncertain whether developments such as these have substantially reinforced the intermediate tier of government within the Danish political system. At the time of writing (May 2003) the future of regional government is subject to intense political and administrative scrutiny under the auspices of the Danish Commission on Administrative Structure (*Strukturkommissionen*), established by central government to review the pros and cons of the current three-tier system. Regional policy may have been decentralized, but until now this would not seem to have created a 'Denmark of the Regions' where the position of the intermediate tier over government has become impregnable.

Bibliography

Albrechts, L. and Swyngedouw, E. (1989), 'The Challenges for Regional Policy under a Flexible Regime of Accumulation', in L. Albrechts *et al.* (eds), *Regional Policy at the Crossroads – European Perspectives*, Jessica Kingsley, London, pp. 67-89.

Alden, J. and Boland, P. (eds) (1996), *Regional Development Strategies – A European Perspective*, Jessica Kingsley, London.

Amtsrådsforeningen and Kommunernes Landsforening (2000), *Regional erhvervspolitik – en fællespjece fra ARF og KL om visioner og mål i den regionale erhvervspolitik*, ARF/KL, København.

Andersen, N. Å. and Kjær, P. (1996), 'Institutional Construction and Change: An Analytical Strategy of Institutional History', *COS-rapport*, 96/5.

Anderson, J. J. (1990), 'Skeptical Reflections on a Europe of the Regions: Britain, Germany and the ERDF', *Journal of Public Policy*, Vol. 10, pp. 417-47.

Arbejdsministeriet (1997), *Bekendtgørelse om en varslingspulje*, 72, 28 January 1997.

Bachtler, J. (1997), 'New Dimensions of Regional Policy in Western Europe', in M. Keating and J. Loughlin (eds), *The Political Economy of Regionalism*, Frank Cass, London, pp. 77-89.

Bachtler, J. and Taylor, S. (1997), 'EU Regional Development Strategies: Comparisons and Contrasts Among Objective 2 Programmes', in J. Bachtler and I. Turok (eds), *The Coherence of EU Regional Policy. Contrasting Perspectives on the Structural Funds*, Jessica Kingsley, London, pp. 219-45.

Bogason, P. (1982), 'Denmark: The Regional Development Council', in Douglas Yuill (ed.), *Regional Development Agencies in Europe*, Gower, Farnborough, pp. 107-28.

Bogason, P. and Jensen, L. (1991), 'Statens ansvar for regional udvikling i Danmark', *NordREFO*, 1991/3, pp. 51-82.

Borras Alomar, S. *et al.* (1994), 'Towards a "Europe of the Regions"? Visions and Reality from a Critical Perspective', *Regional Politics and Policy*, Vol. 4, pp 1-27.

Bullmann, U. (1996), 'The Politics of the Third Level', *Regional & Federal Studies*, Vol. 6, pp. 3-19.

Cameron, G. and Danson, M. (2000), 'Partnership and Networking in Scotland', in M. Danson, H. Halkier and G. Cameron (eds), *Governance, Institutional Change and Regional Development*, Ashgate, Aldershot, pp. 11-36.

Conzelmann, T. (1995), 'Networking and the Politics of EU Regional Policy: Lessons from North Rhine-Westphalia, Nord-Pas de Calais and North West England', *Regional & Federal Studies*, Vol. 5, pp. 134-72.

Damborg, C. (1998), 'The North Jutland Objective 2 Programme: Coordination and Evaluation', *IQ-NET Occasional Paper*, No. 2.

Damborg, C. and Halkier, H. (1998), 'Regional Development Agencies in Denmark – Towards a Danish Approach to Bottom-up Regional Policy', in H. Halkier, M. Danson and C. Damborg (eds), *Regional Development Agencies in Europe*, Jessica Kingsley, London, pp. 80-99.

Damborg, C., Nielsen, D. Ø. and Halkier, H. (1999), 'The North Jutland Objective 2 Programme: The Final Cut?', *IQ-NET Occasional Paper*, No. 3.

Danson, M., Halkier, H. and Cameron, G. (eds) (2000), *Governance, Institutional Change and Regional Development*, Ashgate, Aldershot.

Direktoratet for Egnsudvikling (1980-87), *Orientering og årsberetninger, 1980-87*, Direktoratet for Egnsudvikling, Silkeborg.

Erhvervs- og Boligstyrelsen (2003) *Regionale tilbud*, http://www.ebst.dk.

Erhvervsfremmestyrelsen (1992-96), *Årsberetning, 1992-96*, Erhvervsfremmestyrelsen, København.

Erhvervsfremmestyrelsen (1996), *Rapport om afgrænsning af støtteberettigede områder*, Erhvervsfremmestyrelsen, Silkeborg.

Erhvervsfremmestyrelsen (1999), *Notificering af områder berettiget til statsstøtte med regionalt sigte 2000-2006*, Erhvervsfremmestyrelsen 29 March 1999, Silkeborg.

Erhvervsfremmestyrelsen (2000), *Danmarks Mål 2-program 2000-2006*, Erhvervsfremmestyrelsen, Silkeborg.

Erhvervsministeriet (1995), *Regionalpolitisk Redegørelse 1995*, Erhvervsministeriet, København.

Finansministeriet (1988-01), *Statsregnskabet*, Finansministeriet, København.

Gaardmand, A. (1988), 'Jobbet til manden eller manden til jobbet? Om dansk regionalpolitik 1945-85', in NordREFO (ed.), *Om regionalpolitikken som politikområde*, NordREFO, Helsinki, pp. 67-108.

Halkier, H. (1997), 'The North Jutland Objective 2 Programme: Institutions and Implementation', *IQ-NET Occasional Paper*, No. 1.

Halkier, H. (1998), 'Danish Regions and the Europeanization of Regional Policy', *European Studies Series of Occasional Papers, European Research Unit, Aalborg University*, No. 27.

Halkier, H. (2000), 'Regional Policy – An Inter-organisational Approach', *Regional & Industrial Policy Research Paper Series, EPRC, University of Strathclyde*, No. 37.

Halkier, H. (2003), 'Discourse, Institutions and Policy Change – The Strange Case of Thatcherism and Regional Policy in Scotland', *Spirit Discussion Papers*, No. 23.

Halkier, H. and Damborg, C. (2000), 'Development Bodies, Networking and Business Promotion – The Case of North Jutland, Denmark', in M. Danson, H. Halkier and G. Cameron (eds), *Governance, Institutional Change and Regional Development*, Ashgate, Aldershot, pp. 92-114.

Halkier, H., Danson, M. and Damborg, C. (1998), 'Regional Development Agencies in the New Europe – Patterns, Issues and Prospects', in H. Halkier, M. Danson and C. Damborg (eds), *Regional Development Agencies in Europe*, Jessica Kingsley, London, pp. 343-57.

Halkier, H., Danson, M. and Damborg, C. (eds) (1998), *Regional Development Agencies in Europe*, Jessica Kingsley, London.

Halkier, H. and Flockhart, J. E. (2002), 'The Danish Cases – Bottom-up Initiatives between Regional and National Environments', in A. Östhol and B. Svensson (eds), *Partnership Responses – Regional Governance in the Nordic States*, Nordregio, Stockholm, pp. 41-84.

Hanf, K. and O'Toole, L. J. jr (1992), 'Revisiting Old Friends: Networks, Implementation Structures and the Management of Inter-organizational Relations', *European Journal of Political Research*, Vol. 21, pp. 163-80.

Heinelt, H. (1996), 'Conclusions', in H. Heinelt and R. Smith (eds), *Policy Networks and European Structural Funds*, Avebury, Aldershot, pp. 294-321.

Heinelt, H. and Smith, R. (1996), 'Introduction', in H. Heinelt and R. Smith (eds), *Policy Networks and European Structural Funds*, Avebury, Aldershot, pp. 1-8

Hood, C. (1983), *The Tools of Government*, Macmillan, London.

Hooghe, L. (1996), 'Building a Europe with the Regions: The Changing Role of the European Commission', in L. Hooghe (ed.), *Cohesion Policy and European Integration. Building Multi-level Governance*, Oxford UP, Oxford, pp. 89-126.

Hooghe, L. and Keating, M. (1994), 'The Politics of European Union Regional Policy', *Journal of European Public Policy*, Vol. 1, pp. 369-92.

Huggins, R. (1996), 'Technology Policy, Networks and Small Firms in Denmark', *Regional Studies*, Vol. 30, pp. 523-26.

Illeris, S. (1989), 'Egnsudvikling i fremtiden', *AKF Nyt*, Vol. 1989, pp. 7-14.

Illeris, S. (1994), *Essays on Regional Development in Europe*, Department of Geography and International Development Studies, Roskilde.

Industri- og Handelsstyrelsen (1988-91), *Årsberetninger 1988-91*, Industri- og Handelsstyrelsen, København.

Industriministeriet (1985), 'Industriens lokalisering', *Arbejdsnotat*, No. 2

Industriministeriet (1987a), 'Lokal erhvervspolitik – debatoplæg om forholdet mellem statslige og lokale initiativer', *Arbejdsnotat*, No. 7.

Industriministeriet (1987b), 'Industriministeriets fremtidige struktur: Rapport fra styregruppen for analyse- og strukturprojektet', *Arbejdsnotat*, No. 8.

Industriministeriet (1990), *Regional erhvervspolitik i Danmark – Rapport afgivet af arbejdsgruppen vedrørende regionalpolitik*, Industriministeriet, København.

Jordan, G. and Schubert. K. (1992), 'A Preliminary Ordering of Policy Network Labels', *European Journal of Political Research*, Vol. 21, pp. 7-27.

Jørgensen, H. and Lind, J. (1987), 'Decentralized Welfare Capitalism: The Case of Employment and Industrial Policies', *Acta Sociologica*, Vol. 30, pp. 313-37.

Keating, M. (1997), 'The Political Economy of Regionalism', in M. Keating and J. Loughlin (eds), *The Political Economy of Regionalism*, Frank Cass, London, pp. 17-40.

Keating, M. and Loughlin, J. (1997), 'Introduction', in M. Keating and J. Loughlin (eds.), *The Political Economy of Regionalism*, Frank Cass, London, pp. 1-13.

Knudsen, J. P. (2002), 'Interview with Bendt Bendtsen', *Journal of Nordregio*, Vol. 2, pp. 13-15.

Lov om kommuners og amtskommuners deltagelse i erhvervsudviklingsaktiviteter, 1991-92, 383, 20 May 1992.

Marks, G. (1996a), 'Exploring and Explaining Variation in EU Cohesion Policy', in L. Hooghe (ed.), *Cohesion Policy and European Integration. Building Multi-level Governance*, Oxford UP, Oxford, pp. 388-422.

Marks, G. (1996b), 'An Actor-Centred Approach to Multi-Level Governance', *Regional & Federal Studies*, Vol. 6, pp. 20-38.

Marks, G., Hooghe, L. and Blank, K. (1996), 'European Integration from the 1980s: State-Centric v. Multi-level Governance', *Journal of Common Market Studies*, Vol. 34, pp. 341-78.

Martin, R. and Townroe, P. (1992), 'Changing Trends and Pressures in Regional Development', in P. Townroe and R. Martin (eds), *Regional Development in the 1990s – The British Isles in Transition*, Jessica Kingsley, London, pp. 13-24.

Maskell, P. (1998), 'Learning in the Village Economy of Denmark: The Role of Institutions and Policy in Sustaining Competitiveness', in H.-J. Braczyk *et al.* (eds), *Regional Innovation Systems*, UCL Press, London, pp. 190-213.

PLS Consult (1997), *Evaluering af regionale erhvervsudviklingsprogrammer – Hovedrapport*, Erhvervsfremmestyrelsen, København.

Regeringen (2001), *Regional erhvervspolitisk redegørelse .reg21*, Erhvervsministeriet, København.

Regeringen (2003), *Den regionale vækststrategi*, Økonomi- og Erhvervsministeriet, København.

Rhodes, R. A. W. (1988), *Beyond Westminster and Whitehall – The Sub-central Governments of Britain*, Unwin Hyman, London.

Rhodes, R. A. W. and Marsh, D. (1992), 'New Directions in the Study of Policy Networks', *European Journal of Political Research*, Vol. 21, pp. 181-95.

Staeck, N. (1996), 'The European Structural Funds – Their History and Impact', in H. Heinelt and R. Smith (eds), *Policy Networks and European Structural Funds*, Avebury, Aldershot, pp. 46-73.

Stöhr, W. (1989), 'Regional Policy at the Crossroads: An Overview', in L. Albrechts *et al.* (eds), *Regional Policy at the Crossroads – European Perspectives*, Jessica Kingsley, London, pp. 191-97.

Tömmel, I. (1998), 'Transformation of Governance: The European Commission's Strategy for Creating a "Europe of the Regions"', *Regional & Federal Studies*, Vol. 8, pp. 52-80.

Waarden, F. van (1992), 'Dimensions and Types of Policy Networks', *European Journal of Political Research*, Vol. 21, pp. 29-52.

Windhoff-Héritier, A. (1987), *Policy-Analyse – Eine Einführung*, Campus, Frankfurt.

Wishlade, F. (1996), 'EU Cohesion Policy: Facts, Figures and Issues', in L. Hooghe (ed.), *Cohesion Policy and European Integration. Building Multi-level Governance*, Oxford UP, Oxford, pp. 27-58.

Yuill, D. *et al.* (1981ff), *European Regional Incentives, 1981-*, Bowker-Saur, London.

Östhol, A., Svensson, B. and Halkier, H. (2002), 'Analytical Framework', in A. Östhol and B. Svensson (eds), *Partnership Responses – Regional Governance in the Nordic States*, Nordregio, Stockholm, pp. 23-39.

Interviews

Bjprn Westh, former MP for the Social Democrats and industrial policy spokesperson, 30 June 1998.

Ib Frederiksen, formerly Chief Executive of the Regional Development Directorate, 16 June 1998.

Torben Nørkjær Hansen, Head of Department, DATI, 30 June 1998.

Chapter 10

Europeanization and Beyond Regional Development through Partnership in Norway and Denmark

Henrik Halkier and Arild Gjertsen

Regional policy is as prone to 'fashions' as any other policy area, and in recent years the notion of 'partnership' has often been used to describe how regional development is being promoted by public actors, or as a prescription for how it ought to be promoted (Östhol and Svensson, 2002a, pp. 15ff). But like most positive buzzwords, partnership has ended up being used in so many different contexts that, rather than highlighting similarities, its omnipresence threatens to obscure significant differences. Since 1988 the European Structural Funds have integrated inter-tier and cross-sectoral partnership as its preferred mode of operation, and while various forms of inter-tier co-ordination have long been practiced in (semi-) federal countries like Austria, Spain and Germany (Yuill *et al.*, 1999, pp. 43-54), recently also more centralized European countries such as England and Sweden have tried to promote co-ordination of regional development efforts through partnership arrangements as part of major national initiatives (Benneworth, 2001; Östhol and Svensson, 2002b). Given the overarching presence of the European Structural Funds for more than a decade, it is of course tempting to assume that 'partnership' in regional policy throughout most of Western Europe will essentially have been modelled along the same EU lines so that although the concept of partnership in itself is perhaps not completely clear, then at least we know that in practice the Structural Funds have provided the underlying model. Comparative studies have, however, demonstrated that even within the presumably unified policy system that is the Structural Funds, member states administer European programmes in rather different ways – more or less centralized and with a variety of roles assigned to non-government 'partners' (Hooghe (ed.), 1996; Heinelt and Smith (eds), 1996) – and that differences between regional development partnerships could hence be potentially even more pronounced in forms of regional policy that are not formally part of such a formalized international network of multi-level governance: many bottom-up initiatives preceded the advent of the Structural Funds and some of the major national initiatives were conceived to not only address regional development issues but also to focus on improving co-ordination between segmented policy sectors. In other words it can be assumed that a variety of forces – regional, national and European – must have influenced the way in which individual development partnerships function, and thus it becomes an important task to develop a conceptual framework that is able to distinguish between different forms of partnership and employ this in empirical studies of the organizational framework for regional policy at the beginning of the 21st century.

The aim of this chapter is to investigate the changing nature of partnership in regional policy in two Nordic countries, Norway and Denmark, in order to establish – through two parallel sets of regional case studies – the extent to which a European model has been transferred, adopted or circumvented. The text starts out by outlining an analytical framework for the study of regional development partnerships and briefly charting the role of partnership in changing paradigms in regional policy in Western Europe. Then the case of the Norwegian Regional Development Plans is analysed, focusing on inclusiveness, accountability and coherence in the interplay between key partners and the wider political environment. Following this, a parallel case study of Denmark is presented in order to highlight the importance of both national and regional influences on the ways in which regional development partnerships function, and finally these two cases are placed in a broader context, focusing on the relationship between public and private actors and, not least, the role of European, national and regional tiers of government in the process.

The chapter is based on work undertaken in connection with a study of partnership, regional policy and regional governance in the Nordic countries sponsored by *Nordregio*. In each of the four countries – Norway, Denmark, Sweden and Finland – in-depth studies were carried out in three regions exhibiting different combinations of strengths and weaknesses with regard to public and private resources conducive to regional development, and an extensive series of qualitative interviews was carried out with key actors in the regions. In combination with documentary sources and existing writings on partnership, regional policy and regional governance, this made it possible to identify differences and similarities between the ways in which the notion of partnership has become integrated in this policy area in the four Nordic countries, and identify some of the underlying actors shaping these patterns (see Östhol and Svensson (eds), 2002).

Partnership in Regional Policy – An Analytical Framework

In the context of public policy the term partnership alludes to independent actors working together in pursuance of particular goals, and the definition proposed by Nelson and Zadek captures this when they describe partnerships as made up of people and organizations from some combination of public, business and civil constituencies who engage in voluntary, mutually beneficial, innovative relationships to address common societal aims through combining their resources and competencies (Östhol, Svensson and Halkier, 2002, p. 24). Defined like this, partnership is in other words an example of a network-type mode of social co-ordination in which formally independent actors, on the basis of mutual resource dependencies, co-operate on a medium- to long-term basis (Thorelli, 1986; Powell, 1990; Halkier, 2000). Partnerships may be instituted for a variety of purposes, ranging from short-term collaboration around individual projects, via involvement in individual policy-making or -implementing bodies, to long-term collaboration which attempts to develop and implement an overall strategic approach to an entire area of public policy (Östhol, Svensson and Halkier, 2002, pp. 24f), and it is the latter, the strategic partnerships, that are the main object of study in this chapter.

Partnerships are in other words a particular form of policy network that cuts across traditional political and social lines of division by involving several tiers of government, different policy sectors, and in many cases actors not just from the public but also from the private sector. Clearly the scope for variation is considerable, and even the particular form of strategic partnership which is the organizing principle at the heart of the Structural Funds has been defined in an ambiguous way from the European level. Originally it had been stipulated that 'all stages of the planning and implementation process should involve partnership between the relevant national, regional and local authorities and the Commission' (Wishlade, 1996, p. 33), but on the basis of two rounds of Structural Funds programming the European Commission insisted that this was not merely 'an open invitation to non-governmental actors to become part of the policy networks revolving around EU policy' (Östhol and Svensson, 2002a, pp. 15f) where the 'relevance' of particular actors was a matter of national government discretion. Instead the regulations for the current programming period specify that partnerships should be broadened and highlight the need to include sub-national and non-government actors, and in doing so pay particular attention to issues concerning 'equal opportunities for men and women as well as sustainable development' (EU Commission, 1999, p. 17).

Partnership is in other words not only a variable but also a contested organizational form in relation to the governance of regional policy, and therefore it is necessary to develop an analytical framework capable of distinguishing between different forms that such arrangements may take. The literature on policy networks and inter-organizational relations is vast and growing (Halkier, 2000), and hence there is no shortage of conceptual frameworks which could be chosen as a starting point. From the perspective of this chapter three *dimensions* of partnership are of particular importance (Östhol, Svensson and Halkier, 2002, pp. 27f):

- The *inclusiveness* of partnerships, i.e. who participates and why, can be established by looking at the distribution of roles within the network and how new actors can obtain access. The general expectation here would be that more actors, private as well as public, will become involved when regional policy is no longer a form of top-down government intervention but has instead become embedded in new networks of governance;

- *Accountability* issues are often associated with the introduction of new forms of governance: while government-type political steering had the electoral process as a core means through which decisions maintain legitimacy, once decisions are transferred to semi-autonomous networks other, more functional, forms of legitimacy are likely to move to the fore;
- *Coherence* refers to the ability of a partnership to gain support for a common outlook on regional development policies and mobilize resources necessary for implementation. Setting up partnership committees and organizations is in a sense the easy part of the operation, but these networks may range from being purely symbolic gestures to becoming dynamic drivers of change within the region.

Moreover, within the *policy-making process* these dimensions of partnership are likely to influence each other, and it is therefore possible to put forward two sets of hypothetical ideal types with which the empirical findings can be compared.

Table 10.1 Institutional preconditions and the strategic orientation of regional development partnerships

		Primary resource mobilization	
		External	*Internal*
Initiative	*External*	Induced	Enforced
	Internal	Extractive	Generative

On the one hand the *strategic orientation* of a regional development partnership is likely to be influenced by the institutional preconditions under which it functions, and this in turn will have a bearing on what partners will be involved, the legitimacy of the activities, and the degree of strategic coherence. Within this field of public policy the region as a spatial entity is of course crucial, and thus distinguishing between extra- and intra-regional factors will be important, both with regard to the *agenda-setting initiation* of partnership and the focus for *mobilizing resources* for development projects. As summarized by Table 10.1, a cross-tabulation of the spatial characteristics of the origins of partnership and its resource mobilization produces four different strategic orientations of regional development partnerships, examples of which are immediately recognizable within regional policy. While partnerships within the Structural Funds could be said to be induced by making it a precondition for European co-funding, examples of enforced partnership would include for example central government attempts to increase co-ordination of development efforts within a region. Similarly, concerted efforts of regional actors to attract for example foreign inward investment would belong in the extractive category, while pooling of regional resources in order to stimulate for example innovation within indigenous firms would come under the generative heading. Each set of institutional preconditions would appear to suggest that different sets of actors will be central within the partnership, and that they will be subject to varying forms of accountability arrangements and resource dependencies: the rationales of external actors are likely to be different from those of actors within the region, in terms of accountability the constituencies of external actors in terms of legitimacy will often be out of reach for regional actors, and while external resources will mostly have strings attached in the form of strategic implications, the possibility of mobilizing resources internally may be fairly limited in peripheral regions.

On the other hand the eventual *policy impact* of partnership arrangements would appear to differ along two lines, namely the degree to which *strategic coherence* is achieved in terms of aims and methods, and the extent to which strategies have been backed up by *resources* of the actors involved, and by cross-tabulating variables relating to actor strategies and resources, we arrive at a typology of the impact of partnerships on policy implementation which has been summarized in Table 10.2 (Östhol, Svensson and Halkier, 2002, inspired by Mariussen *et al.*, 2000). The *ritualistic* partnership refers to a situation in which the actors involved have neither a common strategic framework nor the ability or willingness to commit substantial resources to the partnership process, and thus the output of the process may simply be to enhance the image of the region or to comply with requirements imposed from outside the region.

Table 10.2 Policy impacts of regional development partnerships

		Resource available	
		Small	*Large*
Strategic coherence	*Weak*	Ritualistic	Composite
	Strong	Visionary	Synergetic

The *visionary* partnership denotes a situation where actors are able to reach a common perception of challenges, possibilities and solutions in the regional development field but commands relatively few resources through which its strategies can be implemented. The *composite* partnership refers to a situation with an extensive co-operative arrangement and relatively large resources at hand, but where the partnership remains a 'catalogue' of unconnected projects and efforts due to a fragmented perception of goals and strategies, and thus again the immediate impact of such partnerships on regional development activities would appear to be limited. The *synergetic* partnership is used to denote an outcome where large resources are available to the partnership and a high degree of strategic coherence has been achieved by the partners involved. This situation is clearly the one which would appear to involve the greatest potential for the partnership to make a difference in terms of making it possible for actors to jointly implement, possibly innovative policies within the framework of a regionally defined development policy.

On the basis of the three partnership dimensions and the two sets of ideal types regarding the functioning of partnership in the context of regional policy, we can now turn to the empirical analysis of the cases of first Norway and then Denmark.

Partnership in Regional Policy – The Case of Norway

On a general level, it could be argued that Norwegian regional policies have oscillated between a Danish ideal – the idea of the regional level as the important pro-active development agent – and a Swedish ideal where regional development is primarily the responsibility of state-level authorities – implemented by the regional level (Mariussen *et al.*, 2000, p. 13). At the end of the 1980s a new source of inspiration for approaching the question of regional development emerged – the European Union – where the 'partnership-principle' was put in focus. In a White Paper (Kommunal- og arbeidsdepartementet, 1996-97), the challenge for regional policies was not primarily connected to the redistributional aspect of such policies – in other words evening out differences between regions. Rather, the main development challenge was stated as being *regional growth*, hence the focus on entrepreneurship as the driving force in regional development. Consequently, the concept of partnerships was introduced, and tied in with the establishment of regional development programmes (RDPs). A main target for these programmes is to co-ordinate the use of means administered by various development agents at this level, and to make development plans at the county-level *operative*. These programmes will subsequently be the focus for the discussion of partnerships in the Norwegian context.[1]

Three regions have been selected for analysis:

- *Aust-Agder* has had previous experiences with attempts to co-ordinate regional development activities since the region was part of a governmental pilot project with greater regional autonomy. The project was however not continued, which led to a deterioration of relations among the involved actors at the regional level. The RDP process may enable regional actors to re-establish some of these relations;
- *Vestfold* is a region located in the central south-east part of Norway relatively close to Oslo. As such, the region is characterized by the opposite challenges to most other Norwegian regions; the main problems seem to be related to a population influx. As a consequence the available public resources in terms of regional policy are essentially non-existent. Nevertheless, the Vestfold region is engaged in the RDP process, and focuses on the building of partnership;
- *Troms* in Northern Norway is a region that is characterized by relatively high employment in traditional primary industries compared to the national average. Employment in the public sector is also relatively high. The relative share of

1 For details of the three Norwegian case studies, see Gjertsen, 2002.

> the population that resides in peripheral and rural areas is large compared to the national average. Seen from the point of view of regional development, Troms is equipped with a wider range of means and tools compared to the other two cases.

Looking at partnership *inclusiveness*, the range of partners within the context of the RDPs varies between the three regions. In this respect, the *Troms* region stands out as the most inclusive; *Vestfold* has the narrowest range of partners. However, it is necessary to make a distinction between the *formal* partnership, as it appears in documents and plans, and the *actual* partnership in terms of negotiations, meetings and share of the total partnership budget. Looking at the nucleus of partners, the difference between the three regions is evened out. Common to all three regions is the relative importance of the County Council, the SND, the County Governor's agricultural department and, to a lesser extent, the regional labour market authorities. The explanation for this is straightforward enough; these partners control the majority of the regional development tools available.

The links between these partners and the 'end-users' of the RDP process – the private sector and the municipalities in the region – are generally weak. The private sector interests in the partnership process are taken care of by the regional confederations of business/industry and trade unions, respectively. The role of these partners in the RDP process is primarily of an advisory nature. It is not a question of relegating major decision-making to the private sector, although the input on a specific project level might be more substantial. In the case of *Vestfold* for instance, some of the partners on the regional level put it squarely: the private sector does not see the participation in the RDP process as something worth expending valuable time on. The main reason for this is probably the fact that the RDPs contribute very little in terms of fresh resources being put into circulation. While synergy effects of co-ordinating resources might exist, they are not always tangible and obvious, hence the lack of interest on behalf of the private sector. Moreover, this might also lead to a scepticism among the regional partners administering regional development funds, contributing to 'shallow' partnership processes, driven by loyalty and a sense of duty vis-à-vis state level authorities more than anything else.

Previously it was suggested that partnership *cohesion* and the resources available to the partnership are variables conditioned by each other. The evidence from the three regions studied here seems to support this suggestion to some extent. There are obvious differences between the three regions presented here; the *Vestfold* region seems to get a low score on both resources and cohesion. It could be argued that the few regional policy tools available in the case of *Vestfold* limits the need of the actors to think in terms of cohesive partnerships, resulting in a *rhetorical* arrangement that approximates the 'ritualistic' partnership outlined in Table 10.2. On the other hand, the *Troms* and *Aust-Agder* regions have a broader range of resources available for regional development work, and, it would seem, somewhat more cohesive and integrated partnerships. Although it is impossible to draw any distinct lines of demarcation between the partnership typologies referred to in Table 10.2, both the *Troms* and the *Aust-Agder* regions seem to be a long way from being defined as 'synergetic' partnerships. The 'composite' approach seems more fitting for describing these partnerships. The principal explanation as to why these partnerships do not seem to be more closely integrated than they actually are in these two cases, is probably found in the nature of regional – state-level relations. The lack of autonomy experienced by some of the regional partners, does not stimulate more cohesive partnership relations at the regional level.

To the extent that the question of democratic *accountability* can be viewed as problematic in light of partnership arrangements on the regional level, scepticism can arise from at least two aspects. Decision-making and policy formulation can be seen as being conditioned by a supra-national level, for example the European Commission, bypassing the 'accountability assurance' of national/state-level authorities and policies. In the case of Norway, it clearly would be far-fetched and irrelevant to argue that this is the case. It quite simply is not. Another, and possibly more relevant, argument in the Norwegian case is that accountability becomes an issue because decision-making is pulled out of the light of an open and democratic process. The involvement in decision-making of both the private sector and other regional development agents – neither answering directly to the elected political assembly in the region – can be viewed as an accountability problem.

However, looking at the RDP reform as an expression of partnerships being formed at the regional level, little evidence can be found to suggest that this has contributed to the emergence of significant accountability problems. As far as relegating decision-making to the private sector is concerned, the study of the three selected regions show that the involvement of the private sector within the framework of the RDP process is relatively weak. To the extent that private actors are involved in the policy-making process at the regional level, this seems to take place *outside* the framework of the RDP process. This is primarily done through well-established planning processes, for example county plans and strategic business development plans. Admittedly, the RDPs are built on the basis of such planning processes to a considerable degree, but whether these 'subterranean' foundations for the RDP process qualify for using the term 'partnership' is questionable. The input from private actors is more along the lines of 'brain-storming' sessions and conferences for the purpose of informing planners in the county administration. This undoubtedly contributes to securing the legitimacy of planning processes and – eventually – the RDP process, but it is not a question of giving the private sector any *autonomous* role as far as policy-making is concerned. As such, the private sector's involvement can hardly be described as obscuring democratic processes.

A stronger argument for partnerships contributing to accountability problems can perhaps be found in the ambiguous relations between actors on the regional and national level, respectively. Perhaps the most tangible example of this ambiguity (in the context of the RDPs) is the way the regional SND boards have functioned. The democratically elected regional assembly has until recently merely played an advisory role, without the directive powers normally associated with, say, a bank or other financial institutions. Consequently, the RDPs do not seem to have played any significant role as a strategic foundation for the relationship between the partner with a democratically elected leadership (the County Council) and the important partner in terms of business development (the SND). Subsequent to this study, however, changes have been made in terms of strengthening the regional SND boards powers and responsibilities. The possible effects of these changes, remains to be seen, however.

Two main conclusions can be drawn from the cases:

- The RDP processes seem to have been instrumental in creating somewhat closer relations between regional actors, although to a varying degree. The RDP process represents an arena which is given a positive assessment by most of the actors – in terms of a better exchange of information and widened perspectives on regional development. Nevertheless, it would be difficult to label this as a profound reorientation of norms and beliefs among the actors. Consequently, the RDPs do not seem to have resulted in the establishment of genuinely new institutions. The most important effect of the RDP and its partnership seem to be facilitating a better common understanding of regional development challenges;
- The RDPs and their partnerships do not seem to have contributed to significantly more operational regional policies. Few of the actors indicate that the RDP process as such has contributed to developing new and previously unattainable development policies to any substantial degree. The partnership processes seem to be geared towards the 'least common denominator' approach.

Explaining these outcomes of the RDP processes, several aspects of the processes can be pointed to. Firstly, the RDP's function as a policy instrument can be perceived as unclear or ambiguous. Balancing the RDPs between being the outcome of a *strategic* process and being a plan for implementing previously developed strategies, can be difficult. The actors themselves often refer to the RDPs as 'cut-and-paste' products, 'administrative processes' and 'status overviews'. An important reason for this – given by the actors themselves – is a general lack of capacity for entering into substantial partnership processes.

Secondly, the RDP processes generally seem to be founded on consensus. A 'consensual' partnership is in itself not necessarily an impediment to the negotiating dynamics of a partnership, but if the process stops at *mapping agreement* the partnership is in danger of being synonymous with 'the least common denominator' and conflict avoidance – where strategies and priorities easily become rhetorical varnish. Thus, when the RDP processes seem to be characterized by consensus, this does not necessarily imply that the different actors have different approaches to the question of regional development, but it can easily curtail the scope of development policies. Likewise, few conflicts between partners are detectable. Interestingly, where one finds elements of a more substantial negotiating dynamic, this seems to be related to the relationship between the County Council and the SND – concerning the size of the business development fund and the infrastructure budget respectively. Such negotiations are connected to the use and control of resources, and implies that 'dynamic' partnerships require something substantial to negotiate on. This raises the question of what is possible to define as the regional development capital available to the partnership, and what mandate the partnership has for administering this capital. A perceived lack of regional autonomy seems to be a problem in this respect.

Thirdly, while the RDPs are considered an arena for exchanging information and bettering the common perception of development challenges, the co-operation among partners within the context of the RDP process can not be described as something genuinely new to the regional level. Such co-operative relations existed prior to the introduction of RDPs, and the RDPs should be seen as a continuation of this. The RDPs should not necessarily be viewed as a superfluous element, however. The partnership arrangements have contributed to a stronger formalization of co-operation.

Lastly, *vertical* partnership relations – between regional actors and state-level authorities – obviously seem to define the scope of partnership relations at the regional level. Conflicting signals from various state-level bodies are described as problematic across the board. The actors' criticism of vertical relations is primarily directed at the perceived lack of co-ordination between ministries. The best cure for the problems which arise from this situation is suggested as being a greater degree of regional autonomy, rather than unilaterally focusing on bettering relations among ministries. Some point to the paradox that control and guidelines for the use of development means have been emphasized by state-level authorities, while the rhetoric has focused on the opportunities for regionally adapted development through the RDPs.

Partnership in Regional Policy – The Case of Denmark

Danish regional policy has been transformed beyond recognition since the beginning of the 1990s, and so has the role of partnership arrangements within this field of policy-making. While most other countries in Western Europe decreased their expenditure on national grant schemes in peripheral regions, their Danish equivalent, *egnsudviklingsstøtten*, was terminated as of 1991, and thus regional policy came to consist of a plethora of sub-national development initiatives plus the Structural Funds programmes which, although small by European standards, more than substituted the now defunct national subsidy schemes in financial terms (Halkier, 2001). This also implied a shift away from a style of policy-making in which partnership relations were of limited importance, to a situation where network-forms of organization were important, not only in the relatively decentralized management of the Structural Funds programmes but also within the large number of bottom-up development initiatives that emerged from the late 1980s onwards.

For the Nordic study of partnership in regional policy three Danish regions were selected for particular scrutiny on account of their presumed differences with regard to access to development resources:

- *Storstrøm* has a long history of being supported by first central government regional grants and then European Objective 2 monies. The region was hard hit by the decline of shipbuilding, and the scope for innovative policies has been hampered by the absence of major private or public knowledge-based institutions;
- *North Jutland* (Nordjylland) has also been a long-standing beneficiary of national and European regional policy on account of a combination of a low level of industrialization in some parts of the region and the predominance of declining industries in its major cities. Actors within the region have had a strong involvement in development activities dating back to the 1980s, and facilitated by the presence of a university with a strong engineering faculty, new industries have gradually begun to emerge on a large scale, especially around telecommunications and IT;
- *Vejle* exemplifies a region that traditionally has neither been supported by national nor European regional policies to any great extent. Private economic activity, especially associated with a range of export-oriented agro-related manufacturing, has ensured that especially the Fredericia-Kolding-Vejle triangle has become a national growth centre, but since the 1990s public actors have taken an increasing interest in supporting economic development.

All three regions are intermediate-tier administrative units (*amter*) within the Danish political system, and in the following findings will first be reported under the headings inclusiveness, accountability, and coherence, and then compared to the two sets of partnership-process ideal types concerning strategic orientation and policy impact.[2]

With regard to *inclusiveness* public actors have clearly played a proactive role in setting up partnerships and devising policies in all the three case study regions, both with regard to overarching strategies and collaboration, and in relation to individual development bodies. But at the same time partnerships practically always include actors from the private sector on boards and committees, mainly in the shape of representatives from regional/local business or employers organizations, while individual development projects organized along partnership lines often involve individual firms, sometimes even in a proactive role. Most of the overarching strategic partnerships on the regional level include a significant local government representation in order to facilitate inter-tier co-ordination within the public sector, while the voluntary sector is largely absent except in connection

2 For details of the three Danish case studies, see Halkier and Flockhart, 2002a and 2002b.

with individual development projects which fall within their 'sectoral' remit (e.g. anglers and promotion of green tourism). This pattern of inclusion and exclusion could suggest that these partnerships are in fact closed 'iron triangles' on the sub-national level, but all interviewees generally claimed that relevant resources, financial or otherwise, give access to partnership participation, something which would imply that partnerships do actually have a relatively open character. Such an interpretation does of course hinge on what existing partners will in practice consider to be 'relevant' resources in an economic development context, and thus the strategic implications are still unclear: pragmatic inclusion of actors with 'relevant' resources would seem to permit innovation, but at the same time the dominance of traditional interest organizations in strategic partnerships suggests that, perhaps, the source of dynamism should primarily be located at the level of individual projects.

Also with regard to *accountability* the three case study regions presented broadly similar pictures. Political accountability is largely indirect in the sense that the committees and boards responsible for individual partnerships have invariably been appointed or approved by elected politicians, and especially partnerships with a predominantly strategic role often have politicians serving as members of for example its steering committee. Moreover, political accountability in practice is supported by on the one hand legal accountability – partnerships involving monetary relations are governed by normal contractual standards – and indeed by trust which is also claimed by many interviewees to play an important part in ensuring effective and transparent co-operation, something which would seem to be supported by the patterns of inclusiveness noted above. Perhaps the most important lesson to be drawn would be that accountability has not emerged as a major issue in its own right, and thus a 'functional' type of legitimacy would seem to dominate: if partnerships are seen to produce results in terms of regional policy, then the organizational patterns are not seriously questioned.

All in all the situation with regard to inclusiveness and accountability would in other words seem to be characterized by similarities and consensus: the 'rules of the game' are the same in each of the three regions, something that suggests that they reflect national preferences, and thus a 'Danish model' of partnership within regional economic development policy would seem to be in evidence. In the light of these findings it is therefore particularly interesting to note that with regard to the last of the three key partnership dimensions, *strategic coherence*, a completely different picture emerges from the three case studies, as illustrated by Table 10.3.

Table 10.3 Strategic orientation and policy impact of Danish regional policy partnerships

	North Jutland	*Storstrøm*	*Vejle*	
			County	*Triangle*
Strategic orientation	Induced	Induced	Enforced	Generative
Policy impact	Synergetic	Composite	Ritualistic	Synergetic

Firstly, it is interesting to note that in one of the regions, Vejle, two competing strategic partnerships have been identified: a region-wide operation initiated by the county council, and sub-regional network built around the three dynamic cities in the eastern so-called *Triangle* part of the county. While the existence of sub-regional partnerships based on groupings of district councils has been found in all three regions, the limited co-operation between the two major development networks sets Vejle apart from the other case study regions, and thus in the following these spatially overlapping partnerships will be treated as two separate entities.

Secondly, it is evident that the overall strategic orientation differs greatly. In two regions the strategic partnerships can be classified primarily as induced, i.e. being prompted by external demands and to a large extent relying on mobilization of resources from outside the region. In contrast to this the supposedly overarching partnership in Vejle appears to be of a mainly enforced nature, prompted if not outright demanded by co-ordination initiatives from the national level, while the bottom-up partnership in the Triangle region displays a generative strategic orientation, being a local initiative that relies primarily on mobilization of resources within the locality. While significant variations have been identified with regard to the origins and basic resource mobilization strategies of regional policy partnerships in Denmark, it should, however, also be stressed that in terms of specific economic development strategies all four partnerships are overwhelmingly concerned with promoting the growth of indigenous firms and thus even the two regions in which external resources play a crucial role are ultimately using European funds to mobilize resources from private actors within the region.

Thirdly, it is also clear that the *policy impact* of the four strategic partnerships vary greatly, with two of them appearing to be synergetic in the sense of combining considerable resources within a reasonably clear development strategy, one partnership being composite by involving relatively large resources within a looser strategic framework, and one partnership appearing to be of a mainly ritualistic nature with limited impact in terms of policy priorities within the region. In short, having a strategic partnership formally in place does not in itself ensure that it makes much difference in terms of the allocation of policy resources on the ground.

All in all the role of partnerships in Danish regional policy clearly varies between the regions. In North Jutland the main strategic partnership may have been largely induced by the European Structural Funds, but nonetheless still appears to have been able to maintain a potentially controversial strategic emphasis on industrial modernization while at the same time keeping at bay inherent tensions between the revitalized core areas around Aalborg and its less well-off peripheries. In Storstrøm the main function of the partnership would appear to be to facilitate the spending of the European funds available, something which was complicated by the absence of a dynamic Aalborg-style regional core, although this at the same time also made the task of the partnership easier because the question of intra-regional differences remained of limited importance. Finally, Vejle is the only case in which contending strategic partnerships have been identified, with a weakly resourced region-wide partnership coexisting with several sub-regional partnerships of considerable dynamism.

Taken together the three cases would seem to suggest that several potentially conflicting factors may influence the way in which regional development partnerships function and their potential for having a tangible impact on regional policy. On the one hand external funding gives the fund holder – the County in the case of the Structural Funds in Denmark – considerable leverage over other actors, but as in the diverging experience of North Jutland and Storstrøm, this may or may not result in a high degree of strategic coherence. On the other hand intra-regional polarization may make it more difficult to establish strategic coherence because of diverging interests, but at the same time the presence of a regional core with dynamic firms and knowledge institutions may facilitate the emergence of new economic growth potentials which could eventually benefit the entire region. From this perspective the outcome of some of the case studies are perhaps less surprising. In Storstrøm the absence of territorial tensions and a perception of limited indigenous potential resulted in a peaceful process because spending external funding was the main preoccupation, whereas in Vejle the combination of intra-regional polarization and absence of large-scale external funding produced a situation where sub-regional territorial particularism could flourish. North Jutland may in a sense be the most interesting case in that a longstanding perception of 'common fate' of industrial decline has generated partnership structures with a reasonably clear strategic focus that – on the back of significant amounts of European monies – appear to be able to manage tensions between the increasingly successful core and the less well-off parts of the region. This would seem to imply that while the environment in which a partnership operates is of course important – e.g. presence/absence of external funding or intra-regional polarization – the partnership process itself can also make a difference by establishing a framework for longer-term interest mediation.

Partnership and Regional Development – Beyond Europeanization?

The analysis of cases from Norway and Denmark has shown that both national and regional factors would seem to influence both the strategic orientation and policy impact of partnerships for regional development. While the national and supra-national levels define the general rules of the game, individual regions subject to the same rules may still vary both with regard to strategic orientations and the impact of partnerships on regional policy.

Table 10.4 provides a summary of the case studies by positioning individual regions according to the key variables, and this cross-tabulation would appear to highlight two results.

Table 10.4 Strategic orientation and policy impact of regional policy partnerships in Norway and Denmark

		Policy impact			
		Ritualistic	*Visionary*	*Composite*	*Synergetic*
	Enforced	N, D			
Strategic orientation	*Induced*			2N, D	D
	Extractive				
	Generative				D

Firstly, the Danish partnerships seem to be more different from one another than their Norwegian counterparts, something which could reflect varying degrees of centralization in the two countries. Interestingly, although the Danish model has been influenced by the advent of the European Structural Funds, this has not lead to homogenous results across the regions with regard to partnership as the organizational framework for regional policy, probably reflecting a tradition for decentralized management of many welfare policies. In contrast to this, partnerships in Norway may have been inspired by the Structural Funds but obviously lack the associated financial tools and direct enrolment in a multi-level governance structure, and consequently a vertical partnership relation between regions and the supra-national level – possibly contributing to a strengthening of the regional level – has not been institutionalized. Add to this that the Norwegian oil-economy contributes to a considerable pressure on the redistributional aspects of policies and hence a climate of detailed state-level control, and the 'signing away' of policy-making to the regional level is not easily put on the agenda. In short, here the national framework clearly matters.

Secondly, it would also appear that there is no simple correspondence between different aspects of the partnership process, as is sometimes assumed in the literature (e.g. Cooke and Morgan, 1998, pp. 218ff). In the three Danish case-study regions a resource-reallocating synergetic impact has resulted both from collaborative arrangements of a generative nature and on the basis of a partnership created in response to the availability of the European Structural Funds. Conversely, an induced strategic orientation does not necessarily result in a synergetic impact, as the example of Storstrøm with its composite policy impact shows. From an analytical perspective the implication of this is that it is indeed necessary to investigate the partnership process in its entirety because it is difficult to make assumptions about impact on the basis of strategic orientations, however tempting this might otherwise be in terms of economizing with scarce research resources. From a policy perspective the implication would seem to be that the partnership process on the regional level clearly matters in terms of influencing the eventual outcome and, indeed, that successful experience with externally induced collaboration could potentially establish patterns of collaboration that may outlast the availability of the European Structural Funds. This would also seem to be the implication of the Norwegian case studies in that in some regions the process has been more successful in establishing collaborative relations than in others, although it is of course interesting to note that externally enforced partnerships would invariably appear to result in ritualistic partnerships, i.e. words rather than action.

Finally, the question of accountability of partnerships and their relationship to regional democracy is on the agenda in both countries, albeit in ways that are rather different from the thinking in other Nordic and European countries. While the Danish partnerships seem to be surrounded by functionalist forms of legitimacy – focusing on the perceived economic results rather than the role of elected representatives – the more limited role of the Norwegian partnerships would seem to explain absence of conflicts concerning the involvement of private actors while instead the uneasy relationship between regionally elected and central government appointed bodies is more salient. It is, however, interesting to note that in both cases this has *not* been tied to notions of extending democracy through stakeholding, as would seem to have been the case in Sweden and the UK for instance. Partnerships for regional development are of course also inscribed in the ongoing positioning strategies of the various tiers of government in Norway and Denmark, but essentially they are not seen as vehicles of democracy or stakeholding, but about something rather more limited: regional level intersectoral co-ordination prompted by national authorities or mobilization of financial resources within a multi-level governance setting.

All in all the analysis clearly demonstrates that although the growing role in regional policy of strategic partnerships between public and private actors and different tiers of government may have been inspired or prompted by the post-1988 Structural Funds, the way this organizational device operates in practice also reflects national and regional circumstances. While the combination of extensive horizontal and vertical networks are at the core of the EU approach to partnerships for regional development, this principle still leaves ample room for manoeuvre, and thus speaking of a European 'model' may indeed be misleading. In order to understand the structure and workings of partnership-type of organizations within the field of regional policy, our analysis has, hopefully, suggested that much more detailed forms of enquiry are called for in order to establish the extent to which such organizational changes can be interpreted as instances of Europeanization.

Bibliography

Benneworth, Paul (2001), *Regional Development Agencies – The Early Years*, RSA, Seaford.

Cooke, Philip and Morgan, Kevin (1998), *The Associational Economy*, Oxford UP, Oxford.

European Commission (1999), *Reform of the Structural Funds 2000-2006 – Comparative Analysis (June 1999)*, European Commission, Brussels.

Gjertsen, Arild (2002), 'The Norwegian Cases – Partnership Out of Step? The Regional Level under Pressure', in Anders Östhol and Bo Svensson (eds), *Partnership Responses – Regional Governance in the Nordic States*, Nordregio, Stockholm, pp. 203-34.

Halkier, Henrik (2000), 'Regional Policy – An Inter-organizational Approach', *Regional and Industrial Policy Research Paper Series*, EPRC, University of Strathclyde, No. 37.

Halkier, Henrik (2001), 'Regional Policy in Transition – A Multi-level Governance Perspective on the Case of Denmark', *European Planning Studies*, Vol. 9, pp. 323-38.

Halkier, Henrik and Flockhart, John Evan (2002a), 'Partnership and Regional Development – The Case of Denmark', *European Studies Series of Occasional Papers*, European Research Unit, Aalborg University, No. 31.

Halkier, Henrik and Flockhart, John Evan (2002b), 'The Danish Cases – Bottom-up Initiatives between Regional and National Environments', in Anders Östhol and Bo Svensson (eds), *Partnership Responses – Regional Governance in the Nordic States*, Nordregio, Stockholm, pp. 41-84.

Heinelt, Hubert and Smith, Randall (eds) (1996), *Policy Networks and European Structural Funds*, Avebury, Aldershot.

Hooghe, Liesbet (ed.) (1996), *Cohesion Policy and European Integration. Building Multi-level Governance*, Oxford UP, Oxford.

Kommunal- og arbeidsdepartementet (1996-97), *Om distrikts- og regionalpolitikken*, St.meld. nr. 31.

Mariussen, Åge et al. (2000), 'Evaluering af regionale udviklingsprogram i Norge', *Nordregio Report*, R2000/5.

Nelson, J. and Zadek, S. (2000), *Partnership Alchemy – New Social Partnerships in Europe*, The Copenhagen Centre, Copenhagen.

Powell, Walter W. (1990), 'Neither Market nor Hierarchy: Network Forms of Organization', *Research in Organizational Behaviour*, Vol. 12, pp. 295-336.

Thorelli, Hans B. (1986), 'Networks: Between Markets and Hierarchies', *Strategic Management Journal*, Vol. 7, pp. 37-51.

Wishlade, Fiona (1996), 'EU Cohesion Policy: Facts, Figures and Issues', in Liesbet Hooghe (ed.), *Cohesion Policy and European Integration. Building Multi-level Governance*, Oxford UP, Oxford, pp. 27-58.

Yuill, Douglas et al. (1999), *European Regional Incentives 1999*, 18th edition, Bowker Saur, London.

Östhol, Anders and Svensson, Bo (2002a), 'Introduction', in Anders Östhol and Bo Svensson (eds), *Partnership Responses – Regional Governance in the Nordic States*, Nordregio, Stockholm, pp. 13-22.

Östhol, Anders and Svensson, Bo (2002b), 'The Swedish Cases – Partnership by State-led Design', in Anders Östhol and Bo Svensson (eds), *Partnership Responses – Regional Governance in the Nordic States*, Nordregio, Stockholm, pp. 85-134.

Östhol, Anders and Svensson, Bo (eds) (2002), 'Partnership Responses – Regional Governance in the Nordic States', *Nordregio Report*, R2002/6.

Östhol, Anders, Svensson, Bo and Halkier, Henrik (2002), 'Analytical Framework', in Anders Östhol and Bo Svensson (eds), *Partnership Responses – Regional Governance in the Nordic States*, Nordregio, Stockholm, pp. 23-39.

Chapter 11

Conclusion: Europeanization as a Means to Strengthening the Regions within the State

Søren Dosenrode and Henrik Halkier

If this study had been undertaken before the referendum on Finnish, Norwegian and Swedish EU membership in 1994 – or in the years just after it – it would have revealed a clear picture of four centralized states which are all in the process of moving away from strong centralization towards varying degrees of decentralization. According to Bullman's terminology (1997), we would have been dealing with a change from a classic unitary state towards a devolving unitary state (Norway) or even beyond that, towards a regionalized unitary state (Denmark, Finland, Sweden). After the Norwegian population turned down the proposal for EU membership in 1994, the Norwegian regions lost power as a consequence (cf. Chapter 4). But it is important to stress here that these processes of decentralization began before European integration gained momentum in the middle of the 1980s. But the European integration process has added dynamics to the process of decentralization (Denmark, Sweden); and it has worked as a catalyst and has delivered the necessary arguments for reforms (Finland, Norway). Let us turn to the question of Europeanization of the Nordic regions.

Considering the dynamics of the European integration process and the strength of the mere presence of the European Union, it is not surprising that all the Nordic regions were 'Europeanized'. It is equally close to a truism that we find the strongest Europeanization in the regions belonging to the EU member states, and the smallest degree of Europeanization in the Norwegian regions – still, it does take place as a consequence of Norway's participation in the Interreg programmes. In the sense of 'quiet' regional Europeanization, Norway is a parallel to Switzerland (cf. Dosenrode, 1995).

Considering the *question of Europeanization* within the regions, we can conclude that *passive* Europeanization takes place in all Nordic regions, including the Norwegian (albeit to a lesser extent). *Mental* Europeanization including the learning aspect is present, too, but in a less homogenous way. This picture is repeated and strengthened when looking at *active* Europeanization, where the picture is one of significant diversity between the Nordic regions.

Within the regions it is quite obvious that *active* Europeanization, to the extent it has taken place, was initiated during the first years almost exclusively by the administrative elite, and concentrated on a few administrative units. Now the regional politicians also take initiatives, but their main role is still to confirm or follow up on initiatives proposed by civil servants. The civil servants often have better education, for example they speak foreign languages, and through their daily work they see possibilities that politicians do not realize. Still, it is to be expected that as mental Europeanization develops, the increased knowledge will influence regional politicians in such a way that they begin to include the European dimension in their thinking and actions in the same way as politicians on the national level do (cf. Dosenrode, 1997). This will be especially true for politicians and civil servants in the many regions which maintain offices in Brussels.

What motives do we find when searching for the reasons for pursuing a strategy of active Europeanization? The two main motives, in order of priority, were regional development and larger autonomy *vis-à-vis* the national centre. Adding to this were other, but inferior, motives such as the promotion of understanding amongst people, staff development, etc, but in the following we will concentrate on the two major motives.

This main motive for active Europeanization is similar in all Nordic regions, both on the individual regional level, and on the level of the national associations of regions: to promote regional development, for instance, by creating better framework conditions for businesses within the region, by helping to create contacts to potential partners in individual EU projects, etc., and to a lesser extent by trying to influence the policy-making process of the EU, either directly or through the national channels. This is a very pragmatic approach to European integration, but it is important to remember that the main tasks of the Nordic regions have been of an implementing nature. These tasks depend on the taxes the regions can collect; social welfare, healthcare, secondary education and infrastructure all demand resources (read: money). In return, taxes are dependent on local economic activity. From this perspective it is hardly surprising that the two 'forerunners' concerning Europeanization among the Danish regions have been Storstrøms Amt and Nordjyllands Amt because these two regions are located in the periphery and have experienced high unemployment rates. This also explains why Roskilde Amt, within comfortable reach of Copenhagen and enjoying a low rate of unemployment, belongs to the least Europeanized region in Denmark. It does not, however, explain why Skåne and Århus Amt pursue active Europeanization; to get a better understanding of this, we have to look at the second main motive: Brussels as the alternative bargaining chip in the national game.[1]

1 It goes without saying, that Europeanization is pursued out of other motives than the above mentioned, too (cf. chapters 1 and 2), and that there is no one-to-one causality between the amount of resources received from the EU and the degree of Europeanization in a region.

This important but secondary motive is the wish to establish a more equal *relationship with the national centre*. Although some regions deliberately pursue this aim themselves, is it often left to the national associations of regions to develop this strategy in its interactions with the EU and with the national governments. As we see in the three EU member states, the region-state relationship has undergone a development in the direction of larger autonomy for the regions. This development has been supported by increased integration on the European level. But the extent to which the regions, on an individual basis, or united in a national association, have used the EU as a lever for further autonomy varies considerably. There is considerable difference among the countries: in Norway, most initiatives have traditionally come from above; in Sweden, which is in a transition phase, the initiatives come partly from the regions, and in Denmark and Finland 'the road to Brussels' is used consciously to strengthen the position of the regions *vis-à-vis* the state.

The above-mentioned motives go for both the individual region and the national associations of regions in the four countries. They constitute a significant part of the explanation of why regions pursue an active strategy of Europeanization, but when looking at individual regions, additional explanations for pursuing a strategy of active Europeanization must be considered. When we talk of active Europeanization as the project of the region's elite, especially the administrative one, it becomes clear that the individual factor gains importance in terms of explaining why some regions have a high level of activity and others a low one. As the process of integration progresses and with it the learning process of the regional politicians, the role of the civil servant will decline, but remain important.

Inspired by theoretical considerations, Olsson and Åström (2003) call attention to three additional factors which might explain whether *strong* Europeanization is to be expected: a separate cultural identity, historical links to other European countries, and a minimal dependence on the state. Olsson and Åström conclude that this kind of strong Europeanization in the form of regionalist tendencies is not at work in Sweden. Can we extend this conclusion to the rest of the Nordic countries?

The cultural thesis which Olsson and Åström refer to (large cultural heterogeneity promotes regionalism) is useful in our case, in the sense that a fairly outspoken cultural homogeneity on the national level does not promote regionalism (compared to other European states). Even when considered together, one could cautiously argue that at least Denmark, Norway and Sweden are more homogeneous than Spain or Italy for instance when looking at language, the common welfare state model, etc. This homogeneity within the Nordic countries does, on the other hand, facilitate cross-border co-operation, in case other factors should trigger off such an endeavour (e.g. an EU project on regional development demanding cross-national participation).

When looking at the historical thesis (close historical links to other European countries promotes regionalization), it also seems reasonable to include the geo-political variable. Contacts with other European regions are often a matter of geographic proximity. Scandinavia is to a very large extent bordered by the sea which, in spite of easy communication by means of ships, does limit close everyday contacts with other regions, especially in the case of Norway and Jutland. Where close geographic proximity existed, recent (political) history has limited the explanatory factor of this aspect, at least concerning the Nordic regions contacts to non-Nordic regions. The Finnish experiences with Karelia and the Kola peninsula in connection with World War II and the following Soviet annexation, and the Danish experiences with Germany in the Schleswig-Holstein question between 1848 and 1921 followed by the 1940-45 occupation have limited the utility of the potentially valuable common historic roots. As an example of the latter, the creation of a cross-border Euro-region did upset significant parts of the population on the Danish side of the border to Germany, in spite of the hundreds of years of common history as part of the combined duchies of Schleswig-Holstein. Thus we may conclude that the historical factors, as stipulated in the hypothesis, are not present in a significant amount. But inside Scandinavia cross-border co-operation grows and geographic proximity may be an explanation in the case of Skåne which is working together closely with Copenhagen (Copenhagen and Malmö were connected by a bridge in 2001).[2]

The question of the dependence of the regions on the state has been touched upon (the hypothesis that a minimal dependence on the state fosters regionalism). We found, on the contrary, that dependence was an important factor in explaining why Nordic regions actively pursue a strategy of active Europeanization. If we consider Europeanization as a lower level on a scale, on which the next level is regionalism, followed by separatism, then we slowly approach an explanation of why we do have Europeanization, but also why it is not pursued as vigorously, in the form of regionalization, as in Germany or Austria. Factors such as the pursuance of regional development and prosperity and the quest to establish a less one-sided relationship with the national centre are important for the Nordic regions, not the dreams of a Europe of Regions. For the Nordic regions, the all-important frame of reference remains the nation-state.

What impact can we ascribe the degree of Europeanization concerning the basic administrative structures and processes of the regions? In Finland and Norway the adaptation process before the expected EU membership triggered off structural reforms at the regional level. They stopped in Norway, but were continued in Finland. Concerning the administrative routines and processes, there has, to varying degrees, been small adjustments made, for example particular administrative units have been assigned the responsibility for EU-regional funds or the procedures of public procurement for instance. This does not, however, change the picture of an overall stability; the European integration process has not challenged the administrative systems fundamentally, although the marginal administrative adjustments do not imply that the regions do not participate in the Europeanization

2 Another example is the Haparanda (S)-Torneå (SF) cross-border co-operation initiative which is one of the most successful ones of this type in the EU, with wide-reaching shared administration, service provision and development activity.

process; quite the contrary. As Chapters 4 and 8 show, even some Norwegian regions pursue active involvement on the Brussels scene. There are very pragmatic reasons for this phenomenon. To the individual region it seldom matters much whether it is implementing a regulation passed by the national parliament or by the EU; as long as it is a directive, the regional administrator cannot even see the difference, because he receives the new regulation from the national ministry concerned. This apparent tranquility does not have to last eternally; in most regions 'Europe' begins to be present in the minds of regional politicians and regional administrators when looking at new issues or projects. Considering the comparatively short period of time since the implementation of the Single Market Programme, one could reverse the argument and be surprised as to how large an extent 'Europe' is present in the minds of regional authorities. The mental aspect of the Europeanization process should not be underestimated, neither in the regions nor in the national associations of regions.

For the regions of the federal EU states (Austria, Belgium, Germany) it has been fairly easy to get substantial influence on parts of the national EU decision-making. These regions had rights secured in their constitutions, rights that were partly diminished by the ongoing integration, but as their respective national centres needed their consent to ratify the various treaties (SEA, Maastricht, Amsterdam, Nice), they had a good bargaining position. Not so in the case of the Nordic regions embedded in their respective centralized states.

It comes as no surprise that the Norwegian regions are the least involved in the national EU decision-making, considering that Norway only has a peripheral role in the EU decision-making system as a member of the European Economic Area. For the regions of the other three Nordic states, the situation has been better; Denmark has been a member of the EU far longer than Finland and Sweden. This implies on the one hand that the Danish regions have had time to get used to the EU, but on the other hand it also means that the integration process has come about quietly, incrementally, not forcing the regions to deal with the question of European integration before the beginning of the 1990s. The Danish regions have been integrated in the national part of the decision-making process mainly because they had experience and knowledge which the national centre needed. But there have been additional reasons, too. Firstly, the general problem of 'selling' the European idea, that the EU was perceived as very far away from the ordinary citizen, has pressed for the participation of the lower levels (legitimation and democracy). A second factor was the *fait accompli* reason; the regions had already begun cultivating contacts in Brussels, both on a united basis (ADR) and individually. These contacts could of course be ignored by the Danish central administration until 1992, but from then on came the third factor, the Maastricht Treaty, with the Committee of Regions which officially includes the regions in the EU system. These are altogether reasons why the Danish regions have been involved on the national level of the EU decision-making process for a while; an involvement kept consciously on a low level by the national centre to the great dissatisfaction of the regions. If the strategy was to keep the regions away from influence, the strategy has backlashed rather badly; due to the perception of being ignored and kept out of the Danish decision-making process, the regions have increased their European engagement with success, to the chagrin of the national centre. These processes have certainly affected the Swedish administrations, especially when it comes to regional development policy. The partnership concept of the EU Structural Funds is widely accepted and the Swedish Government now uses it as a way of making its own regional policy more 'democratic' in the Swedish regions in general. The Government has a programme for growth agreements between institutions in the regions (CC, CA and LA) in which the partnership concept is important, although the democratic ambition seems rather superficial. Within Finland the partnership arrangements are most visible in the Structural Funds programmes, as well as in the national programmes such as the Centres of Expertise and Regional Centres Development Programme, that display advanced forms of the so-called 'Triple Helix' dynamics in the form of co-operation between public authorities, universities, polytechnics and research institutes, as well as the business community. On the national level the Association of Local and Regional Authorities ('Kuntaliitto') also acts as an interest organization vis-à-vis the national government.

The five thematic chapters examining specific aspects of the changing position of Nordic regions in a wider European context would certainly seem to confirm the general picture outlined above. First and foremost it is abundantly clear that Nordic regions are indeed actors in their own right, taking initiatives that transgress their traditional territorial and functional roles when setting up offices in Brussels, engaging in trans-border co-operation projects, or embarking on new ventures in 'bottom-up' economic development. It is also evident that many of these activities aim at or result in improving the position of the regions *vis-à-vis* central government *within* the unitary political system, for example by getting access to sources of information, by securing European funding for activities within the region, especially with regard to economic development, or simply by creating political capital through involvement in politics on a larger territorial scale.

These developments do not, however, make the Nordic regions comply with the 'Europe of the Regions' scenario, neither in terms of the current state of affairs or the underlying development trends. Initiatives taken on the regional level do not generally fundamentally challenge the authority of central government – which is hardly surprising, given that these initiatives are driven by sub-national governments and do not reflect regionalist or nationalist political ambitions. In addition to this the concurrent trends of Europeanization and regionalization are neither cause nor consequence, nor necessarily processes that run counter to central government interest, cf the positive encouragement by national governments of Nordic trans-border co-operation or the active decentralization of regional policy in the case of Denmark. Rather than 'Europe of the Regions', the process of Europeanization of the Nordic regions would seem to result in a 'mosaic' of multi-level governance in which the nation-state continues to play a pivotal role. From the European level the Structural Funds have clearly played an important facilitating role in many of these processes, and thus whether the momentum can be maintained after the coming enlargement of the EU towards the east will be interesting to see.

Europeanization is both a *de facto* condition that the regions will have to live with and it is, for the regions in Denmark, Finland, Sweden and to a smaller degree in Norway, a potential means to acquiring additional resources. In Denmark, Finland and Sweden it is also a means to create a more symmetric interdependent relationship between region and state. This does imply more influence for the regions in Denmark, Norway and Sweden, but the ongoing integration process also has another potential implication running counter to this development. Due to the process of integration, an increasing number of policy decisions are made at the supranational level. This implies that tasks normally performed at the national level are pushed up one level, thus setting resources free at the national level. Now this is not necessarily greeted with enthusiasm by the bureaucrats in the national centres as politicians could get the idea that one could cut budgets and reduce staff. The implications for the regions are that: 1) the central government searches for new tasks to avoid cuts in 'their' resources (bureaucratic survival), new tasks that basically are of sub-national nature; and that 2) more resources are set free to control the regions. These influences are felt in the Danish and Swedish regions as well as in the Norwegian ones (although to a lesser extent), and have to be added to the picture. In the Finnish case the programme-based development ideology is visible both in the national and European programmes that mobilize an important amount of development resources, as well as in some important legal and administrative changes. These are connected to the idea of a regional level co-ordinating financial resources for regional development in a cross-sector fashion, as well as to some additional administrative experiments, such as the Kainuu regional experiment starting in 2005 where a directly elected regional level will be introduced for the first time. Still, we found no evidence whatsoever of regions wishing to see their national state fade away, being replaced by the regions: the state is still the primary target of the loyalty of the regions. The Europeanization process is, however, a useful means in the day-to-day policy when dealing with the national centres. The outspoken Euro-scepticism in all Nordic states will, as an additional factor, prevent regional politicians from pursuing too many European dreams.

Bibliography

Bullmann, Udo (1997), 'Regional Integration in the EU – a German Perspective', paper at the *Conference on Local and Regional Integration in the EU*, Odense, 7-8 March.

Dosenrode, Søren (1995), 'Going NUTS: amter, delstater og kantoner i Europa' in *Nordisk Administrativt Tidsskrift*, No 2, pp. 149-167.

Dosenrode, Søren (1997), 'Denmark – The Testing of a Hesitant Membership' in Kenneth Hanf and Ben Soetendorp, *Adaptation to European Integration*, Longman, London.

Olsson, Jan and Åström, Joachim (2003), 'Why Regionalism in Sweden?' in *Regional and Federal Studies* (forthcoming), Frank Cass, London.

APPENDICES

Appendix A: Denmark

1) Regions in the national context are called Counties (amter), official translation: Regions.
2) The number of counties: 14.
3) The main tasks of the Danish regions:
   - Hospitals;
   - Public healthcare;
   - Education (grammar schools) and culture;
   - Regional planning including infrastructure and environment;
   - Administration.

4) The budgetary share of the regions in comparison with the total public sector: 11%.
5) Degree of the regions' self-financing: 94%.
6) The organization of the national and sub-national levels.

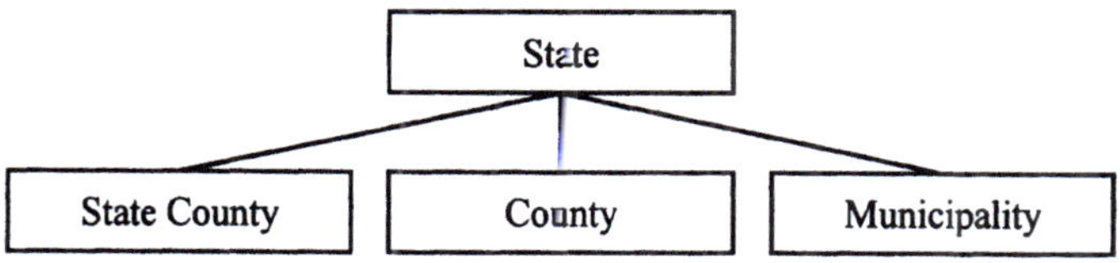

Figure A-1 Complementary tasks and equal submissiveness to the state

7) Participation in EU decision-making process:

   National level:
   - Membership of the relevant EU Special Committees;
   - Membership of the parliamentary contact committee;
   - Membership of the administrative co-ordination committee;
   - Regular semi-annual meetings with the Permanent Representation in Brussels.

   Supra-national level:
   - Member of the Committee of Regions;
   - The Association of Danish Regions has an office in Brussels;
   - Several regions have an office in Brussels;
   - The Association of Danish Regions is a member of several EU-interest organizations.

Appendix B: Finland

1) Regions in the national context are called *Maakunta* (Regions, institutionally organized in regional councils), which function as Joint Municipal Boards for regional development, official translation: Regions.
2) The number of regions: 19 + 1 (Ahvenanmaa = Åland an autonomous region with special status).
3) The main tasks of the Finnish regions:
   - Regional planning and management of regional development;
   - International functions. (In addition to developing international contacts on a wider front key organizational functions such as proposing members for the Committee of the Regions and participating in the activities of similar international bodies).

Note that as the Finnish regional level is made up of municipalities (joint municipal boards), the financial comparisons only make sense in *municipal* terms (Sources: The Association of Finnish Local and Regional Authorities 2003 and Statistics Finland).

4) The budgetary share of the regions in comparison with the total public sector: approximately 62% (2002).
5) Degree of self-financing: 73% (30 January 2001).
6) The organization of the national and sub-national levels (see figure B-1).
7) Participation in EU decision-making process:

   National level:
   - On the national level the organizational structure for decision-making and co-ordination of EU affairs are dominated by the central government actors;
   - Regions are central to EU Structural Funds decision-making and implementation.

   Supra-national level:
   - Members of the Committee of Regions;
   - The Association of Finnish Local and Regional Authorities, as well as several individual regions or their alliances have offices in Brussels and engage actively in international projects and networks;
   - Members in several EU-or pan-European interest organizations for regions, including Congress of Local and Regional Authorities of Europe (CLRAE), Assembly of European Regions (AER), Conference of

Peripheral Maritime Regions of Europe (CPMR) and the Association of European Border Regions (AEBR).

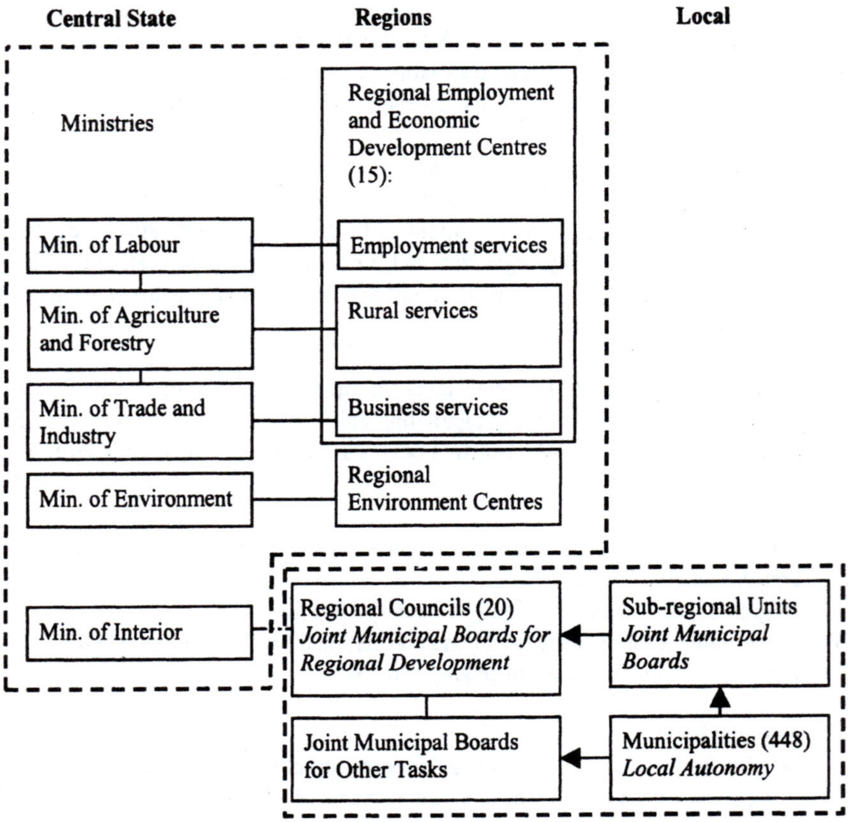

Figure B-1 Administrative structure in Finland: central state, regions and local level

Source: Virkkala, Seija (2002), 'The Finnish Cases: Combining "top-down" and "bottom-up" Partnership Formation' in Östhol and Svensson (eds), *Partnership Responses: Regional Governance in the Nordic States*, Stockholm, Nordregio, R2002:6.

Appendix C: Norway

1) Regions in the national context are called Counties (Fylker), official translation: County.
2) The number of counties: 19.
3) The main tasks of the Norwegian regions:
   - Education (upper secondary);
   - Transport and communication;
   - Specialized social services (care for children, alcohol and drug addicts);
   - Regional planning.

4) The budgetary share of the regions in comparison with the total public sector: 5%.
5) Degree of the regions' self-financing: Variable between 10% and 15%.
6) The organization of the national and sub-national levels.

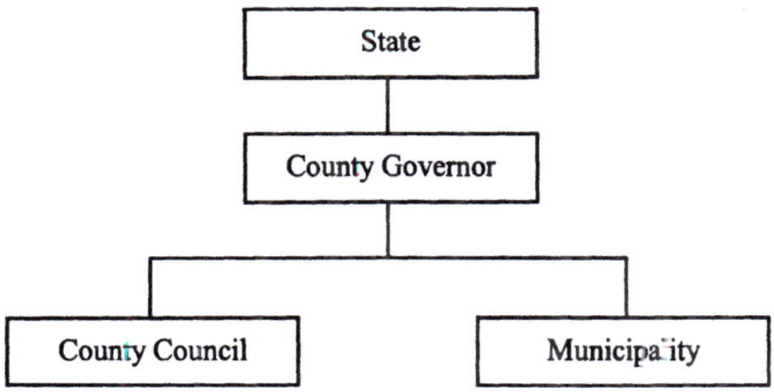

Figure C-1 Complementary tasks and equal submissiveness to the state

7) Participation in EU decision-making process:
   None, as far as Norway is not a member of the European Union and the European Economic Area (EEA) Agreement does not involve participation in EU decision-making processes.

Appendix D: Sweden

1) Swedish 'regions' consists of 18 counties, two regions and one municipality without a county council.
2) The total number of regions: 21.
3) The main tasks of Swedish regions:
   - Health and medical care;
   - Dental care;
   - Education, culture and public transport.

4) The budgetary share of the regions in comparison with the total public sector: about 7% of total public expenditures (not investments).
5) Degree of regions self-financing: 82%.
6) The organization of the national and sub-national levels:

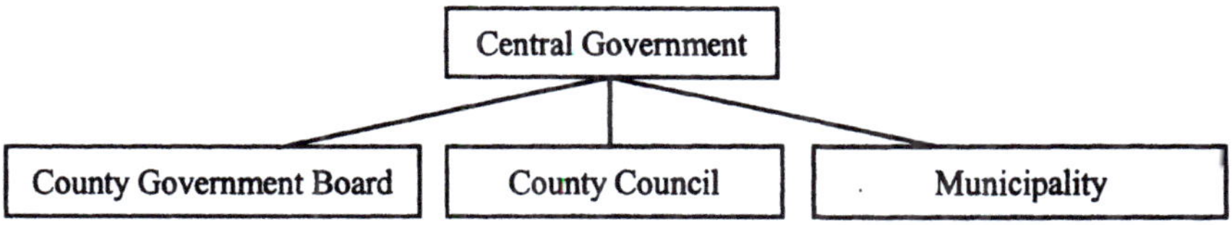

Figure D-1 The regional political system of Sweden

7) Participation in EU decision-making process:

   National level:
   The national process of consultation is quite informal, but is nevertheless important. Some examples:
   - Ongoing contact with the Ministry of Environment concerning environmental issues;
   - Ongoing contact with Parliament's Committee for Trade and Industry regarding growth and business development;
   - Ongoing contact with Parliament's European Committee concerning all kinds of EU-related questions;
   - Ongoing contact with the permanent representation in Brussels.

   Supra-national level:
   - Member of the Committee of Regions;
   - The Association of Swedish Regions has an office in Brussels;

- Several regions have an office in Brussels;
- The Association of Swedish Regions is a member of several EU-interest organizations.

Index

For Product Safety Concerns and Information please contact our EU representative GPSR@taylorandfrancis.com Taylor & Francis Verlag GmbH, Kaufingerstraße 24, 80331 München, Germany

Batch number: 10725883

Printed by Printforce, the Netherlands